RESEARCH AND PRACT

Wayne Joi

MW01008564

Post-Pandemic Social Studies:
How COVID-19 Has Changed the World and How We Teach
WAYNE JOURNELL, ED.

Teaching History for Justice:
Centering Activism in Students' Study of the Past
CHRISTOPHER C. MARTELL & KAYLENE M. STEVENS

Post-Pandemic Social Studies

How COVID-19 Has Changed the World and How We Teach

Edited by

Wayne Journell

FOREWORD by JOEL WESTHEIMER
AFTERWORD by TYRONE C. HOWARD

TEACHERS COLLEGE PRESS

TEACHERS COLLEGE | COLUMBIA UNIVERSITY

NEW YORK AND LONDON

Published by Teachers College Press,® 1234 Amsterdam Avenue, New York, NY 10027

Front cover images: Micrograph of a coronavirus, courtesy of the Center for Disease Control; Earth as seen from the Apollo mission, courtesy of NASA.

Library of Congress Cataloging-in-Publication Data

Names: Journell, Wayne, editor.
Title: Post-pandemic social studies : how COVID-19 has changed the world
   and how we teach / edited by Wayne Journell ; foreword by Joel
   Westheimer ; afterword by Tyrone C. Howard.
Description: New York : Teachers College Press, [2021] | Series: Research
   and Practice in Social Studies Series | Includes bibliographical
   references and index.
Identifiers: LCCN 2021047445 | ISBN 9780807766255 (Paperback : acid-free
   paper) | ISBN 9780807766262 (Hardcover : acid-free paper) | ISBN
   9780807780688 (eBook)
Subjects: LCSH: Social sciences—Study and teaching (Elementary) | Social
   sciences—Study and teaching (Middle school) | Social sciences—Study
   and teaching (Secondary) | Social sciences—Study and
   teaching—Curricula—United States. | Curriculum planning—United
   States. | COVID-19 Pandemic, 2020–
Classification: LCC LB1584 .P665 2021 | DDC 372.89—dc23/eng/20211103
LC record available at https://lccn.loc.gov/2021047445

ISBN 978-0-8077-6625-5 (paper)
ISBN 978-0-8077-6626-2 (hardcover)
ISBN 978-0-8077-8068-8 (ebook)

Printed on acid-free paper
Manufactured in the United States of America

Contents

Foreword

Toward the end of April 2020, a popular meme circulated on social media noting that the year seemed exceptional, calendrically speaking:

> 2020 is a unique leap year. It has 29 days in February, 300 days in March, and 5 years in April.

Readers of this book will no doubt relate: Australian wildfires (remember those?); an assault on the Michigan State Capitol; impeachment; Brexit; police shootings of unarmed Black, Indigenous, and People of Color (BIPOC); radical increases in economic inequality worldwide; and of course, the worst global health emergency in more than 100 years. And it was not yet June.

One year later, we are still reeling from more than 4 million pandemic-related deaths worldwide. Spiking infection numbers around the globe and the appearance of potent new variants mean that the COVID-19 pandemic is not over. The climate crisis continues with potentially catastrophic consequences. Despite the important conviction of former police officer Derek Chauvin for the murder of George Floyd, state-supported violence against BIPOC communities continues. And the 2020 attack on the Capitol building in Lansing, Michigan, seems to have foreshadowed the January 6, 2021, assault on the U.S. Capitol building in Washington, D.C., that left five people dead, many more injured, and a world wondering whether democracy can survive.

Yet here is the interesting thing about this particular moment in history: Many things that were impossible before the pandemic suddenly (and perhaps briefly) became possible. Crises have a way of doing that. In the United States, before the pandemic, calls to find one trillion dollars for healthcare were ridiculed and deemed naïve. Today, three trillion dollars (and more to come) are being spent for the social and economic benefit of ordinary citizens. Almost overnight, homeless people in some communities were suddenly sheltered in hotels and empty residential spaces. Prisoners were released from overcrowded jails and funneled into alternatives to incarceration. Commitments to social spending on criminal justice are now competing with ideas about social spending on reducing inequalities, addressing mental health and well-being, and creating infrastructure that benefits everyone.

In education, too, the impossible became possible. Teaching—under assault for years—suddenly became once again commendable as politicians clamored over one another to praise teachers' selfless devotion to students and their families. Destructive public obsessions with standards and accountability (based on the deluded assumption that the only thing teachers need to succeed is public scrutiny) were curbed overnight as standardized tests were swiftly cancelled across the nation. Anything is possible.

This message—that anything is possible—is the inspiring and buoyant throughline of *Post-Pandemic Social Studies*. Wayne Journell and his contributors rightfully place social studies at the center of not only educational but also social, political, and economic reform. Social studies, after all, is concerned with that most radically progressive question: How should we live? Social studies makes learning meaningful and relevant as it connects knowledge and skills with life outside of school. In this moment of opportunity, then, how can social studies educators respond? How could we refashion social studies and schools more broadly in the service of justice and societal improvement? How could the conjoined crises we face nationally and globally be addressed by young people learning about how to effect change? How does political polarization impact our ability to work together toward solutions to intractable social, ecological, and economic problems, and what can social studies curriculum do to change that? How do our emotions and community attachments to one another hinder or help our efforts to live together, to improve social policy, and even to agree on the relevant evidence that informs our decisions? How do current assessment practices limit our educational imagination? These questions and more are the concern of the thoughtful contributions that follow.

The COVID-19 pandemic has functioned like an x-ray, exposing already-existing fault lines in our nation and the world: poverty and economic inequality, unequal access to high-speed Internet and computers, inadequate resources for those most in need, and the proliferation of misinformation and conspiracy theories that threaten the foundation of civic life. Online learning meant that we were transported into our students' homes, and they were transported into ours. The problems were difficult to ignore. Some students had parents nearby with resources and enough education to demand their kids follow the curriculum, maybe even get ahead. Other parents were frontline workers, or holding down two jobs, or working at home with little time for other activities. Some students shared their computers or their rooms with siblings, while others had quiet and spacious work areas. Some students were homeless or had no access to computers at all.

None of these is a new challenge, but they are newly spotlighted for all to see—"pinned," in the vernacular of the now-ubiquitous video conferencing platforms. Education has long been heralded as a key to addressing persistent inequality, stimulating social mobility, decreasing unemployment, teaching about sustainable living, strengthening democratic institutions, and reducing violence. But this book goes further than noting the importance of education for students' social mobility. Taken together, the vision these chapters advance is one not satisfied with education that benefits individuals. They suggest, rather, the possibility of social studies curriculum and teaching that foregrounds issues of social justice, builds communal ties, and embraces and advances the habits and dispositions of democratic life.

Remember that old saying about the two Chinese characters that comprise the word "crisis." One is the character for "danger" and the other the character for "opportunity." Whether this is a correct interpretation of the Chinese etymology or not (and it is likely not), the lesson rings true: With every crisis comes an opportunity. Having confronted the danger of a global pandemic in unprecedented ways, we should also now turn to the opportunity. But opportunity is not the same as destiny. Positive change is not guaranteed. If we hope to make meaningful changes to the curriculum, we will have to seize this moment. For social studies educators, let this volume be your guide.

—Joel Westheimer

Preface

As a social studies educator, I am often fond of reminding my family, friends, and students that we are all constantly "living through history." Certainly, in my 41 years on this planet, I have witnessed events that have felt historic—the fall of the Berlin Wall, the Clinton impeachment, the September 11th attacks, Obama's election, the recent insurrection at the U.S. Capitol—and while they have been permanently etched into my memory, none of them ever impacted me personally outside of the emotions that come from watching something profoundly inspiring or unspeakable. I came to those events as a spectator, knowing that I was watching history unfold but viewing it at arm's length.

The COVID-19 pandemic was the first event that made me *feel* as though I was living through history. My wife and I regularly talk about when our world, as we knew it, ended. The last weekend of February 2020, we had just spent 3 days in Miami, traveling through airports, dining in crowded restaurants, and taking in a performance of *Hamilton*. We had heard about this strange virus that had been found in China, but on that weekend, it was the furthest thing from our minds.

Less than 2 weeks later, everything changed. My daughter's school district closed, and my days were spent proctoring 1st-grade remote learning. My university switched to fully online courses and sent all students home. Masks became standard issue any time we left the house, which was not often. Nasal swabs, temperature checks, and quarantines soon became a regular part of our daily existence.

I would imagine everyone reading this book has a similar story, which is what makes this pandemic so unique and transformative. None of us could avoid it. Even if we were fortunate enough to escape the wrath of the virus itself, the societal response to the pandemic upended our lives in ways few could have possibly anticipated. Moreover, this disruption that was originally forecasted to last only a few weeks has now, as of this writing, passed the 1-year mark. We are truly living through history.

History also tells us that this pandemic will eventually end. On social media, I see people proudly showing off their vaccine cards, and it is a constant reminder that there is a light at the end of this long, dark tunnel we have been traveling through. This book is concerned with what lies on the other side. The authors in this book have approached this work with the understanding that the post-pandemic world in which we will live is still being shaped. With that, we offer a vision of what the social studies curriculum can, and should, be in the wake of COVID-19.

I would like to thank the talented team at Teachers College Press for making this book a reality, particularly the vision of Brian Ellerbeck, whom I have enjoyed working with over the past few years. Of course, this book would not exist without the talented scholars who agreed to write chapters, all of whom did so while balancing Zoom teaching, homeschooling, and other realities of pandemic life. I am honored that they have agreed to lend their voices to this project. Finally, this book, as with all aspects of my professional life, would not have been possible without the support of my wife, Kitrina, and my daughter, Hadleigh, who is always the motivation behind my scholarship.

Finally, I know I speak for all the authors in this volume in dedicating this book to the over four million people worldwide who have died from this horrible virus. May this book honor their memory.

—*Wayne Journell*

Post-Pandemic Social Studies

Introduction

Wayne Journell

In late 2019, as the first cases of COVID-19 were being diagnosed in Wuhan, China, few could have imagined the amount of devastation this novel coronavirus would inflict on the world. Even as Wuhan, a city of over 11 million people, began draconian lockdown measures in late January 2020, much of the Western world viewed these actions as an overreaction by an authoritarian regime. It was only after the virus had reached U.S. shores and we saw how quickly it ravaged healthcare systems in Italy and Spain did we make the unprecedented decision to shut down most aspects of American life.

It is impossible to fully quantify the damage created by COVID-19. As of this writing, over 700,000 people have died from COVID-19 in the United States alone, and the worldwide figure exceeds four million. The U.S. economy, which at the start of 2020 saw the stock market reach previously unthinkable heights, plummeted to depths not seen since the Great Depression. Businesses deemed nonessential were forced to shut down, with many predicted to sustain losses that will prevent them ever from reopening, forcing over 65 million Americans to file for unemployment since the start of the pandemic.

Taken-for-granted aspects of U.S. daily life were also impacted. K–12 schools, colleges, and universities shut their doors and transitioned to remote learning, forcing millions of parents to juggle homeschooling while working from home. Sports, concerts, conferences, and other large-scale gatherings became relics of the immediate past, with no one sure when or how such events would return. Even basic human interaction has been affected, as many Americans are still afraid of leaving their houses and congregating with others for fear of either catching the virus or transmitting it to vulnerable loved ones.

In short, life as we knew it before 2020 ceased to exist. Although vaccines have given the world hope of ending the pandemic, it is still unclear if or when we will be able to return to anything resembling pre–COVID-19 normalcy. It seems clear that that the fallout from the pandemic will be felt within society for the foreseeable future.

ENVISIONING A POST-COVID-19 SOCIAL STUDIES CURRICULUM

This book was conceived in that space between the destruction of our old way of life and what comes next. As states began closing schools and universities, the immediate focus of educators was, rightly, the transition to remote learning and issues related to student welfare, such as ensuring that students who relied on schools for meals would still be able to receive breakfast and lunch services. Then, as any hope of returning to finish the 2019–2020 school year faded, attention turned to finding creative ways to safely reopen schools in the fall and forming contingency plans for when future waves of the virus struck.

Here, we are focused on that time in the future when concerns over how to fill classrooms end and we can resume debates over best practices for teaching and learning. Even after social distancing retreats into our collective memory, the lessons learned from COVID-19 should remain, particularly for a discipline like social studies that is so influenced by the world around us. In just a few short months, an invisible virus brought the most powerful nation in the world to its knees like no other event in recent memory, and in doing so, it exposed the systemic inequalities and economic instability that too often remain hidden beneath the veneer of American exceptionality within the social studies curriculum.

The pandemic offers an opportunity to push the social studies curriculum toward a more justice-oriented, critical examination of U.S. society. The history of social studies education, however, suggests that such change will not come easily or automatically. In fact, many of the major world events of the 20th and 21st centuries have had the opposite effect. World War I (Barton, 2016; Weber & Montgomery, 2019), World War II and the Cold War era (Nelson, 1986; Thornton, 2008, 2017), and the attacks of September 11, 2001, and the ensuing War on Terror (Journell, 2016; Stoddard & Hess, 2016), for example, resulted in a more nationalistic social studies curriculum in which the study of U.S. history was prioritized over other social studies disciplines. A civic republican discourse promoting patriotism and service to the nation also was emphasized over more global and critical approaches to civic education.

A common theme running through each of those examples, though, is the notion of an Other that allows us to frame ourselves in contrast to extremism. The social studies curriculum has been able to maintain the appearance of American exceptionalism for the past century because the narrative of the United States as the defenders of democracy against fascism/communism/terrorism has helped whitewash early atrocities of our own making, such as slavery and Native American relocation, as well as systemic issues (e.g., White supremacy, sexism, classism) that continue to oppress many Americans despite the illusion of progress (Brown & Au, 2014; Miller-Lane et al., 2007).

COVID-19, however, does not offer an easily identifiable foil, which may be why the Trump administration continued to push the theory that the novel coronavirus was created in a Chinese laboratory despite most scientific evidence pointing to a natural transmission between animals and humans. In the same way that Hurricane Katrina was a natural disaster that exposed the inequities between rich and poor and Blacks and Whites in New Orleans, specifically, and in urban areas more broadly, the coronavirus has laid bare cracks in the myth of American exceptionalism on a national scale. No amount of finger-pointing will change the fact that the deaths and economic woes that have occurred since the start of the pandemic happened on our watch and were not the result of foreign aggression or global economic strife.

Perhaps, then, it is instructive to look at how the social studies curriculum responded to another recent national crisis—the Great Recession of 2008. There was no Other to blame then; it was a crisis of our own making. The recession was largely a product of unregulated capitalism and corporate greed, two elements that, ironically, have helped position the United States as the most powerful economy in the world. The actions of banks, mortgage companies, and other corporations that were "too big to fail" ultimately led to a financial crisis in which millions of Americans lost their jobs, and economic growth declined to the worst point since the Great Depression. Yet the government responded to the crisis by bailing out the banks and mortgage companies instead of the folks on "Main Street" who had been most directly affected.

The fallout from the Great Recession, arguably, altered U.S. domestic policy more significantly than even the September 11th attacks. On one side of the political spectrum, the Tea Party formed in opposition to the use of government spending to bail out the economy, and on the other, the Occupy Wall Street movement and increased calls for democratic socialist economic policies appeared among the far left. Yet the social studies curriculum remains largely the same as it was in 2007. Even the economics curriculum remains unchanged; neoclassical economic theory remains the official, and oftentimes the only, approach to economic education, without any real acknowledgement of its limitations (Adams, 2019; Shanks, 2019). Some states have also created or required courses in financial literacy in the decade since the recession (Ogden, 2019), which suggests that those in power want to place the onus of responsibility for the economic collapse on individual Americans' decision-making rather than a failure of the system (Lucey et al., 2016).

It is important that this type of selective framing does not occur in the aftermath of the pandemic. Amid the chaos wrought by COVID-19, it seems unthinkable that it would not lead to substantive changes in the curriculum. Particularly when compared to other nations throughout the world, the virus has exposed failures in U.S. leadership, federal preparedness, and the American health care system. The varying responses by states, determined largely on ideological lines, on when to shut down and reopen have illustrated the limitations of federalism, as well as the harmful consequences of extreme partisanship and regionalism. The protests against shutdown orders reflected not only the dangers of political echo chambers and science skepticism, but also the fragile state of the U.S. economy in which millions of people live paycheck to paycheck and have no reliable safety net when tragedy strikes.

COVID-19 also illuminated inequitable social stratifications within U.S. society and our inability or unwillingness to protect our most vulnerable citizens. Disproportionate numbers of African Americans and Latinxs, particularly those living in poor urban areas, have succumbed to the virus when compared to Whites and those in the upper and middle classes, even when accounting for age disparities. These unequal mortality rates are not due to genetics but rather to structural issues, the roots of which are often embedded in racism and xenophobia, that have resulted in decades of poverty, poor nutrition, and lack of health care access.

It would be naïve to expect K–12 education to bring these aspects of the crisis to students' attention in critical or substantive ways. Schools, as Foucault (1978/1991) noted, are "apparatuses of security" for the state, designed to instill social norms within the population (p. 102). As we have seen throughout history, those norms are decided by those in power, meaning that within the official canon, the story of COVID-19 will likely be one that fits the narrative of American exceptionality: the resilience of the American people, the bravery of our healthcare workers, the ingenuity that resulted in a vaccine, and so on.

That is not to say that these inspirational aspects of the crisis are unimportant. They are, and they should be recognized, both within schools and in society at large. However, avoiding a critical look at the pandemic and what it has illustrated, or reconfirmed, about the limitations of U.S. society would be more than a wasted pedagogical opportunity; it would be a moral failing.

This book is designed to be a thought experiment about how social studies teachers could teach about COVID-19 in the future, as well as how this crisis should impact the social studies curriculum more broadly. Although history suggests that the formal curriculum will likely not take the critical approach advocated here, teachers have considerable influence over how the curriculum is presented to students. It is our hope that this book can serve as a starting point for helping teachers reshape the way they think about their instruction in a post–COVID-19 world.

STRUCTURE OF THE BOOK

The book is divided into two parts. The first focuses on providing guidance on how to teach about the COVID-19 crisis as a recent historical event.

Even as the impact of the coronavirus on daily life wanes, it will remain a focal point of societal discourse. Teachers will inevitably be forced to wade into the debates over whether governments overreacted or underreacted, whether mitigation strategies were preferable to more lax approaches, and whether the attempts to save lives were worth the economic devastation that ensued. Constructing these "first drafts" of history (Stoddard et al., 2011) can be challenging, particularly when the emotional toll of the crisis is still fresh in the societal mindset. The first six chapters offer teachers a roadmap for navigating this difficult, and potentially traumatic, terrain.

In Chapter 1, Catherine Mas provides a historical context for teaching about the COVID-19 crisis. While this novel coronavirus is the most disruptive pandemic in recent memory, it is far from the only disease to lead to widespread death and alter daily life. COVID-19 is often compared to the 1918 Spanish flu that resulted in over 50 million deaths worldwide and required many of the same social distancing measures we see today; however, there have been other pandemics since then that have also been deadly but did not result in significant societal changes. An understanding of this history provides the necessary depth for students to formulate nuanced opinions about what they just lived through.

However, there is an inherent danger in discussing COVID-19 and other pandemics in the abstract. As the COVID-19 death toll steadily began to rise, it became fashionable in the media to make statements like "U.S. COVID-19 deaths now surpass Vietnam War fatalities" or "COVID-19 is now the leading cause of death in the United States." As we start comparing numbers of deaths, either among historical pandemics or between COVID-19 and other events that led to mass casualties, it is easy to forget that each one of those deaths represents a family member or a friend to someone. As the COVID-19 death toll continues to climb, it is exceedingly likely that many students will personally know someone who has succumbed to the virus. In Chapter 2, Rebecca C. Christ, Bretton A. Varga, Mark E. Helmsing, and Cathryn van Kessel provide guidance on how to situate the teaching of COVID-19 within the context of death and grief, which is an aspect of K–12 social education that has long been ignored.

Chapters 3 and 4 offer examples of approaches for teaching about the COVID-19 crisis that align with the *C3 Framework* (National Council for the Social Studies, 2013) and use the Inquiry Design Model (Swan et al., 2018). In the first, Carly Muetterties and Holly Wright outline a project for middle and high school students that combines inquiry-based instruction and social–emotional learning principles and culminates in students creating an artifact that represents the realities of living through the tumultuous year of 2020. In the second, Lisa Brown Buchanan, Cara Ward, Tracy Hargrove, Amy Taylor, Maggie Guggenheimer, and Lynn Sikma describe an interdisciplinary unit designed for young learners that situates the pandemic within content standards for social studies, math, and science.

In Chapter 5, Christopher H. Clark argues that to truly understand how the pandemic unfolded in the United States, students need an awareness of political polarization and the role of ideology in political and social decision-making. He dissects how the pandemic quickly became a "red state" versus "blue state" issue, with the sides framing COVID-19 in different ways. The result was a wide gap between individuals of different party and ideological adherence in their attitudes to the virus and, more generally, in their propensity to trust scientific data.

In Chapter 6, Sandra Schmidt advocates for spatial thinking as a way for students to better understand both the local and global impact of the pandemic. She argues that by framing inquiry about COVID-19 around dynamics of place, space, and social data, teachers can help students become more aware of systemic issues, both globally and within the communities in which they live, that have led to unequal outcomes among different groups within society.

The second part of the book moves away from teaching about COVID-19 as an event and instead argues for using the pandemic to critically examine K–12 social studies curriculum and instruction. In Chapter 7, Wayne Journell argues that COVID-19 shattered the myth of American exceptionalism that is so prevalent within the social studies curriculum. The pandemic has illuminated the fragile nature of many aspects of U.S. society, from our healthcare system to our democratic process, which can be used to counter the traditional narrative of exceptionalism.

In Chapter 8, Cathryn van Kessel furthers Journell's argument by noting that COVID-19 laid bare longstanding "diseases" within American society, namely intersecting systemic racism, classism, and sexism. She argues that social studies educators can use COVID-19 to illuminate the nexus of personal and collective responsibility for interlocking structural violence to foster a sense of personal, and yet interconnected, responsibility to make fundamental changes necessary for U.S. society to hurt less moving forward.

The pandemic also illuminated vast economic and political disparities, both in the United States and around the world. In Chapter 9, Leonel Pérez Expósito and Varenka Servín Arcos argue that in light of the COVID-19 crisis, questions related to economic and political inequity should be central to the social studies curriculum moving forward. They suggest fostering skills related to what Allen (2016) has termed "participatory readiness" to help students from unequal polities and marginalized communities develop civic agency.

Within the United States, Black Americans have historically been the victims of systemic economic and political inequity, and thus it is unsurprising that they have also borne the brunt of the COVID-19 crisis. The combination of the pandemic and the harrowing video of George Floyd being murdered by members of the Minneapolis police department (on the heels of the murders of Ahmaud Arbery and Breonna Taylor in the weeks before) may have started a movement for equality that the nation has not seen since the 1960s. In Chapter 10, Kristen E. Duncan and Amber M. Neal argue that the widespread impacts of both the COVID-19 pandemic and the Black Lives Matter protests call for a critical reexamination of how we historize events within the social studies curriculum.

The circumstances surrounding the origin of the novel coronavirus also led to the marginalization of another group of Americans: those of Asian descent. From President Trump repeatedly referring to COVID-19 as the "Chinese virus" to a sharp rise in anti-Asian violence, Asian Americans have faced widespread discrimination since the start of the pandemic. Sohyun An and Noreen Naseem Rodríguez argue in Chapter 11 that COVID-19 is just the latest incident of anti-Asian sentiment due to a public health crisis. In their chapter, An and Rodríguez chronicle the history of racializing disease in the United States and suggest that COVID-19 should lead to greater urgency for teaching Asian American history and racial literacy in social studies education.

As these chapters attest, for most people, the pandemic was an emotional experience, and in Chapter 12, Jennifer Hauver argues that educators should more critically analyze the role emotion can have and ought to have in social studies education. Hauver recounts her experience teaching in a high school social studies classroom during the pandemic and the powerful role that emotion played in helping her students contextualize their feelings as they lived through history. She then argues that by embracing the emotional act of teaching, social studies teachers can help students better understand aspects of the formal curriculum.

In Chapter 13, Katherina A. Payne and Anna Falkner make a similar argument for the teaching of elementary social studies. They argue that COVID-19 reinforced the essential question at the heart of elementary social studies education: "How do we live together?" Payne and Falkner believe that the ideal way to broach this question is by taking a sociological approach that centers people's relationships with one another, the places they inhabit, and the institutions they create within those places. This type of approach affords elementary students the means not only to examine the historical roots that led to the events of 2020 but also to think about a different, better way of living together.

The question of how we live together is also at the heart of the COVID-19 crisis. The pandemic forced many Americans to give up some of their basic freedoms in order to protect the most vulnerable among us. Yet, as the "rallies to reopen" that occurred in many state capitals attest, not all Americans agreed with that approach. In Chapter 14, Yun-Wen Chan and Ya-Fang Cheng examine this relationship between public safety and personal freedom in U.S. society and argue that freedom should be built upon altruism. They further this argument by comparing the U.S. response to COVID-19 with two successful cases of coronavirus prevention, Taiwan and New Zealand, and argue that social studies education should seek to foster altruistic dispositions in students.

The COVID-19 crisis has also forced us to reconsider longstanding tenets of civic education. Even as technology and increased transportation have made the world more interconnected than ever before, the social studies curriculum in the United States and other Western nations has maintained a nationalistic focus. Yet the coronavirus does not recognize national borders, and the (in)actions of some nations impacted others as the virus quickly spread across the world. As such, Sarah Mathews argues in Chapter 15 that COVID-19 is the quintessential example for why social studies education should broaden its conception of civic education to include global learning so that we are better poised to deal with the challenges of living together as part of a global community.

COVID-19 also provided an extreme case study in the limitations of federalism, which Karon LeCompte, Brooke Blevins, and Kevin R. Magill explore in Chapter 16. As with national borders, the coronavirus had no regard for state boundaries or policies, creating the need for a nationwide response. Without a strong federal response to the virus, state governors became the decision-makers on when to shut down, what to shut down, and when to reopen. These decisions varied from state to state, and sometimes county to county, creating confusion and resentment while rendering ineffective earnest attempts at slowing the spread of the virus.

Finally, as Stephanie van Hover, Michael Gurlea, Tyler Woodward, David Hicks, and David Gerwin argue in Chapter 17, any transformation of social studies teaching and learning requires an accompanying change in assessment practices. COVID-19 forced states to cancel their high-stakes tests, giving districts and teachers more autonomy to determine what students learned and how they met the expectations in state standards documents. The authors argue that the COVID-19 crisis provides an opportunity to rethink assessment practices in social studies education, and they urge the field to consider "ambitious" assessment that moves beyond privileging recall of factual content.

Many pundits and prognosticators have said that COVID-19 will lead to a "new normal," a phrase that typically bears negative connotations. Certainly, the pandemic has led to hardships that few could have fathomed, and some cherished aspects of society may be altered forever. At the same time, however, the pandemic offers an unprecedented opportunity for us to reflect on all facets of American life, including the way in which we educate our students. This book challenges social studies educators to use the pandemic to advocate for a more critical learning experience, one that challenges traditional ways of looking at the world and seeks a better, more equitable path forward.

REFERENCES

Adams, E. C. (2019). Twenty years of economics curriculum: Trends, issues, and transformations? *The Social Studies, 110*(3), 131–145. https://doi.org/10.1080/00377996.2019.1581725

Allen, D. S. (2016). *Education and equality*. University of Chicago Press.

Barton, K. C. (2016). International conflict and national destiny: World War I and history teaching. In W. Journell (Ed.), *Reassessing the social studies curriculum: Promoting critical civic engagement in a politically polarized, post-9/11 world* (pp. 1–13). Rowman & Littlefield.

Brown, A. L., & Au, W. (2014). Race, memory, and master narratives: A critical essay on U.S. curriculum history. *Curriculum Inquiry, 44*(3), 358–389. https://doi.org/10.1111/curi.12049

Foucault, M. (1991). Governmentality. In G. Burchell, C. Gordon, & P. Miller (Eds.), *The Foucault effect: Studies in governmentality* (pp. 87–104). University of Chicago Press. (Original work published 1978)

Journell, W. (Ed.). (2016). *Reassessing the social studies curriculum: Promoting critical civic engagement in a politically polarized, post-9/11 world*. Rowman & Littlefield.

Lucey, T. A., Agnello, M. F., & Laney, J. D. (2016). Financial literacy in the wake of the great recession. In W. Journell (Ed.), *Teaching social studies in an era of divisiveness: The challenges of discussing social issues in a non-partisan way* (pp. 159–174). Rowman & Littlefield.

Miller-Lane, J., Howard, T. C., & Halagao, P. E. (2007). Civic multicultural competence: Searching for common ground in democratic education. *Theory & Research in Social Education, 35*(4), 551–573. https://doi.org/10.1080/00933104.2007.10473350

National Council for the Social Studies. (2013). *College, career, and civic life (C3) framework for social studies state standards*. Author.

Nelson, M. R. (1986). Some possible effects of World War II on the social studies curriculum. *Theory & Research in Social Education, 14*(4), 267–275. https://doi.org/10.1080/00933104.1986.10505526

Ogden, T. (2019, April 23). More states are forcing students to study personal finance. It's a waste of time. *The Washington Post*. https://www.washingtonpost.com/outlook/2019/04/23/more-states-are-forcing-students-study-personal-finance-its-waste-time/

Shanks, N. (2019). Against 'economic man': A feminist challenge to prevailing neoclassical norms in K–12 economics education. *Theory & Research in Social Education, 47*(4), 577–603. https://doi.org/10.1080/00933104.2019.1647904

Stoddard, J., & Hess, D. (2016). 9/11 and the war on terror in American secondary curriculum, fifteen years later. In W. Journell (Ed.), *Reassessing the social studies curriculum: Promoting critical civic engagement in a politically polarized, post-9/11 world* (pp. 15–27). Rowman & Littlefield.

Stoddard, J., Hess, D., & Hammer, C. M. (2011). The challenge of writing 'first draft history': The evolution of the 9/11 attacks and their aftermath in school textbooks in the United States. In L. Yates & M. Grumet (Eds.), *World yearbook of education 2011: Curriculum in today's world: Configuring knowledge, identities, work and politics* (pp. 223–236). Routledge.

Swan, K., Lee, J., & Grant, S. G. (2018). *Inquiry design model: Building inquiries in social studies.* National Council for the Social Studies and C3 Teachers.

Thornton, S. J. (2008). Continuity and change in social studies curriculum. In L. S. Levstik & C. A. Tyson (Eds.), *Handbook of research in social studies education* (pp. 15–32). Routledge.

Thornton, S. J. (2017). A concise historiography of the social studies. In M. M. Manfra & C. M. Bolick (Eds.), *The Wiley handbook of social studies research* (pp. 9–41). John Wiley & Sons.

Weber, C. A., & Montgomery, S. E. (2019). The emergence of elementary citizenship education: Insights from Iowa's rural schools, 1910–1935. *Theory & Research in Social Education, 47*(2), 261–293. https://doi.org/10.1080/00933104.2018.1501449

PART I

TEACHING ABOUT THE COVID-19 PANDEMIC

CHAPTER 1

Putting COVID-19 Into Historical Context

Catherine Mas

When a novel coronavirus broke out across the world in 2020, many turned to historians for some sense of control or comfort in the knowledge that we have been here before. The truth is, we haven't. The biological character of COVID-19 has generated a specific set of fears and challenges for 21st-century society. Its highly contagious and unpredictably pernicious nature has led to an abrupt halt to everyday economic and social activities that hinged on our close contact with one another in a dense and interconnected world.

Notwithstanding this rupture, looking to the past can deepen our understanding of the social conditions, political responses, and human actions that have shaped (and continue to shape) the course of the pandemic. The current crisis has revealed aspects of the human condition that have surfaced many times before in the face of epidemic outbreaks. The threat of contagion has provoked patterns of thought and behavior, including panic, scapegoating, and xenophobia, that tend to sharpen existing divisions. At the same time, the shared experience of illness has forged deep social bonds, demonstrating humans' capacity for community, care, and innovation.

We saw these dueling tendencies play out in the early phases of the pandemic—even before it was characterized as such. On February 11, 2020, at a press conference of the World Health Organization (WHO), the novel coronavirus and the disease it causes were given names: SARS-CoV-2 and COVID-19. This act of naming brought into being a new threat, one requiring immediate international attention. More than 40,000 cases had already been confirmed in China, along with hundreds more in 24 other countries. WHO Director-General Tedros Adhanom Ghebreyesus urged the world's leaders to ramp up efforts at detection and containment, taking advantage of what he called a "window of opportunity" to "shut down the virus" before widespread community transmission rendered the problem uncontrollable (WHO, 2020, pp. 4, 13). Attempting to convey the severity of COVID-19, Tedros commented that "viruses can have more powerful consequences than any terrorist action." He continued, "If the world doesn't wake up and consider this enemy virus as public enemy number one, I don't think we will learn from our lessons" (WHO, 2020, p. 9). Despite his warning, the virus quickly got ahead of prevention efforts. Exactly one month later, on March 11, the WHO declared a pandemic.

It has been commonplace to hear leaders describe being "at war" with the virus. Tedros, for instance, equated public health preparedness with more high-profile global counterterrorism efforts in the hopes of unifying diverse nations and mobilizing vast resources and expertise against a common enemy. Individual nations have done the same, albeit with varying intentions and emotional registers. In the United States, for example, President Trump referred to the pandemic in March as "our big war"—against what he was then calling "the Chinese virus." Of course, a pandemic cannot have a nationality. Viruses do not recognize the arbitrary borders humans have drawn around nations or ethnic groups. Yet history shows us that political ideas filter all too easily into our understanding of contagion. While the ways in which individuals, communities, and nations experience and deal with outbreaks is rooted in a specific temporal and spatial context, the war metaphor evokes a basic reality—that of a disease ecology that unites the human species, as well as the political structures and cultures that divide us.

In what follows, I offer a historical context for COVID-19, looking first at patterns of human migration and ecological change that have facilitated epidemic outbreaks in the past. I then turn to the history of modern public health to understand shifting political responses to contagious disease. Next, I examine international efforts to control and prevent influenza pandemics in the 20th century to contextualize widespread assumptions that scientific and technological prowess will bring an end to the current pandemic. Finally, I note how COVID-19 has exposed dangerous fractures in our public health systems, including the fragility of medical infrastructures and health disparities that have deep historical roots.

WHEN PEOPLE AND PATHOGENS MOVE

The first reports of a coronavirus outbreak came from Wuhan, China, in the final days of 2019. In January 2020, the Chinese government issued a lockdown order in Wuhan, signaling the severity of the situation and sparking sensational stories and conspiracy theories about the disease's origins. Many involved gruesome descriptions of wet markets and people with uncommon eating habits. A video of a Chinese woman eating "bat soup"—although filmed in 2016—went viral on social media platforms, stoking anti-Asian racism from people who were eager to assign blame for the outbreak (Palmer, 2020). While scientists have discredited such sensationalized origin stories, they affirm an underlying truth: that the novel coronavirus "jumped" from animals to humans. COVID-19, like SARS, Zika, and MERS, is a zoonosis, a disease caused by a pathogen (in this case, a virus scientists have named SARS-CoV-2) that has "spilled over" from an animal host to humans. The frequency and virulence of these spillovers have amounted to global crises in the 21st century (Quammen, 2012). Such animal-borne infections—which have wreaked such havoc because humans lack immunity to them—become increasingly frequent as humans encroach onto wildlife environments and as transportation technologies allow for their rapid global spread.

The spillover event that sparked the COVID-19 pandemic is part of a historical process that has been centuries in the making. The intermingling of peoples and pathogens has accompanied the rise and fall of empires, the growth of industrial capitalism, and more recent forces of globalization. The bubonic plague, a zoonosis from rodents caused by the bacterium *Yersinia pestis*, is responsible for one of the earliest and most deadly pandemics. Before antibiotics were available, the death rate was 50%, and it killed within days of the onset of symptoms. The first of three pandemic cycles was known as the Justinian Plague, after the 6th-century emperor under whom it started. Constantinople was an ideal crossroads through which plague could spread across Africa, Europe, and Asia via the vast trade networks and military routes of the Byzantine empire (Orent, 2004).

The second cycle, known as the Black Death, originated in Central Asia in the 1330s, with outbreaks continuing up until the 1830s. Italy, the center of Mediterranean trade during the Renaissance, became the center of the pandemic. In port cities most vulnerable to the plague, authorities instituted one of the earliest public health measures: quarantine. First practiced in Venice, the term derives from the word *quaranta*, or forty, for the number of days in which passengers and goods aboard incoming ships would be confined. The duration resonated with Christian notions of purification, calling to mind the 40 days of Lent before Easter—a usable framework for sanctioning a drastic measure. It worked; strictly enforced isolation allowed cities to contain the problem (Snowden, 2019).

The globalization of disease was more fully realized in the 15th and 16th centuries with the ecological transformations set in motion by Christopher Columbus's voyage to the New World. Due to the driving force of imperialism, a diverse set of plants, animals, and microbes sailed alongside the people, technologies, and ideas that traveled from Europe and Africa to the Americas and back. Through the "Columbian exchange," populations that had been geographically separated for centuries were now brought into close contact, and the health consequences were enormous (Crosby, 1972). This time, it was not zoonotic pathogens but those carried by European hosts that were uniquely devastating for Indigenous Americans. With no previous exposure to diseases like smallpox, whooping cough, and measles that were endemic in Europe, a series of epidemics decimated approximately 90% of the Indigenous population. The enormous loss of life disrupted local political systems. In 1520s Peru, a smallpox outbreak destroyed Incan society, as the death of the emperor and others in power created a vacuum of leadership.

For the Aztecs, where the onslaught of disease coincided with military conflicts with European invaders, smallpox was a form of biological warfare. One Aztec testimony recalled the terrifying nature of the illness, describing smallpox victims who "could not move; they could not stir . . . And if they stirred, much did they cry out. Great was its destruction" (quoted in Crosby, 1972, p. 56). Meanwhile, Spanish conquistadors, who emerged largely unscathed, interpreted the crumbling of Indigenous societies to disease as a sign of divine intervention. A Dominican friar on Hernán Cortés's expedition commented, "When the Christians were exhausted from war, God saw fit to send the Indians smallpox, and there was a great pestilence in the city" (quoted in Crosby, 1972, p. 48). British colonists voiced similar interpretations of epidemics, painting colonization as a "natural" and rightful process. In colonial New England, Puritan minister Cotton Mather believed that disease worked to clear the lands to which they were entitled (Crosby, 1972).

The transatlantic slave trade was also part of the Columbian exchange, as New World colonies relied on the labor of enslaved Africans to extract resources. Africans carried not only biological materials such as plants and microbes to the Americas, but also medical knowledge that would shape public health practices. For instance, Mather learned about the technique of smallpox inoculation from his African slave, Onesimus, and later read about the practice among Turks (Minardi, 2004). It involved taking a small amount of material from the pustules of an infected individual and introducing it into a healthy individual. The goal was to produce a much milder infection that would induce immunity. While this idea formed the basis of modern vaccination, the medical elite at the time resisted inoculation, worrying it would hasten disease spread. Mather, however, was convinced that mass inoculation might help contain smallpox and prevent future outbreaks.

When a smallpox epidemic broke out in Boston in 1721, Mather embarked on an inoculation crusade. Attempting to convince skeptics of inoculation's benefits, he drew on Onesimus's explanation, European reports of the practice, and additional African slave testimony (Minardi, 2004). Ultimately, Boston physicians and a divided public ended Mather's campaign. However, in the wake of this failure, he would develop a theory of how epidemics—and, in turn, the body—worked. Owning and using one of the few microscopes in colonial New England, Mather concluded in 1724 that the atmosphere was teeming with "unseen Armies of Numberless Living Things, ready to Seize and Prey upon us!" (Mather, 1972, p. 47). Mather's perception of disease as a militant invasion led him to think of the body as a fortress, with immunity offering protection against foreign threats (Cohen, 2009). This idea of health security took shape in the context of New World colonization and a plantation economy, as well as the conflicts and collaborations that followed encounters between peoples and pathogens.

THE SCIENCE AND POLITICS OF PUBLIC HEALTH

Contemporary responses to COVID-19 have varied dramatically across the globe and over the course of the pandemic. Some governments have taken aggressive measures, including lockdowns, large-scale testing, and the use of new digital technologies, especially smartphone apps, to facilitate contact tracing. Others have had a laxer response, keeping businesses open while encouraging physical distancing and the use of face masks. Different responses reflect difficult questions about what role government should play in regulating health and controlling disease. They reflect longer-standing debates around how to protect the welfare of nations, economies, and the general public, as advances in science, medicine, and technology redefine both problems and solutions.

Cholera pandemics in the 19th century offer a useful vantage point on these debates. The disease thrived in the conditions that gave rise to industrial capitalism: a tightly interwoven global economy with crowded cities, worsening poverty, and steam-powered ships and trains that moved microbes at new speeds from one hotspot to the next. Cholera traveled along colonial trade routes from India to Western Asia and Europe and then to the Americas, causing panic wherever it went.

When cholera raged in Europe in the 1830s, residents of New York City—a major port notorious for its crowds and filth—anxiously awaited information as they prepared for an imminent outbreak. Affluent New Yorkers fled for the countryside, while those who stayed stocked up on supplies and quack-promoted remedies. Business stagnated as shops closed and incoming ships were quarantined. Cholera arrived in 1832, and in the absence of knowledge or clear solutions for the problem, the city's merchants, physicians, and political leaders often placed the onus on individuals to deal with the epidemic. They often assigned blame to what they considered the immoral behaviors of those most frequently stricken with the disease—the poor who lived in the city's densely populated and unsanitary districts. Medical authorities posted an advisory to "be temperate in eating and drinking" and abstain from alcohol. They later assured citizens that the disease was limited to areas where "the intemperate and the dissolute" resided (Rosenberg, 1987, p. 42). Disproportionate suffering and scapegoating mapped onto racial and ethnic divisions, as Irish immigrants and African Americans were among the groups targeted as ignorant, intemperate, dirty, and diseased (Rosenberg, 1987).

Over the course of subsequent outbreaks, cholera would capture the attention of new institutions of public health and communities of experts that developed around them. In a pioneering epidemiological study, British physician John Snow created extensive maps of cholera cases during an 1854 outbreak in London. His mapping project led him to identify the Broad Street Pump as the source of the outbreak. With the knowledge that cholera was a water-borne illness, it soon became clear that poor and marginalized groups suffered, not because they behaved badly or were inherently susceptible, but because of poorly maintained sewage systems and water supplies. Government authorities acted to improve the decrepit infrastructures that had allowed cholera's uncontrolled spread. Cholera—and the broader relationship between infectious disease and poverty—became an indictment of society. Medical experts began to acknowledge that good health for all citizens hinged on political decisions, especially those that would alleviate conditions of poverty. As social medicine pioneer Rudolf Virchow stated in 1848, "Medicine is a social science, and politics is nothing but medicine at a larger scale" (Mackenbach, 2009, p. 181).

Meanwhile, cholera came under the jurisdiction of international systems of public health. The International Sanitary Conferences convened to create regulations for travel and quarantine, standardize prevention efforts, and share information—negotiating a balance between the needs of commerce and public health (Huber, 2006). The first conference took place in Paris in 1851, and most countries sent two delegates: a diplomat and a physician. As physicians shed new light on disease transmission, delegates favored new strategies to control cholera, including strengthened information networks, facilitated by the telegram, and the use of disinfectants on ships, over older quarantine measures that stifled trade. Even as more scientifically informed solutions came about, a Eurocentric view continued to shape the portrayal of cholera as an Asian menace, as well as to promote quarantine measures and travel restrictions that, often contemptuously, targeted Mecca pilgrims (Huber, 2006). The 14 conferences that would take place between 1851 and 1938 formed a key precedent for major global health institutions that exist today, like the WHO.

By the turn of the 20th century, public health figured prominently in Progressive Era efforts to build a more organized, rational society. A growing faith in science and statistics would guide policymaking and empower experts with solutions to some of society's greatest problems, from poverty and corruption to unsafe labor conditions and, of course, disease. In the controlled space of the laboratory, scientists proved the "germ theory"— that microorganisms caused infection—and were able to isolate microbes and to develop new vaccines, serums, and antitoxins. Germany and Japan were some of the first nations to implement compulsory vaccination laws, which soon swept across Europe and the United States as nations hoped to conquer the problem of disease. Yet such laws met with resistance, sparking new understandings of a conflict between public health and personal liberty (Willrich, 2008).

Indeed, public health breakthroughs gave rise to the antivaccination movement. In the United States, some Americans decried state intervention in people's lives as a form of "medical tyranny" (Colgrove, 2005). Antivaccinationists seeded doubt in the science and safety of vaccines, suggesting that they had not actually been responsible for public health improvements or that they caused permanent injury in children. Compulsory vaccine laws were challenged in courts around the country, one of which, *Jacobson v. Massachusetts*, reached the Supreme Court in 1905. The case involved a Massachusetts resident who refused to be vaccinated in accordance with state law. Ultimately, the Court ruled in favor of Massachusetts, deciding that the state has the authority to restrict individual behavior when the collective well-being is at stake. Yet the public debate was not resolved, with antivaccinationism persisting to this day as a powerful force against public health efforts. As of this writing, the United States has not been able to achieve herd immunity to COVID-19—despite having more than enough vaccines to inoculate the entire population—because many adults have refused to get vaccinated.

HOW NOT TO PREVENT A PANDEMIC

At the outset of the COVID-19 pandemic, the question "When will there be a vaccine?" came to occupy the minds of many. The question implies a dual assumption that a vaccine would come about relatively quickly and that it would put an end to the pandemic. That assumption is shaped by relatively recent historical developments: first, the outbreak of novel influenza viruses, some of which have produced pandemics, and second, advances in virology and vaccine production to understand and confront them.

The pandemic era we live in today began in 1918 (Morens et al., 2009). The "Spanish influenza" virus (H1N1 Influenza A) that spread across the globe that year spawned a lineage of flu viruses with varying gene structures. The 1918 virus likely had avian origins and mutated along the way. In 1918, however, little was known about the virus that would kill an estimated 50–100 million people around the world. The pandemic spread during the First World War. It got its name because Spain—neutral during the war—had reported on the epidemic in newspapers while other countries censored information that might hurt soldier morale. War allowed not only for such misconceptions to flourish, but also for influenza's sudden and rapid spread with traveling troops and in crowded army barracks. When the war ended, influenza continued its worldwide spread. Recent advances in bacteriology were of little use, as viruses largely eluded scientific observation before the invention of electron microscopes in the 1930s. A futile race for a vaccine made nonpharmaceutical interventions necessary to mitigate the impact, including the closure of schools, theaters, churches, and other crowded gathering spaces, as well as the use of face masks (Tomes, 2010).

In the decades following the Spanish flu, medical experts and political leaders promised to prevent another devastating pandemic from happening again. The League of Nations Health Organization (LNHO) was created in the wake of both a global war and a pandemic on the premise that "the prevention and control of disease" were "matters of international concern," requiring international cooperation (League of Nations, 1919, p. 11). Although the LNHO itself was short-lived, its work would continue with the creation of the WHO in 1948 in the aftermath of World War II. The WHO was bolstered by the overwhelming optimism of the postwar period in which breakthrough medical technologies, such as penicillin and insecticides, and conditions of peaceful collaboration made the goal of eradicating infectious disease from the world seem both possible and urgent.

As the WHO initiated programs for the global eradication of malaria, yaws, tuberculosis, and smallpox, it also funded the World Influenza Centre. Established in 1948, the World Influenza Centre's tasks focused on research and surveillance rather than on distributing medical resources. Scientists had begun to recognize the complexity of influenza's epidemiology and how "antigenic drifts" occurred to create new strains and new epidemics. Scientists understood that even if influenza had disappeared from one country, it was always present somewhere in the world. Closely tracking the emergence of new flu strains through a network of more than 60 watch laboratories affiliated with the WHO would allow international health workers to intervene in the chain of events that led to a pandemic (Andrewes, 1952).

As virologists made progress in understanding the nature of viruses, the prospect of a vaccine became an increasingly achievable goal. When scientist Jonas Salk developed an experimental vaccine for poliomyelitis (polio) in 1953, the widely publicized breakthrough gave him an almost celebrity status. The poliovirus had been perhaps the most dreaded virus in postwar America, causing life-threatening and disabling disease in those infected. That polio mainly affected children added to the fears of parents who did not let their toddlers play outside during the wave of outbreaks that swept the nation prior to Salk's discovery (Oshinsky, 2005). So when Salk needed to prove the vaccine's quality and safety, parents eagerly volunteered their children in field experiments. A total of 1.6 million schoolchildren enrolled in what became one of the largest clinical trials ever undertaken in American history. The vaccine was ultimately determined safe and up to 90% effective in preventing paralytic polio. A program of mass immunization followed, and annual polio cases dropped dramatically—from around 15,000 cases in the 1950s to fewer than 100 in the 1960s.

The polio vaccine's success—both as a scientific feat and as a social phenomenon—set the stage for a technical response to a new strain of influenza virus that would wash over the globe in 1957. When the "Asian influenza" (H2N2) emerged, American public health experts were, for the first time, confronted with a novel flu strain that surveillance networks had identified early enough to allow for preventive measures (Trotter et al., 1959). Virologists had developed the first flu vaccine in the 1940s, and with 15 years of trials behind them, immunization was seen as the obvious means to confront pandemic influenza. In fact, leading virologist Joseph Smadel (1958) admitted that the public's acceptance of a large-scale flu vaccination program that year might not have been possible if it were not for "the highly successful campaigns for immunization against poliomyelitis" (p. 129). Whereas the story of the polio vaccine showed how willing Americans were to place their faith in science and their trust in modern medicine, the Asian flu pandemic revealed the limited extent to which new surveillance systems, together with emerging research on viruses and vaccines, made it possible to predict and prevent a possible pandemic.

Although the World Influenza Centre had spent years building a global surveillance network, the WHO was delayed in its detection of the novel H2N2 virus. It likely originated in China's Yunnan Province in February 1957, but it took until April for the WHO to issue a pandemic alert, allowing a lapse of 2 months in which the undetected virus spread rapidly throughout Asia and the Middle East. Over the course of 1957 and 1958, H2N2 would reach nearly every part of the world, causing approximately two million deaths worldwide. In the United States, it caused 66,000 excess deaths, making it the most significant outbreak in the country since 1918.

In turn, it presented an opportunity to test new strategies for pandemic prevention. Once the threat was clearly established in April 1957, an international group of virologists mobilized to isolate the flu strain and track its spread. As soon as laboratory reports suggested that the virus had all the necessary attributes to produce a pandemic—novel antigenic structure, high transmissibility, and virulence—researchers got to work developing a vaccine. The U.S. Surgeon General, who anticipated massive epidemics in the fall and winter months, urged pharmaceutical companies to make large batches of vaccine as quickly as possible for the immunization of Americans on an unprecedented scale (Smadel, 1958).

While health officials sounded the alarm and pressured drug manufacturers to take swift action, it had been decided that there would be no federal involvement in the development and distribution of a vaccine program. As a contemporary report described, "The consensus of opinion was that governmental regulation should be avoided unless absolutely necessary and that the usual doctor–patient relationship be maintained" (Jenson et al., 1958, p. 193). Such reasoning reflected a disdain for anything that resembled "socialized medicine" during the Cold War. In this climate of anticommunist anxiety, rather than implementing a centralized vaccination program, public health authorities relied on private companies to voluntarily follow their advice. In many ways, pharmaceutical companies rose to the challenge. By June and July, companies were in the experimental phase of vaccine development, and they were able to manufacture millions of doses for use in August, September, and October. Yet, with no government subsidy, companies had to assume the financial risk that such mass production entailed. Moreover, there was no federal intervention to ensure the widespread and equitable distribution of vaccine supplies.

So even though researchers succeeded in producing a safe and effective vaccine, with short supply and a lack of government action, the vaccine was not able to stop the nationwide surge in influenza cases that came with the opening of schools in September 1957. Only seven million people had received vaccines by the time the epidemic peaked in October. In the absence of nonpharmaceutical interventions—there were no quarantine measures, no school closures, no cancelation of large gatherings—communities had little protection from the virus's rapid spread (Henderson et al., 2009). As demand for the vaccine began to outweigh the supply, companies abandoned plans to prioritize distribution to health care workers and high-risk groups. Then, by the time manufacturers were able to get the vaccine to market in bulk, the epidemic already subsided, and companies were burdened with the costs of unsold vaccines (Dehner, 2012).

Cold War geopolitics were an obstacle to rapid response, both in 1957 and again in 1968 with the virus dubbed "Hong Kong influenza" (H3N2) that caused one million deaths worldwide. Both of these flu pandemics originated in China, the world's most populous country, which had been largely cut off from global politics. Throughout the 1950s and 1960s, the United Nations (UN) refused to recognize the People's Republic of China, founded by Communist revolutionary Mao Zedong. Western countries that dominated the UN sought to limit the influence of Communist leaders, insisting that the administration of the Republic of China in Taiwan (ousted by Mao's revolution) was China's only true government. As a UN agency that relied heavily on the United States' financial and technical support, the WHO followed suit. Ultimately, Cold War ideological battles overpowered the spirit of objectivity and neutrality that scientists and international health workers so valued. With political barriers limiting the reach of the WHO's surveillance unit, delays in the detection and intervention created huge setbacks for pandemic prevention.

The flu pandemics of 1957 and 1968 showed the world the speed at which viruses could travel in the age of air travel. Vaccine programs attempted in both events were imperfect, and virologists began to doubt the financial and logistical feasibility of continually chasing a vaccine for the next new flu strain, to quickly bottle and distribute it "just in time" (Eyler, 2006). Still, many remained optimistic about the technical solutions in their arsenal. The pandemics furthered confidence in scientists' ability to isolate novel viruses and quickly develop protective vaccines. Public health officials were convinced that more research, a quicker manufacturing process, and government-led coordination would allow them to stave off the next pandemic (Dehner, 2012).

The opportunity arrived in February 1976, when the Centers for Disease Control and Prevention (CDC) learned of an influenza outbreak at Fort

Dix in New Jersey. The CDC's leadership included strong proponents of preventive medicine with a keen awareness of the failures of 1957 and 1968. Therefore, when reports from Fort Dix showed a novel flu strain had killed a healthy young man, they saw the need to act fast while the advantage was on their side. Not only had they caught the virus early—before vaccine manufacturers shut down their seasonal flu vaccine production lines in spring to await the predictions for the following year—but new production techniques allowed for even better vaccines and faster production schedules. It also helped that President Gerald Ford was up for reelection, and the imagined political damage a pandemic might cause motivated swift action. Public health officials and Washington politicians agreed that universal vaccination was needed to prevent a possible pandemic from occurring in the fall flu season, and this time, they would not rely on private enterprise to shape the response (Dehner, 2012). In March, Ford authorized the National Influenza Immunization Program, which he announced to the American public with Jonas Salk and Albert Sabin—the scientists behind the famed polio vaccine—by his side.

The program, however, ran into major problems. At the outset, critics lamented the kind of political intervention the program called for, with some advocating a military-style effort of stockpiling vaccines rather than large-scale preventive immunization (Lakoff, 2017). Then, in the summer, drug companies halted vaccine production, announcing they would not bottle the vaccine unless the government offered liability insurance against the risk of potential side effects. Congress passed legislation to indemnify companies, and distribution followed. Further problems arose as states were tasked with the rollout. A handful of states halted programs when three elderly people died shortly after receiving the vaccine. Reports of multiple cases of Guillain-Barré syndrome further amplified fears, even though no link could be established between the vaccine and this severe neurological condition. By the end of the year, around 40 million people had been immunized. However, the anticipated pandemic never came, and the program was suspended. The media would refer to the failed program as the "swine flu fiasco" (Dehner, 2012; Lakoff, 2017). The experience revealed that with no clear threat of a pandemic, the benefits of a vaccine would not be deemed worth the risks. For years to come, this dilemma—the uncertainty of risk—would continue to undermine efforts at preventing pandemics that had not yet occurred.

COVID-19 is an illustrative example of how failure to account for the possibility of a pandemic can result in tragic outcomes. Despite both Presidents George W. Bush and Barack Obama publicly warning of the possibility of a future pandemic, Congress had cut funding for pandemic preparedness by 50% between 2003 and the start of the COVID-19 pandemic (Greenberg, 2020). President Trump went even further; in 2018, his administration disbanded the Global Health Security and Biodefense unit created under President Obama, and in the following year—just 2 months before COVID-19 was first detected in China—the administration ended a pandemic early-warning program designed to train scientists around the world to respond to pandemic threats (Baumgaertner & Rainey, 2020; Reuters, 2020).

DISEASE, DENIAL, AND DISPARITY DURING A PANDEMIC

Leading global health experts would continue sounding the alarm that a catastrophic disease event—of the likes of the 1918 pandemic—was not a matter of *if*, but *when*. By the late 1980s, they described the threat of "emerging infections," such as HIV/AIDS and multidrug-resistant tuberculosis, to which the world was becoming increasingly vulnerable thanks to the economic, ecological, and political conditions of late-20th–century globalization. The early HIV/AIDS pandemic, in particular, offers a more recent context for the COVID-19 pandemic, most notably the politics of denial and the disparity of disease burden.

When the first cases of HIV/AIDS were reported in the United States in 1981, physicians labeled the disease "Gay Related Immune Disorder" as they struggled to understand the mysterious illness appearing in otherwise healthy gay men. Eventually they learned that the zoonotic disease attacked the immune systems of those infected. However, the perception that AIDS affected certain groups who were already marginalized—most glaringly, the gay community, but also intravenous drug users and Haitian immigrants—allowed for widespread denialism and delay in responding to the outbreak. President Ronald Reagan remained notoriously silent on the issue for years. He did not publicly utter the word "AIDS" until 1985, let alone fund research or health programs to mitigate the suffering of tens of thousands diagnosed with the deadly disease (Brier, 2009). The WHO began monitoring the worldwide spread of HIV/AIDS in 1985, offering guidance to developing countries that lacked the laboratory infrastructure to test HIV antibodies.

By the early 1990s, new antiretroviral drugs revolutionized AIDS treatment, transforming HIV/AIDS from a so-called "gay disease" to a disease of poverty, disproportionately impacting poorer populations around the world that cannot afford expensive antiretrovirals. New forms of activism around global health equity have called for international treaties to lower drug prices, especially as poorer countries face the uneven burden of disease—in the face of opposition from large pharmaceutical companies. Unequal access to life-saving medicines presents a central paradox in global health security: While the surveillance inputs of poor and marginalized areas are necessary in preparing for global health crises, the prevention and treatment outputs are largely distributed to powerful and wealthy countries.

The problem of how to get individuals to care about global health—enough to do something to prevent a crisis—is intimately tied to the problem of how to get care to people in an equitable fashion. When COVID-19 erupted in 2020, world leaders and public health systems found themselves tragically unprepared, even though infectious disease experts had been warning of the "next big one" for decades. Instead, this pandemic has exposed fatal flaws in our health infrastructures, from failures in testing to overcrowded hospitals and medical supply shortages. In the United States, staggering rates of COVID-19 deaths among Black, Indigenous American, and Latinx populations—more than double that of White Americans—lay bare the impact of historically rooted systemic inequalities (APM Research Lab, 2020). Moreover, as the COVID-19 pandemic recession leads to high unemployment and the loss of employer-based health insurance, the lack of a social safety net puts large swaths of the population at even greater health risk.

History can be useful in the sense that knowledge of the past can help us imagine alternative futures. COVID-19 will not be the last pandemic we see in our lifetimes—and the next one could be worse. Rather than waiting for a crisis (or conjuring a foreign threat) to mobilize resources and justify public health spending, what if, in the wake of the current pandemic, we placed a higher value on *maintaining* the well-being of our communities? That approach might mean rebuilding solidarity across political borders and embracing an outlook of welfare rather than warfare in the realm of health security (Lakoff, 2017). It might mean committing to prevention of all kinds of health problems, infectious and chronic. It must certainly involve investing in a more equitable health care system rather than mere preparedness for an as yet unknown catastrophe. Doing so may lessen the death and grief that are inherent to pandemics, the subject of the next chapter.

REFERENCES

Andrewes, C. H. (1952). The work of the World Influenza Centre. *The Journal of the Royal Institute of Public Health and Hygiene, 15*(12), 309–318.

APM Research Lab Staff. (2020). *The color of coronavirus: Covid-19 deaths by race and ethnicity in the U.S.* Author. https://www.apmresearchlab.org/covid/deaths-by-race

Baumgaertner, E., & Rainey, J. (2020, April 2). Trump administration fired entire pandemic response team in 2018. *Los Angeles Times.* https://www.latimes.com/science/story/2020-04-02/coronavirus-trump-pandemic-program-viruses-detection

Brier, J. (2009). *Infectious ideas: US political responses to the AIDS crisis.* University of North Carolina Press.

Cohen, E. (2009). *A body worth defending: Immunity, biopolitics, and the apotheosis of the modern body.* Duke University Press.

Colgrove, J. (2005). "Science in a democracy": The contested status of vaccination in the Progressive Era and the 1920s. *Isis, 96*(2), 167–191. https://doi.org/10.1086/431531

Crosby, A. W. (1972). *The Columbian exchange: Biological and cultural consequences of 1492.* Greenwood Publishing.

Dehner, G. (2012). *Influenza: A century of science and public health response.* University of Pittsburgh Press.

Eyler, J. M. (2006). De Kruif's boast: Vaccine trials and the construction of a virus. *Bulletin of the History of Medicine, 80*(3), 409–38. https://doi.org/10.1353/bhm.2006.0092

Greenberg, J. (2020, March 30). *Federal pandemic money fell for years. Trump's budget didn't help.* Politifact. https://www.politifact.com/article/2020/mar/30/federal-pandemic-money-fell-years-trumps-budgets-d/

Henderson, D. A., Brooke, C., Inglesby, T. V., Toner, E., & Nuzzo, J. B. (2009). Public health and medical responses to the 1957–58 influenza pandemic. *Biosecurity and Bioterrorism: Biodefense Strategy, Practice, and Science, 7*(3), 265–273. https://doi.org/10.1089/bsp.2009.0729

Huber, V. (2006). The unification of the globe by disease? The International Sanitary Conferences on cholera, 1851–1894. *The Historical Journal, 49*(2), 453–476. https://doi.org/10.1017/S0018246X06005280

Jenson, K. E., Dunn, F. L., & Robinson, R. Q. (1958). Influenza, 1957: A variant and the pandemic. *Progress in Medical Virology, 1,* 165–209.

Lakoff, A. (2017). *Unprepared: Global health in a time of emergency.* University of California Press.

League of Nations. (1919). *Covenant of the League of Nations.* Author. https://www.refworld.org/docid/3dd8b9854.html

Mackenbach, J. P. (2009). Politics is nothing but medicine at a larger scale: Reflections on public health's biggest idea. *Journal of Epidemiology and Community Health 63*(3), 181–184. https://doi.org/10.1136/jech.2008.077032

Mather, C. (1972). *Angel of Bethesda* (G. W. Jones, Ed.). American Antiquarian Society and Barre Publishers.

Minardi, M. (2004). The Boston inoculation controversy of 1721–1722: An incident in the history of race. *The William and Mary Quarterly, 61*(1), 47–76.

Morens, D. M., Taubenberger, J. K., & Fauci, A. S. (2009). The persistent legacy of the 1918 influenza virus. *New England Journal of Medicine, 361*(3), 225–229. https://doi.org/10.1056/NEJMp0904819

Orent, W. (2004). *Plague: The mysterious past and terrifying future of the world's most dangerous disease.* Free Press.

Oshinsky, D. M. (2005). *Polio: An American story.* Oxford University Press.

Palmer, J. (2020, January 27). Don't blame bat soup for the coronavirus. *Foreign Policy.* https://foreignpolicy.com/2020/01/27/coronavirus-covid19-dont-blame-bat-soup-for-the-virus/

Quammen, D. (2012). *Spillover: Animal infections and the next human pandemic.* W. W. Norton & Company.

Reuters. (2020, March 25). *Partly false claim: Trump fired entire pandemic response team in 2018.* Author. https://www.reuters.com/article/uk-factcheck-trump-fired-pandemic-team/partly-false-claim-trump-fired-entire-pandemic-response-team-in-2018-idUSKBN21C32M

Rosenberg, C. E. (1987). *The cholera years: The United States in 1832, 1849, and 1866.* University of Chicago Press.

Smadel, J. (1958). Influenza vaccine. *Public Health Reports, 73*(2), 129–132.

Snowden, F. M. (2019). *Epidemics and society: From the Black Death to the present.* Yale University Press.

Tomes, N. (2010). "Destroyer and teacher": Managing the masses during the 1918–1919 influenza pandemic. *Public Health Reports, 125*(3), 48–62.

Trotter Jr., Y., Dunn, F. L., Drachman, R. H., Henderson, D. A., Pizzi, M., & Langmuir, A. D. (1959). Asian influenza in the United States, 1957–1958. *American Journal of Hygiene, 70*(1), 34–50.

Willrich, M. (2008). "The least vaccinated of any civilized country": Personal liberty and public health in the Progressive Era. *Journal of Policy History, 20*(1), 76–93. https://doi.org/10.1353/jph.0.0003

World Health Organization (2020, February 11). *Coronavirus press conference.* Author. https://www.who.int/docs/default-source/coronaviruse/transcripts/who-audio-emergencies-coronavirus-full-press-conference-11feb2020-final.pdf?sfvrsn=e2019136_2

CHAPTER 2

Situating COVID-19 Within the Context of Death and Grief

Rebecca C. Christ, Bretton A. Varga,
Mark E. Helmsing, and Cathryn van Kessel

During a social studies methods course in the fall semester of 2020, undergraduate students were given (virtual) class time to engage with the various ways grief—stemming from COVID-19 and the global pandemic—has impacted their lives. While most students expressed feeling a deep/heavy sense of loss (i.e., grief) about specific aspects of life (e.g., canceling travel plans, reimagining of social life, rescheduling of major life occurrences), for some, grief included the death of a pet, a family member, or a friend. As the conversation unfolded, intersections of grief, death, and social studies began to reveal themselves. Specifically, students began to discuss the roles that subjectivities (e.g., religious affiliations, cultural worldviews, political orientations) and identity markers (e.g., heritage, sexuality, gender) play in how people process grief and make sense of death (Cline, 1997). One student noted that all cultures have their own way of dealing with death, and another expressed how women oftentimes shoulder the burden of navigating a family through grief. Grief and death[1] proved to be generative in pushing students' thinking beyond their personal experiences toward the consideration of grief and death as intricate concepts that cultivate a range of thoughts, emotions, and (re)actions. This position is particularly important given that we live "in a grief-phobic and death-denying society" (Weller, 2015, p. xvii).

Grief and death are often unspoken in educational spaces (e.g., Stylianou & Zembylas, 2021). Notwithstanding how social studies, as a discipline, is replete with death (Helmsing & van Kessel, 2020), educators frequently circumvent direct acknowledgment or engagement with grief and death beyond the inclusion of long-deceased historical figures, ancient spiritual practices, and encounters in which death (indirectly) takes center stage, such as in lessons on war, assassinations, or genocide (Caswell, 2010; Mellor, 1993). In this way, death—with its perpetual companion, grief—is flattened and reduced to a passive aspect of both historical and contemporary inquiry. All too often, death and grief remain muted in class conversations, mirroring its avoidance in our institutions and broader society. With this in mind, we ask: How may teachers confront grief and death with their students in relation to COVID-19 (and beyond)? How might social studies help students develop a complex understanding of grief and death that could be productive in fostering connectivity and impact (future) death-related decisions?

As the relationship between grief and death is perplexingly complicated and entangled, we do not provide a pedagogical checklist for addressing it. Rather, we are interested in maneuvering grief and death away from their current banal positioning and into an active condition of/within social studies education. To do this, we introduce *mortality salience* (Pyszczynski et al., 2015) and Butler's (2009) concept of *grievability* as theoretical perspectives for teachers' and students' experiences and understandings relating to grief and death. Following these theoretical positionings, we briefly situate the ethicalities of teaching about grief and death in K–12 social studies, as well as social studies teacher education, before providing examples of death and grief in student learning within the context of COVID-19 and beyond.

We view this chapter as an invitation for educators to engage with mortality salience and grievability in ways that challenge the curricular/pedagogical positionality and possibilities of grief and death. We acknowledge that engaging with grief and death can be difficult for students and teachers, especially as teachers may wish to avoid the unpredictable dialogic space in classrooms that may be the result from such conversations. However, we believe that by confronting death and grief, teachers will foster communities and territories of healing, understanding, empathy, compassion, and respect. Moreover, we are of shared mind that such a pivot will help teachers cultivate a nuanced perspective toward grief and death that supports students in confronting the inescapability of both death and grieving over loss.

CONCEPTS TO THINK ABOUT DEATH AND GRIEF WITH(IN) SOCIAL STUDIES

COVID-19 has made people grieve things they never thought they could lose (e.g., in-person graduations, hugs, and haircuts) as well as things they continue to anticipate losing (e.g., future holiday gatherings, vacations, and face-to-face meetings). Additionally, COVID-19 requires considering alternative and restrictive grieving practices (e.g., virtual funerals) while simultaneously compelling individuals to (re)think and (re)consider *how* grief can be confronted. Providing adequate educational space and time for students to process grief will be an essential component of any teaching praxis post–COVID-19. How might educators become attuned to noticing when death and associated grief come up in their classrooms?

Mortality Salience

One way is for educators to consider insights about mortality salience (the state of having death on our minds) from *terror management theory* (TMT) about the subtle and overt ways people can react when death is a classroom topic or murmuring in the background (Burke et al., 2010). The "terror" in TMT is the existential anxiety humans feel about their mortality because we (humans) have the ability to imagine our eventual death even in the absence of an imminent threat, an ability that can trigger unhelpful, or even destructive, tendencies: "The irony of man's [sic] condition is that the deepest need is to be free of the anxiety of death and annihilation; but it is life itself which awakens it, and so we must shrink from being fully alive" (Becker, 1973, p. 66). In the context of COVID-19, such tendencies can include hoarding scarce resources, clinging to unproven (or even dangerous) miracle cures, denying risk and behaving recklessly (e.g., gathering in large numbers without a mask), and increased stereotypic thinking and discriminatory actions (see Menzies et al., 2020).

TMT was developed to test the conceptual work of anthropologist Ernest Becker (1973, 1975; Greenberg et al., 1986), particularly his identification of death anxiety as a significant root of human action. If humans were to experience unmitigated existential anxiety, it would interfere with many effective forms of thought and action, so they developed a defensive psychological system to keep thoughts of human mortality away from their consciousness (Solomon et al., 2015). Over the last 30 years, there have been over 500 experiments in countries with divergent cultural belief systems, testing three main hypotheses regarding mortality salience, death-thought accessibility, and anxiety-buffering (Pyszczynski et al., 2015; Schimel et al., 2018).

The various effects of mortality salience are of particular interest to the context of this chapter. The mortality salience hypothesis posits that reminding people of death temporarily increases their need for protective psychological structures that provide feelings of meaning and permanence, such as self-esteem and a consistent worldview (Burke et al., 2010). Mortality salience manipulations usually involve priming participants with either the idea of death or a control topic that also evokes anxiety and discomfort (e.g., dental pain, social exclusion, uncertainty) and then observing the effects. These mortality salience primes can be an overt reminder (e.g., writing about death), something subtler (e.g., being interviewed in front of a funeral parlor), or even a subliminal message (e.g., the word "death" quickly flashed on a computer screen) (Pyszczynski et al., 2015).

These experiments have revealed that mortality salience can affect individuals in a variety of ways, some logical, but some not. People might (ironically) behave in ways that put them in more danger, such as driving recklessly when their self-esteem is tied to driving (Taubman-Ben Ari & Findler, 2010). Another possible effect is that individuals might place more value on the physicality of sexual activity instead of their personal connection with the person with whom they are experiencing the physical act because of their body-centered sense of self-esteem (Goldenberg et al., 2000). People might adhere more rigidly to their worldviews, becoming more intolerant of other views in subtle ways (e.g., decreased reading comprehension; Williams et al., 2012) or in more directly observable ways such as increased support for prejudicial views articulated by those like them (Greenberg et al., 2001) and antagonism toward others (Fa & Kugihara, 2020). Not all reactions are deleterious, thankfully: Individuals might do such things as take better care of their health and form meaningful and supportive personal and community connections (Vail et al., 2012).

Death anxiety impacts health-related decision-making (Arndt & Goldenberg, 2017), and major health concerns, like a pandemic, provoke such anxieties directly (e.g., the deaths of friends and colleagues) and indirectly (e.g., through media coverage). According to psychologist Rachel Menzies and colleagues, the COVID-19 pandemic negatively impacts people's abilities to confront and process grief. Death anxiety can negatively impact mental health, death-related losses are exacerbated by other losses (e.g., financial) that also impact mental health, common "attachment buffers" are limited by social distancing, and death from COVID-19 challenges aspects of the world linked to self-efficacy and a sense of fairness (Menzies et al., 2020, p. 112).

Because conscious and unconscious fears of death (i.e., mortality salience) affect behavior, being in a situation where individuals are constantly reminded of their bodies' vulnerability to disease and death—currently, the COVID-19 pandemic (Greenberg & Solomon, 2020)—will affect any lesson during or about such a situation. Teachers may lose the content in their curriculum-as-planned to the effects of mortality salience that can shape the curriculum-as-lived (Aoki, 1991/2005). As social studies scholar Jim Garrett (2020) aptly stated: "When significant upheaval occurs, there will be an equally significant demand placed on the capacity for individuals to accommodate it, and much of that demand is best understood as an emotional one" (p. 353). TMT tells educators that they need to be aware of harmful effects of mortality salience and work to prevent or thwart them while encouraging more positive trajectories to cope with death anxiety, particularly when teaching about topics in which death is prominent. To work toward this end, pairing TMT with other concepts can be helpful for developing a more complete understanding of death as a form of difficult knowledge (e.g., radical love, see van Kessel & Saleh, 2020).

Grievability

Political philosopher and critical theorist Judith Butler has helped shape conversations about death and loss through the theoretical concept of grievability (2004a, 2004b, 2009, 2020). Social studies educators can use Butler's perspectives when considering how to create spaces to better allow for grief in their classrooms. In order to consider how grievability may play out in classrooms, we first need to follow how Butler explains what affects grieving over the loss of others. Butler's theory helps consider how social forces allow some to grieve more than others while, at the same time, making some lives worthier of grief over others. Butler's ideas of precarity and grievability enable educators to see which lives are valued through their grievability and which lives are valued less, as grief over their loss may be marginalized or ignored altogether.

First, Butler noted that humans are interdependent upon each other. This interdependence makes individuals vulnerable to the actions and attitudes of others, as some people may cause harm, distress, and injury while others provide help through access and assistance to shelter, food, and other resources. For Butler, the "precariousness" of all life means that humans are vulnerable and our lives are subject to change in an instant as a result of forces and people external to ourselves.

Second, Butler stressed how the precariousness for humans (and, we would argue, also nonhumans) is not always equally and universally the same. The precariousness of a person's life may make them more vulnerable through experiences of poverty, abuse, and food and home insecurity—conditions exacerbated through human-made catastrophe such as climate change, war, genocide, forced migration, and other forms of what may be called humanitarian and planetary crises. For example, different societies value some lives over others as observed through enactments of violence, which come in obvious forms like in war and genocide, as well as in subtler forms of intersecting structural violence made evident in unequal access to resources, health, and a standard quality of life. Students are no exception to this witnessing, as they see both contemporary and historical instances of precarity daily in news stories and in social studies curriculum.

Many of the lives Butler wrote about are victims, perpetrators, and bystanders of war. These examples foreground how society, governments, and mass media (such as nightly televised news programs) prominently uphold which lives are deemed worthy of grieving (e.g., often soldiers, but not innocent civilians murdered during global conflict). Although our context in this chapter is about the loss of life through a pandemic and not through a war, we urge social studies educators to follow Butler's thinking and challenge how society determines which lives matter more than others in public and pedagogical spaces.

DISCUSSING DEATH AND GRIEF WITH(IN) SOCIAL STUDIES

As a discipline, social studies is teeming with opportunities for teachers and students to engage with the pain of others (e.g., genocide and Holocaust education, engagements with war and coloniality [Mignolo, 2007]) and to interrogate the conditions seeking to undermine the idea that *all* life—and *everything* for that matter—is grievable. Being in a state of mortality salience and grieving from loss (of life) plays an integral role in how humans relate to/with with each other and make sense of the world. By embracing Butler's (2004b) position that grief helps illustrate "the thrall in which our relations hold us" (p. 23), social studies educators can begin to consider how these relations are constructed in their teaching and learning. Moreover, as Hartman (1997) suggested, "pain provides the common language of humanity; it extends humanity to the dispossessed and, in turn, remedies the indifference of the callous" (p. 18). (Re)positioning grief and death in this way unflattens both concepts and reminds us (e.g., teachers, students, and researchers) that there is a tenuousness to the physical and social worlds and that these worlds are experienced, navigated, and commemorated in different ways.

Although there are innumerable conceptualizations of death, we frame this chapter around death being defined as the irrevocable cessation of all somatic/structural functions within an organism (Lamb, 1994; Rosenberg, 1983). Death as a concept (and as a reality/inevitability) is intrinsically contained within the context of COVID-19—inside and outside of our social studies classrooms. An Emergency Medical Technician who loaded corpses onto refrigerated trucks in New York characterized a feeling of grief in which he was submerged each day at work during the first wave of the pandemic, claiming "you didn't really have time to think about it" (Bracken & Rhyne, 2020). Educators must be careful not to create glib lesson plans from the pain and suffering of others that "predict or prescribe what will be done with that learning" (Garrett, 2017, p. 28).

This task, however, is not an easy one. Teaching about a pandemic can be emotionally charged and requires educators to consider their pedagogical decisions in light of mortality salience and worldview threat (van Kessel et al., 2020). So teachers can consider pedagogical ethics alongside educators and scholars who specialize in teaching other traumatic events, such as the Holocaust and genocide. Of course, each person's relationship with the event featuring loss and its effects is different, but it is suggested that "educators approach the Holocaust without repressing grief and suffering, although traces of repression will always already affect our work" (Morris, 2001, p. 11); we find the same considerations helpful while teaching about COVID-19.

Teachers are faced with a myriad of logistical and ethical decisions daily, and they may be facing their own grief and/or attempting to mitigate the effects of their own mortality salience. Therefore, one precondition to teaching any lesson about COVID-19 (or perhaps any lesson in social studies) is recognizing the powerful cognitive effects and bodily affects that death and grief have on students, teachers, and the learning environment. We describe in more detail below a few examples of social studies content related to death and grief with connections to COVID-19—as well as with content beyond COVID-19—to help demonstrate the infinite reach of grief and death.

Death and Grief in Media

Because so much of students' understanding of the world comes to be known through technology and media platforms, social studies also has an obligation to address media literacy, especially in teaching students how to navigate the changing platforms, as well as how to process the speed and abundance of information to which they have access (National Council for the Social Studies [NCSS], 2016). As such, we need to consider media literacy as a way to "teach our students to read and write their worlds" (NCSS, 2016, p. 185). Because death, in the form of the corpse, appears repeatedly in the media (Braidotti, 2013), media (including both news and pop culture) plays an important role in how students conceive of and process death and grief.

Death-related media saturates news stories of COVID-19, featuring images of bodies on ventilators in hospitals, mass graves, and corpses awaiting overflowing morgues. Because "much of our ability to remember depends on images" and "collectively held images thus act as signposts, directing people who remember to preferred meaning by the fastest route" (Zelizer, 1998, pp. 5 & 7), one may then say that people (re)experience COVID-19 through the media; therefore, these images are not to be taken lightly. Educators should help students critically interpret the discourse used for framing in related news stories, such as the rhetorical construct of "killing grandma" by which politicians, pundits, and analysts have suggested an acceptable number of deaths of elderly persons as symbolically sacrificial to ensure economic distress does not deepen (Gandy, 2020; Kost, 2020). Thus, educators should also consider what media they are utilizing in their classrooms in the teaching of COVID-19.

Taking time and care to consider what media teachers are having their students consume should not be done solely in relation to COVID-19, but for all social studies content. For example, Lindquist (2006) advocated for the sparse sharing of graphic images within lessons of the Holocaust and that "careful consideration" should be given to "students' emotional and intellectual maturity" before utilizing any graphic imagery (p. 219). We also have to recognize that most of the photographs we have of Nazi concentration camps were taken by the Nazis themselves for record-keeping and propaganda purposes (Zelizer, 1998). Educators can interrogate these photographs with students, asking them to consider if knowing the origins of an image changes or shifts its meaning or its power over (their) collective memory. Being aware how different media portray death and grief can help educators be more attentive to the past, as well as in the current moment.

Thus, we need to interrogate the role that media plays, not only in our knowledge of COVID-19 and historical (and current) events, but also in our conceptualizations of death and grief by raising questions, such as the one Zelizer (1998) asked: "How have these earlier images changed the way in which we 'see' each new instance of politically sanctioned death and slaughter?" (p. 13).

Death and Grief in Climate Crises

Social studies also places emphasis on "the study of people, places, and environments [which] enables us to understand the relationship between human populations and the physical world . . . This enables them [students] to acquire a useful basis of knowledge for informed decision-making on issues arising from human–environmental relationships" (NCSS, 2008, para. 8). Part of that relationship between humans and the environment/Earth includes death and grief, especially when considering climate change and climate crisis.

The relationship that humans had with their immediate (and extended) environment shifted—in some cases, dramatically—at the beginning of the COVID-19 pandemic. Many countries (and different U.S. states) instituted restrictions on travel, "safer at home" initiatives, and/or varied levels of lockdown. Once humans stayed inside, talk of "nature coming back" began, providing hope in a sea of grief and death. Yet due, in part, to mortality salience, during the early stages of the pandemic, many were quick to accept this information uncritically; people tend to accept worldview-confirming information (and equally swift to reject disconfirming information; Williams et al., 2012). While many of these reports have been debunked (e.g., Daly, 2020), it is undeniable that lockdown had an effect on Earth and the human and nonhuman beings on it; environmental researchers Tanjena Rume and S. M. Didar-UI Islam (2020) outlined some positive impacts (e.g., reduced water and air pollution, reduced noise pollution), as well as negative environmental impacts (e.g., increased biomedical and municipal waste, reduced recycling) that have come from changes in human behavior due to COVID-19. These negative effects, in particular, impact living beings' abilities to thrive and/or live on Earth—for example, wildlife may ingest or get caught in the discarded disposable masks containing plastic (e.g., Parkinson, 2020). Thus, COVID-19 provides educators an opportunity to interrogate the relationship that humans have with the environment and nonhuman beings on Earth, which may result in increased exposure to death and grief, revealing "the undeniable reality of our bond with the world" (Weller, 2015, p. 8).

Beyond COVID-19, people individually and collectively are affected emotionally by climate change in states of climate grief (e.g., Scher, 2018). As Weller (2015) argued,

> it is our job to openly grieve for the disappearance of wetlands, the destruction of forests, the shrinking whale populations, the erosion of soil, and on and on. We know the litany of loss, but we have collectively neglected our emotional response to this emptying of our world. (p. 114; see also Mas, this volume)

To this point, we call upon social studies (teacher) educators to teach our students (and/or themselves) to grieve environmental, water, fauna, and flora losses as well as to *grieve with* and *stand up with* Indigenous and environmental movements/protests (i.e., #IdleNoMore, #NoDAPL, etc.), especially considering how capitalist, neoliberal, and/or colonial orientations threaten and/or harm delicate ecologies (and sacred sites).

Entwined relationships between human and nonhuman entities on the planet that can evoke grief, although perhaps exacerbated during the time of COVID-19, are omnipresent. Given this situation, it is vital for social studies educators to consider these issues in light of mortality salience and grievability: How are people coming to know and trying to understand the climate crisis situation, and how might we understand layers of (potential) grief when they allow ourselves to recognize all that could be grieved?

CONCLUSION

Through a stream of tears, a preservice teacher thanks her peers and the professor at the conclusion of the grief-related class conversation. Through direct discourse with grief and death, preservice teachers undeniably were able to begin the process of healing. Despite the need for more research into whether this introspection will manifest into classroom practices, we remain optimistic and hopeful that engaging with grief and death will be generative and help prepare students civically.

Recently, we were taken aback by the way an article in a prominent journal began by discussing COVID-19–related deaths and then failed to confront how those deaths impact the landscape of educational research(ers). While we appreciate the wink to death, unfortunately, we see this prevailing—and problematic—casual positioning of death to be another missed opportunity to directly confront and engage with the inevitability of grief and death. In this chapter (and beyond), we resist the "two primary sins of Western civilization: *amnesia* and *anesthesia*—[where] we forget and we go numb" (Weller, 2015, p. xx). When we began working on this chapter, the death toll from COVID-19 in the United States was around 200,000, but by the time we finished the chapter, this number had grown to over 700,000, showing the rapid mass loss of life during the pandemic. Accordingly, we are of the collective positionality that educators must directly initiate conversations with students about the ways in which grief and death have impacted their own unique and intersectional experiences during the global pandemic. Perhaps then, students will be primed to reflect on this current epoch before making connections to the ubiquity associated with grief and death within the context of historical/contemporary inquiry.

NOTE

1. Throughout this chapter, we purposefully vary the order of *grief* and *death* to remind readers that, while they are often connected, grief is not experienced solely as a result of death.

REFERENCES

Aoki, T. T. (2005). Teaching as indwelling between two curriculum worlds. In W. Pinar & R. Irwin (Eds.), *Curriculum in a new key: The collected works of Ted T. Aoki* (pp. 159–165). Lawrence Erlbaum. (Original work published 1991)

Arndt, J., & Goldenberg, J. L. (2017). Where health and death intersect: Insights from a terror management health model. *Current Directions in Psychological Science, 26*(2), 126–131. https://www.doi.org/10.1177/0963721416689563

Becker, E. (1973). *The denial of death.* Free Press.

Becker, E. (1975). *Escape from evil.* Free Press.

Bracken, K., & Rhyne, E. (2020, May 22). 'Lord have mercy': Inside one of New York's deadliest ZIP codes. *The New York Times.* https://www.nytimes.com/video/us/100000007097093/coronavirus-st-johns-hospital-far-rockaway.html?referringSource=articleShare&fbclid=IwAR2dcHWQSFKhjVHyTXwXNi-1bOhZxgkQLPI_jpBGdthrJs3zKhyMTTGMO-3I

Braidotti, R. (2013). *The posthuman.* Polity Press.

Burke, B. L., Martens, A., & Faucher, E. H. (2010). Two decades of terror management theory: A meta-analysis of mortality salience research. *Personality and Social Psychology Review, 14*(2), 155–195. https://doi.org/10.1177/1088868309352321

Butler, J. (2004a). *Undoing gender.* Routledge.

Butler, J. (2004b). *Precarious life: The powers of mourning and violence.* Verso.

Butler, J. (2009). *Frames of war: When is life grievable?* Verso.

Butler, J. (2020). *The force of nonviolence: An ethico-political bind.* Verso.

Caswell, G. (2010). Teaching death studies: Reflections from the classroom. *Enhancing Learning in the Social Sciences, 2*(3), 1–11. https://doi.org/10.11120/elss.2010.02030009

Cline, S. (1997). *Lifting the taboo: Women, death, and dying.* New York University Press.

Daly, N. (2020, March 20). *Fake animal news abounds on social media as coronavirus upends life*. National Geographic. https://www.nationalgeographic.com/animals/2020/03/coronavirus-pandemic-fake-animal-viral-social-media-posts/

Fa, H., & Kugihara, N. (2020). How collective and personal mortality salience impacts antagonism against worldview-threatening others. *Death Studies*. Advanced online publication. https://doi.org/10.1080/07481187.2020.1796842

Gandy, I. (2020, May 25). *Texas' COVID-19 response: Ban abortion, kill grandma*. Rewire News. https://rewire.news/ablc/2020/03/25/texas-covid-19-response-ban-abortion-kill-grandma/

Garrett, H. J. (2017). *Learning to be in the world with others: Difficult knowledge and social studies education*. Peter Lang.

Garrett, H. J. (2020). Containing classroom discussions of current social and political issues. *Journal of Curriculum Studies, 52*(3), 337–355. https://doi.org/10.1080/00220272.2020.1727020

Goldenberg, J. L., McCoy, S. K, Pyszczynski, T., Greenberg, J., & Solomon, S. (2000). The body as a source of self-esteem: The effect of mortality salience on identification with one's body, interest in sex, and appearance monitoring. *Journal of Personality and Social Psychology, 79*(1), 118–130. https://doi.org/10.1037//0022-3514.79.1.118

Greenberg, J., Pyszczynski, T., & Solomon, S. (1986). The causes and consequences of a need for self-esteem: A terror management theory. In R. F. Baumeister (Ed.), *Public self and private self* (pp. 189–212). Springer-Verlag.

Greenberg, J., Schimel, J., Martens, A., Solomon, S., & Pyszczynski, T. (2001). Sympathy for the devil: Evidence that reminding whites of their mortality promotes more favorable reactions to white racists. *Motivation and Emotion, 25*, 113–133. https://www.doi.org/10.1023/A:1010613909207

Greenberg, J., & Solomon, S. (2020, May 21). Coronavirus reminds you of death—and amplifies your core values, both bad and good. *The Conversation*. https://theconversation.com/coronavirus-reminds-you-of-death-and-amplifies-your-core-values-both-bad-and-good-137588

Hartman, S. V. (1997). *Scenes of subjection: Terror, slavery, and self-making in 19th century America*. Oxford University Press.

Helmsing, M. E., & van Kessel, C. (2020). Critical corpse studies: Engaging with death and corporeality in curriculum. *Taboo: Journal of Culture and Education, 19*(3), 140–164.

Kost, R. (2020, May 19). 'Age is a sloppy proxy': Older adults push back on idea that staying safe from coronavirus means staying isolated. *San Francisco Chronicle*. https://www.sfchronicle.com/bayarea/article/Age-is-a-sloppy-proxy-Older-adults-push-15278933.php

Lamb, D. (1994). What is death? In R. Gillon (Ed.), *Principles of health care ethics* (pp. 1027–40). Wiley.

Lindquist, D. (2006). Guidelines for teaching the Holocaust: Avoiding common pedagogical errors. *The Social Studies, 97*(5), 215–221. https://doi.org/10.3200/TSSS.97.5.215-221

Mellor, P. (1993). Death in high modernity: The contemporary presence and absence of death. In D. Clark (Ed.), *The sociology of death* (pp. 11–30). Blackwell.

Menzies, R. E., Neimeyer, R. A., & Menzies, R. G. (2020). Death anxiety, loss, and grief in the time of Covid-19. *Behaviour Change, 37*(3), 111–115. https://www.doi.org/10.1017/bec.2020.10

Mignolo, W. D. (2007). Delinking: The rhetoric of modernity, the logic of coloniality, and the grammar of de-coloniality. *Cultural Studies, 21*(2-3), 449–514. https://doi.org/10.1080/09502380601162647

Morris, M. (2001). *Curriculum and the Holocaust: Competing sites of memory and representation*. Lawrence Erlbaum Associates.

National Council for the Social Studies. (2008). *National curriculum standards for the social studies: A framework for teaching, learning, and assessment*. Author. https://www.socialstudies.org/standards/national-curriculum-standards-social-studies

National Council for the Social Studies. (2016). Media literacy. *Social Education, 80*(3), 183-185.

Parkinson, J. (2020, September 13). *Coronavirus: Disposable masks 'causing enormous plastic waste.'* BBC. https://www.bbc.com/news/uk-politics-54057799

Pyszczynski, T., Solomon, S., & Greenberg, J. (2015). Thirty years of terror management theory: From genesis to revelation. *Advances in Experimental Social Psychology, 52*, 1–70. https://doi.org/10.1016/bs.aesp.2015.03.001

Rosenberg, J. (1983). *Thinking clearly about death*. Prentice Hall.

Rume, T., & Islam, S. M. D-U. (2020). Environmental effects of COVID-19 pandemic and potential strategies of sustainability. *Heliyon, 6*, 1–8. https://doi.org/10.1016/j.heliyon.2020.e04965

Schimel, J., Hayes, J., & Sharp, M. (2018). A consideration of three critical hypotheses. In C. Routledge & M. Vess (Eds.), *The handbook of terror management theory* (pp. 1–25). Academic Press.

Scher, A. (2018, December 24). *'Climate grief': The growing emotional toll of climate change*. NBC News. https://www.nbcnews.com/health/mental-health/climate-grief-growing-emotional-toll-climate-change-n946751

Solomon, S., Greenberg, J., & Pyszczynski, T. (2015). *The worm at the core: On the role of death in life*. Random House.

Stylianou, P., & Zembylas, M. (2021) Engaging with issues of death, loss, and grief in elementary school: Teachers' perceptions and affective experiences of an in-service training program on death education in Cyprus. *Theory & Research in Social Education, 49*(1), 54–77. https://doi.org/10.1080/00933104.2020.1841700

Taubman Ben-Ari., O., & Findler, L. (2010). Reckless driving and gender: An examination of a terror management theory explanation. *Death Studies, 27*(7), 603–618. https://doi.org/10.1080/07481180302898

Vail, K. E., Juhl, J., Arndt, J., Vess, M., Routledge, C., & Rutjens, B. (2012). When death is good for life: Considering the positive trajectories of terror management. *Personality and Social Psychology Review, 16*(4), 303–329. https://doi.org/10.1177/1088868312440046

van Kessel, C., den Heyer, K., & Schimel, J. (2020). Terror management theory and the educational situation. *Journal of Curriculum Studies, 52*(3), 428–442. https://doi.org/10.1080/00220272.2019.1659416

van Kessel, C., & Saleh, M. (2020). Fighting the plague: "Difficult" knowledge as sirens' song in teacher education. *Journal of Curriculum Studies Research, 2*(2), 1–20.

Weller, F. (2015). *The wild edge of sorrow: Rituals of renewal and the sacred work of grief.* North Atlantic Books.

Williams, T. J., Schimel, J., Hayes, J., & Faucher, E. H. (2012). The effects of existential threat on reading comprehension of worldview affirming and disconfirming information. *European Journal of Social Psychology, 42*(5), 602–616. www.doi.org/10.1002/ejsp.1849

Zelizer, B. (1998). *Remembering to forget: Holocaust memory through the camera's eye.* University of Chicago Press.

CHAPTER 3

How Should We Remember COVID-19?

Designing Inquiry for Social–Emotional Learning

Carly Muetterties and Holly Wright

Political scientist Miranda Yaver tweeted in May 2020: "You know, I always wanted to know what it would be like to simultaneously experience the Spanish Flu, Great Depression, and 1968 mass protests while Andrew Johnson was president." Thousands of people shared her tweet, not only because it reflected a comedic exaggeration, but also because of how well it captured the current moment. These notable historical events, separated by decades, had distinct parallel events in the first several months of 2020.

In 2020 or otherwise, students' lived experiences can contain decades' worth of history. As educators, we recognize our responsibility to embrace our students' whole selves—harnessing their assets and building the agency they need to address the challenges before them. The consequences of 2020 events are widespread. Students need systems, structures, and content to process these events in the context of their local and global communities. The ongoing protests in response to systemic racial disparities, coupled with the far-reaching implications of COVID-19, highlight the weaknesses in various social, economic, and political systems. While students need a structured opportunity to process recent history, our work also acknowledges students' own transformative, if not traumatic, experiences of 2020. This historical moment requires educators to address students' wellness, fully incorporating physical, social, emotional, mental, and academic needs.

The pandemic and resulting impacts on our diverse student populations inspired us to consider how to better construct social–emotional learning (SEL) opportunities in academic pursuits. We cast a critical eye on our own curriculum and instructional design processes to consider the ways in which curriculum can address the needs of students. Centering on COVID-19 and 2020 events, we designed projects to help students grapple with their own experiences as they return to school. Grounded in project-based learning

(Larmer et al., 2015), inquiry pedagogy (Grant et al., 2017), and social–emotional learning needs (Farrington et al., 2012; Stafford-Brizard, 2016), this chapter explicates the design and development of a "Re-Launch" inquiry project to support students' return to in-person learning in a COVID-19 world.[1] Through an inquiry process, students develop content knowledge around COVID-19 using an increasingly complex analytical lens. Complementing this process are social–emotional learning principles, represented in the Summit Learning program's "Habits of Success." Based upon the *Building Blocks for Learning* framework (Stafford-Brizard, 2016), the Habits of Success reflect a framework to address students' social–emotional skill development.

The Re-Launch project uses project-based learning elements, with the *C3 Framework* and Inquiry Design Model (IDM) as the design structure (Grant et al., 2017; Larmer, 2018; National Council for the Social Studies, 2013). Framed by the compelling question *How should we remember COVID-19?*, students' inquiry investigations reflect a balance of social studies disciplinary content and skills, as well as students' experiences, highlighting the social–emotional strengths and growth edges of students. Students progress through a series of supporting questions and formative performance tasks. They reflect on their experiences in a supportive environment, connecting their personal experiences to the larger 2020 and COVID-19 context. The project centers on the identification of an artifact that represents the historic era and the realities of living through a pandemic. Based on students' interests (or needs), teachers can provide students the opportunity to build connections and share with their classmates through a class museum.

Though COVID-19, 2020 events, and students' related experiences are the focus of the project, this chapter demonstrates how learning experiences grounded in disciplinary content can intentionally incorporate students' lived experiences and social–emotional learning. To these ends, educators can consider students' specific needs to prepare them to connect classroom learning to the real world.

THE ACADEMICS OF SOCIAL-EMOTIONAL LEARNING

As educators seek to teach in a context where students can learn, they must not ignore the way the brain works. Emotion comes from the brain. Learning and feeling cannot occur separate from one another. The brain organizes stimuli into frameworks called schemata. These schemata promote efficient processing by the brain. When taxed by the stress and trauma of an experience, the schema frees up working memory by placing information into representative frames, allowing for new learning to occur (Tversky, 2019).

Understanding how this mental processing works supports effective project design. If we tap into how students process their experiences, we can support their ability to process new information.

Emotion can drive students toward learning goals, but only if learning design acknowledges how students compartmentalize new information. Otherwise, students can be triggered and retraumatized (Jennings, 2018). Triggers that alarm the brain move students into the fight-or-flight position, which increases levels of cortisol and, ultimately, hinders learning. A project that ties to trauma or places of unrest and instability can hinder a student from growing and developing. Conversely, if we provide the right learning frames that acknowledge students' mental schemas, we can promote deep thinking, problem solving, and optimal learning that are responsive to students' experiences (Tversky, 2019). Addressing the contexts within which students learn can impact both academic and social–emotional development (Jones & Khan, 2017).

Students' academic needs, therefore, cannot be separated from social–emotional needs. Emotions cannot be completely separated from the classroom, nor should they be (Reidel & Salinas, 2011). Rather, the relationship between emotions and learning requires thoughtful consideration of the pedagogical possibilities toward empowering students through social studies education by *carefully* centering emotions. Emotions can lead to powerful connections with content, but they can also be traumatic; teachers need to be aware that certain topics can be triggering for some students but not others (Sheppard et al., 2015). Likewise, programs that address students' social–emotional needs have long-term effects on students' educational experiences (Elias et al., 2003). When teachers and school leaders create opportunities for SEL in classroom instruction, it provides students practice in learning and applying social skills in an authentic way (Morris et al., 2017). Thus, the marriage of academic and social–emotional needs provides a pathway for holistic student development.

In the Re-Launch COVID-19 project, students are challenged to think of the far-reaching impacts of the pandemic. Centering their experiences provides a pathway to deeper learning. As students situate themselves in the events of the world and their lives, they make connections and build relevance, considering how the pandemic affects them similarly and/or differently than anyone else. For example, if a student identifies as a young Black male living in Brooklyn, these realities are intrinsically linked with how he experiences COVID-19, and they differ from a White female's experience in a rural community. By providing space for students to grapple with their thoughts and feelings in the midst of crisis, educators can help students learn how to recognize stress, change their patterns to restore balance, and then reflect on the impacts of the stress and their reaction to it (Costa & Kallick, 2009; Jewell & Durand, 2020).

Accordingly, students are challenged to see facts through their lens of personal experience. They must identify the way this understanding shapes their perspective, affects their emotion, and triggers even more questions to discover. We also wanted to position students as experts on their own experiences, bringing their expertise into an academic dialogue. It is worth noting that students more likely to be viewed from a deficit stance by educators are, likewise, more likely to be adversely impacted by COVID-19 (Delpit, 1995; Tai et al., 2020).

Navigating Trauma and Triggering Content

Though the challenges of 2020 may feel unique, students' carrying trauma into the classroom is nothing new. To address students' SEL needs, programs should approach all school contexts as potentially emotionally charged, where students have acute or chronic challenges impacting their educational experiences (Pawlo et al., 2019). Many academic topics are potentially traumatic or triggering for students, particularly students who come from marginalized communities (Goodman & West-Olatunji, 2010; Sheppard et al., 2015). The impacts of COVID-19 highlight many economic and social disparities in the United States. Marginalized groups, including Black Americans, Latinx Americans, and Indigenous communities, have been disproportionately affected by the illness in terms of the disease itself and of the economic fallout. To be a successful SEL program and meet the students' needs, the context of learning should adjust, including by creating SEL opportunities in academics (Elias et al., 2003). As all learning is potentially in a powerful emotional context, curriculum and instructional design should consistently aim to meet these demands.

Nonavoidance in SEL

The pressing nature of current events during 2020, coupled with the increased levels of anxiety associated with COVID-19 and its spread, demonstrates the acute need to create learning opportunities that address social–emotional development alongside academic endeavors. Rather than avoid topics that can perpetuate trauma and so leave students unprepared to grapple with their own and others' lived experiences, we wanted to create opportunities to incorporate trauma-informed social–emotional learning within the curriculum (Brunzell et al., 2016; Reisman et al., 2020). Integrating academic content with themes or "habits" that address social and emotional skills is a potentially effective way to create supportive learning environments. Recognizing the need to put "Maslow before Bloom"—place students' emotional and physical safety before their formal education needs (Doucet et al., 2020)—our goals were to *balance* Maslow and Bloom, providing a template for future design work.

Guiding questions for our work included:

- How can we surface students' diverse lived experiences?
- How can we give space for students to grapple with their lived experiences without retraumatizing them?
- How can we intentionally build opportunities for complementary academic and social–emotional learning?
- How can we elevate student voices and embolden students to take action around the things impacting them?

HABITS OF SUCCESS FRAMEWORK

To support students' social–emotional learning, the Summit Learning program constructed a conceptual framework called "Habits of Success." The Habits of Success are a collection of 16 foundational social–emotional concepts, organized into 5 categories: healthy development, school readiness, mindsets for self and school, perseverance and independence, and sustainability. The Habits of Success provide a lens through which our team develops curriculum and instruction strategies that support whole-child development and in which the classroom's communal and relational context is considered (Stafford-Brizard, 2016). For this project design work, we focused on five core Habits of Success that support students' well-being: *sense of belonging, stress management, resilience, attachment,* and *agency.* See Table 3.1 for all 16 habits in the 5 categories.

Addressing Pressing Issues in Social Studies

Social studies provide the appropriate academic space for crafting learning experiences that incorporate social–emotional principles, like the Habits of Success. The concepts and skills within social studies address students' needed social understandings and dispositions toward promoting the common good (Barton & Levstik, 2004; Brophy & Alleman, 2007). When educators weave in explicit opportunities to address social–emotional learning needs in social studies curriculum, students have opportunities to voice how they engage with learning and connect it to their out-of-classroom lives (Glew et al., 2020). In a period of political and social unrest, teachers need the tools to mitigate students' trauma while also preparing them to engage in democratic practices and civic spaces (Sondel et al., 2018). Giving classroom space to a triggering or traumatic topic requires, then, that students are engaging in an academic pursuit that not only intentionally mitigates harm and addresses students' social and emotional learning needs, but also provides a tangible opportunity to take action and to share their informed perspectives.

Table 3.1. Habits of Success

Categories	The Habits of Success	Definition
Healthy Development	Attachment	A deep and enduring emotional bond that connects one person to another across time and space (Ainsworth, 1973).
	Stress Management	Constantly changing cognitive and behavioral efforts to manage specific external and/or internal demands that are appraised as taxing or exceeding the resources of the person (Kraag et al., 2006).
	Self-Regulation	Regulation of attention, emotion, and executive functions for the purposes of goal-directed actions (Blair & Ursache, 2011).
School Readiness	Self-Awareness	The ability to accurately recognize one's emotions and thoughts and their influence on behavior. This includes accurately assessing one's strengths and limitations and possessing a well-grounded sense of confidence and optimism (Payton et al., 2008).
	Empathy/ Relationship Skills	Empathy: The ability to take the perspective of, and empathize with, others from diverse backgrounds and cultures, to understand social and ethical norms for behavior, and to recognize family, school, and community resources and supports (Payton et al., 2008).
		Relationship Skills: The ability to establish and maintain healthy and rewarding relationships with diverse individuals and groups. This includes communicating clearly, listening actively, cooperating, resisting inappropriate social pressure, negotiating conflict constructively, and seeking and offering help when needed (Payton et al., 2008).
	Executive Function	The cognitive control functions needed when one has to concentrate and think, when acting on one's initial impulse would be ill-advised. Core executive functions include cognitive flexibility, inhibition (self-control, self-regulation) and working memory. More complex executive functions include problem-solving, reasoning, and planning (Diamond & Lee, 2011).

Table 3.1. Continued

Mindsets for Self and School	Growth Mindset	Wherein students ascribe to the belief: my ability and competence grow with my effort (Farrington et al., 2012).
	Self-Efficacy	The perception that one can do something successfully (Farrington et al., 2012).
	Sense of Belonging	A sense that one has a rightful place in a given academic setting and can claim full membership in a classroom community (Farrington et al., 2012).
	Relevance of School	A student's sense that the subject matter he or she is studying is interesting and holds value (Farrington et al., 2012).
Perseverance	Resilience	Positive adaptation during or following exposure to adversities that have the potential to harm development: (a) developing well in the context of high cumulative risk for developmental problems (beating the odds, better than predicted development), (b) functioning well under currently adverse conditions (stress-resistance, coping) and (c) recovery to normal functioning after catastrophic adversity (bouncing back, self-righting) or severe deprivation (normalization) (Masten, 2007).
	Agency	A student's individual decision-making and autonomous actions (Toshalis & Nakkula, 2012).
	Academic Tenacity	The beliefs and skills that allow students to look beyond short-term concerns to longer-term or higher-order goals, and withstand challenges and setbacks to persevere toward these goals (Dweck et al., 2011).
Independence and Sustainability	Self-Direction	A process in which learners take the initiative in planning, implementing, and evaluating their own learning needs and outcomes, with or without the help of others (Knowles, 1975).
	Curiosity	The desire to engage and understand the world, interest in a wide variety of things, and preference for a complete understanding of a complex topic or problem (Goff & Ackerman, 1992).
	Purpose	A student's understanding of their interests, values, and skills, and the articulation of a credible path after high school for translating those interests, values, and skills into fulfilled lives.

Engage in Social Studies Inquiry

Desiring to create a project that addressed students' SEL needs while also putting them in the driver's seat of their learning led us to create projects using inquiry pedagogies, specifically those captured in the *C3 Framework* and the IDM. The IDM Blueprint is an instructional scaffold that supports teachers and students as they engage in inquiry learning (Grant et al., 2017). Within an inquiry, students complete a series of progressively more complex tasks framed by questions and disciplinary sources. As noted in the *C3 Framework*, inquiry empowers students to ask questions, think deeply, and engage in civic life. These needs are all the more acute when situated within students' experiences of COVID-19 and other 2020 events.

INQUIRY PROJECT DESCRIPTION

In what follows, we describe the inquiry project that positions COVID-19 and students' experiences at the center of learning. The IDM's framework of formative, summative, and civic action tasks support an investigation into COVID-19, as well as emboldens students to contextualize their experiences and take action in a way that elevates their own story. These tasks are represented in formative Checkpoints and summative Final Products in the Summit Learning platform. Framed by the compelling question—*How should we remember COVID-19?*—students investigate the virus's ongoing impact on themselves, their community, and the world. Over the course of the project, students learn about the disease, reflect on their own experiences, and then explore both how their identity affects their perspective on the disease and how their experiences during the pandemic can change how they see themselves—who they are, who they will become, and how they can take action.

During the course of the inquiry project, students explore the facts of the disease itself: its causes, its symptoms, and effective preventative measures. From that common understanding of the virus and its consequences, students begin to reflect more deeply about the impacts it has had on themselves and on those in their community. Using the primary and secondary sources reviewed in the project, students' own personal reflections, and interviews they conduct with others, students select an artifact and draft a narrative that represents the role of COVID-19 in their world. Woven throughout these tasks are social–emotional pedagogies, informed by the Summit Learning Program's Habits of Success. Table 3.2 shows the IDM blueprint for this inquiry.

Table 3.2. The IDM Blueprint for COVID-19 Inquiry

How should we remember COVID-19?	
Standards and Content Angle	D2.Civ.6. Civic and Political Institutions D2.Civ.10. Participation and Deliberation: Applying Civic Virtues and Democratic Principles D2.His.9/12. Historical Sources and Evidence
Cognitive Skills	Selecting Relevant Sources, Informational/Explanatory Thesis, Narrative, Communicating Accurately and Precisely
Habits of Success	Resilience, Stress Management, Attachment, Sense of Belonging, Agency
Staging the Compelling Question	Participate in a gallery walk, viewing pictures that demonstrate different impacts of COVID-19 with complementary reflection questions.

Supporting Question 1	Supporting Question 2	Supporting Question 3	Supporting Question 4
Action: UNDERSTAND	Action: UNDERSTAND	Action: UNDERSTAND	Action: ASSESS
What is COVID-19?	What is COVID-19 to me?	What are artifacts of COVID-19?	How am I a part of COVID history?

Formative Performance Task			
Create an informational flyer similar to the flyers created by the Center for Disease Control (CDC).	Write a narrative to tell the story of COVID-19 from students' own perspective and experience.	Generate a list of different COVID artifacts and write an explanation that connects an artifact back to personal experiences.	Describe how the selected artifact represents students' experiences and the experience(s) of their community, whether local, national, or global in scope.

Table 3.2. Continued.

Featured Sources			
Source A: "Coronavirus is not the flu. It's worse," Vox Media Source B: "What we should know about the coronavirus outbreak," *Washington Post* Source C: "Search speeds up for vaccine . . . " *Science News for Kids*	Source A: "'The Semester of COVID-19': The Toll of the Pandemic on Students," NPR Source B: "Human connection bolsters the immune system . . . " *Washington Post* Source C: "The Class Divide: Remote Learning at 2 Schools, Private and Public," *New York Times*	Source A: "Solving mysteries with archaeologists," Video	Student-generated sources
Summative Performance Task	ARGUMENT: How should we remember COVID-19? Construct an argument (e.g., detailed outline, poster, essay) that evaluates the need to study, remember, and/or celebrate this experience using specific claims and relevant evidence from sources while acknowledging competing views.		
Taking Informed Action	ACT: Share artifacts in a class museum (physical or digital space).		

Situating the Inquiry in SEL Habits

As the project begins, we emphasize the importance of students' *sense of belonging*, both in the classroom space and larger global contexts, in light of COVID-19. Students develop a set of collective norms for their work in the classroom community and bring awareness to their need to be safe, nurtured, and supported as they contribute to the class's learning. In the collective norms-building process, students and adults share values they have for feeling safe, nurtured, and productive in the space. Sharing personal truths moves the group into an exercise of putting words to feelings, which creates order and a way of being that is expected when together. Norms that may result from this process can include behaviors around listening to one another, ways to share feelings (individually or in whole groups), and structures for participating in discussions.

Through discussion and information-gathering, students can share personal experiences about COVID-19. They are also invited to use class

Table 3.3. The Four Keys to Unlock Nonviolent Communication Protocol

	I AM	YOU ARE
Observations	Notice what observations (see, hear, remember, imagine) do not contribute to your well-being.	By listening, notice what observations (see, hear, remember, imagine) do or do not contribute to others' well-being.
	"When I (see, hear, remember, imagine) . . . "	"When you (see, hear, remember, imagine) . . . "
Feelings	Notice the feelings you have in connection to what you observe.	As you listen, notice how the other person feels in relations to what they observe.
	"I feel . . . when I (see, hear, remember, imagine) . . . "	"You feel . . . when you (see, hear, remember, imagine) . . . "
Needs	Notice what you need or value that causes your feelings.	Listen and notice what the other person needs or values that causes their feelings.
	"I feel . . . because I need/ value . . . "	"You feel . . . because you need/ value . . . "
Requests	Identify a request that will enrich your life, without placing a demand on another.	Empathically receive that which would enrich the lives of another without it coming to you with a demand.
	"Would you be willing to . . . ?"	"Would you like . . . ?"

time to reflect on past challenges in order to recognize their own *resilience.* Throughout the project, we provide processing opportunities for students to *manage the stress* of these difficult topics. For example, students learn a protocol for sharing their feelings. This protocol surfaces the basic needs of the human experience by creating a space to say what is often unspoken. Should a moment cause an individual to feel ashamed, for example, the shame is acknowledged as a symptom of a larger need not met. The need for psychological safety is acknowledged, and the emotion can be addressed with actions that lead to security for all. This protocol, titled the *nonviolent communication protocol,* provides students and teachers with a series of steps to aid in processing emotion before reacting to those feelings (Rosenberg, 2003). See Table 3.3.

Through the use of the protocol and the resources provided with the project, students and teachers are able to notice how they feel, find words to describe those feelings, recognize what they need in order to feel differently, and make a request. Coupled with this protocol are instructional supports for teachers to develop the classroom space and student community—a place where students can authentically share themselves.

The project culminates in an opportunity for teachers to create a final product that balances academic content and students' expression of their own experiences. We specifically address the idea of students selecting an *artifact* and the propositions put forth by society around *value* and *worth*. By emphasizing the emotional elements grounded in the disciplinary content, we move away from the possibility of a superficial "show and tell." Instead, students move toward a sharing of themselves, developing their connections to something that will be long-lasting across time and space—a demonstration of the Habit of Success *attachment*. The project prompts students to consider many options for their artifact; weigh the impact or representation of the different items for their experiences, their classmates, and the larger community; and select what is most representative of themselves and their experience. Students demonstrate choice and are encouraged to exercise their own voice and agency when choosing a tangible item to represent their experience. This building of *attachment* through *agency* culminates in an opportunity to communicate an expression of self.

Staging the Inquiry

To introduce students to the academic concepts of the inquiry, we include a staging exercise. Staging an inquiry helps pique students' interests, introduces the inquiry's main themes or ideas, and allows teachers to gather information about students' knowledge and experiences on the topic (Swan et al., 2018). As they open the year's first Re-Launch project, teachers may have had little to no experience with their students. Teachers have students participate in a gallery walk (labeled as an "entry event" in the Summit Learning platform), viewing pictures that demonstrate different impacts of COVID-19 with complementary reflection questions. These pictures include empty streets, stores with boarded-up windows, and a roped-off playground. Teachers are also encouraged to include images of their own community to further connect students' experiences to the project.

To help teachers approach this task responsibly, they are cued to the potentially painful impact the images may have. Teachers are prompted to acknowledge this fact in their task-framing and asked to normalize the range of emotions and experiences people have had during the pandemic. This task is complemented by a series of resources to facilitate a norm-setting exercise. Norms are designed to clarify expectations and provide a sense of predictability for behavior in a space (deLara, 2009). We encourage norms to be developed by the members of a community—in this case, the students and teacher. Norms coauthored by all members of the classroom community make them representative of that collection of individuals. Through instructional materials, teachers can guide students through a series of reflections and then use the sharing of those ideas to generate a set of agreed-upon norms. Using the staging time to engage in this activity demonstrates to students, from the project introduction, that this is a time of learning that is going to be driven by and for them.

Supporting Question 1: What is COVID-19?

After teachers engage students in the staging task, the first supporting question teachers ask students, *What is COVID-19?*, provides students an opportunity to build content knowledge around the virus. This step of the inquiry process is particularly important to address the wealth of misinformation surrounding the virus. Likewise, it provides a disciplinary foundation upon which later supporting questions build. To answer the supporting question, students create an informational flyer similar to those created by the Centers for Disease Control and Prevention. The flyer asks students to draw on provided sources in order to describe the disease, how it spreads, its symptoms, and ways to prevent its spread.

This initial exploration of COVID-19 allows for teachers to intentionally continue to build the classroom community. Throughout instructional notes, teachers are prompted to transition through tasks with sensitivity and flexibility, providing students time to process their emotions, articulate them when desired, and then reflect on the demands those emotions have on internal resources. This explicit teaching of the Habit of Success *stress management* in the beginning of the project paves a path for continued work through the remaining questions in this project.

Supporting Question 2: What is COVID-19 to Me and My Community?

After establishing initial information about COVID-19 with students, the second supporting question, *What is COVID-19 to me and my community?*, provides students an opportunity to situate their experiences within the pandemic. After reading news articles in which other students around the country share their stories, students write a narrative to tell the story of COVID-19 from their own perspective and experience. The purpose of this task is to transfer facts about the pandemic to its human impact, giving students a space to share their personal history with COVID-19. The project's teacher notes encourage teachers to spend time writing their own narrative as a model for students. This personal reflection and willingness to share was designed to foster *attachment* and invite students to develop a *sense of belonging* with their classmates through personal expression.

Providing this space to surface the intersection between emotion and historical study allows students to explore content that connects directly to their lives. Students' personal narratives are positioned as a reference point for learning. The more that students can match what they learn with other knowledge they have, the better they are able to situate that new learning (Gonzalez et al., 2005). By pushing students to connect the events of COVID-19 to their own lives, we enhance these parallel connections in the brain. Moreover, when students associate the information with emotions they experience, they move from *learning to know* to *learning to change* (Sylwester, 1994), providing an opportunity for a transformation of self as a result of experience.

Supporting Question 3: What Are Artifacts of COVID-19?

The third supporting question, *What are artifacts of COVID-19?,* has students connect their experiences to concrete social studies concepts, notably ideas around material culture and artifacts as an historical source. Students explore different types of artifacts from the past and present, then generate a list of a variety of different artifacts (images or physical items) connected to personal experiences during the pandemic. Examples of artifacts can include: an item associated with a loved one whom the student sees less (or more) because of lockdown rules, a picture of a newly adopted pet, a mask or similar medical item, or a common household item that holds new meaning in the COVID-19 context. Students write an explanation that connects their artifact back to personal experiences.

Situating parts within a whole—here, students' experiences within larger community experiences—helps students to focus their attention on understanding their own experiences while simultaneously seeing the perspectives of others. The process of distilling all the complex parts of COVID-19 into a single item (i.e., their chosen artifact) requires higher-order thinking. The logical process of thinking through facts and details to surface memories to consciousness gives a concrete structure to an otherwise abstract process. In order to find a representation of their experience through an artifact, students must define value and meaning for themselves. The defense of this discovery (i.e., their explanation of the artifact) fosters a sense of self-efficacy by creating a place for students to make a claim and confidently share a part of themselves with the world (Reeve & Tseng, 2011). To demonstrate this task, the project materials include an example story of a grandma's slippers:

> My grandma's slippers are worn on the bottom from her walking
> from her bedroom (which she shared with me until she got sick), to
> the bathroom. My family tried to stay away from her to be safe, and I
> remember the shuffling sound as they glided across the floor when she
> became weak. These slippers symbolize her strength, even when her
> body failed her.

This task was designed to nurture a climate of belonging where students can share their experiences and consider the role they play in the world as a result of their experience.

As with the previous questions and tasks, this work has the potential to surface very recent traumas in students' lives. Teachers are encouraged to remind students of collective norms, make thoughtful choices when framing the activity, and be responsive to students' needs by making modifications. For example, teachers can prompt students to select a personal artifact that represents something else about the student's life, such as their experiences in the previous school year.

Supporting Question 4: How Am I a Part of COVID-19 History?

Building directly off the previous question, supporting question four, *How am I a part of COVID-19 history?,* broadens students' understanding of their experiences and historical position. In the formative task, students describe how their selected artifact represents their experiences and the experience(s) of their community, whether local, national, or global in scope. Students construct an evidence-based claim to communicate how their artifact fits into the larger historical narrative of COVID.

Students are expected to consider communal experiences, but they also have space to evaluate inequities. Through research or teacher-provided sources, students can consider the larger context of their experiences reflecting on these key questions:

- How have different communities been affected?
- Are my experiences similar or different from other communities?
- Who has been most affected and what conclusions can I draw?

For example, a student writing about her grandma's slippers may explain how the elderly are disproportionately affected by the virus, how people in her community are affected in comparison to other geographic areas, or the impact of social distancing on families. Students are able to reflect on places of *attachment* in their own lives by drawing on those relationships to narrate the depth of meaning to their artifact. Students use their connections to others to answer the question: "How am I part of COVID-19 history?" They also build connections with their classroom community through their artifact sharing. By engaging with one another and working collectively, students are positioned to navigate the challenges and take action.

Taking Informed Action

By moving through the questions, tasks, and sources of the inquiry project, students progressively build knowledge and disciplinary skills. They are also given opportunities to reflect and share their experiences in a way that is responsive to, and supports, social and emotional needs to maintain academic rigor. The prioritization of psychological safety for students to process improves their ability to think critically and activates their brain through memory and emotion (Higgins et al., 2011; Tversky, 2019). For the summative performance task, students describe how a personal artifact captures their own experiences and their community's experience with COVID-19. This informed action task has students invite others to understand the impacts of COVID-19 for them and their community by sharing their artifact and the meaning it holds.

Informed action tasks use three steps to prepare students for informed action. The steps ask students to understand the issue from the inquiry project, assess the importance and impact of the issue, and act in ways that allow them to share their learning in a real-world context. In this inquiry project, students explore the impacts of COVID-19, then reflect upon and evaluate how it impacted them. The suggested action task is for students to share their artifacts in a class museum (physical or digital space). However, to respond to students' interests and needs, teachers are provided a list of alternative civic actions, ranging from letters to policymakers to creating a time capsule (Muetterties & Swan, 2019).

By providing students an opportunity to take action, we move them into civic spaces: out of the classroom, out of the school building, out of the present, and into the world. Participating in civic life helps prepare students for engaged citizenship, while also developing their civic dispositional commitments. By connecting the academic content to their own experiences and providing an opportunity to apply that learning to a civic context, the inquiry demonstrates the relevance of school, students' experiences, and the ways in which they can use those understandings to take informed action.

CONCLUSION

Grounding our inquiry project design in a pressing modern issue, students' related experiences, and social–emotional learning, teachers can create learning opportunities that consider students' holistic learning needs. When students wrestle with important disciplinary ideas, they are better positioned to understand the current historical era and take action on their learning. At the same time, those topics can surface powerful emotions and potentially traumatic experiences for students. By intentionally addressing students' well-being through social–emotional learning and the Habits of Success framework, teachers can construct learning experiences that mitigate harm and empower students to use their experiences as a springboard for engagement. By opening the doors for students, they can ask questions, set goals, lift their voices, and take action.

NOTE

1. We created three versions of this project to support teacher use (with modified guidance) at the elementary, middle, and high school levels. All three are available to teachers on the Summit Learning platform https://www.summitlearning.org/.

Special thanks to Kathleen Griswell and Justin Hauver, who collaborated in the design and development of this project.

REFERENCES

Ainsworth, M. D. S. (1973). The development of infant-mother attachment. In B. Cardwell & H. Ricciuti (Eds.), *Review of child development research* (Vol. 3, pp. 1–4). University of Chicago Press.

Barton, K., & Levstik, L. (2004). *Teaching history for the common good.* Routledge.

Blair, C., & Ursache, A. (2011). A bidirectional model of executive functions and self-regulation. In R. F. Baumeister & K. D. Vohs (Eds.), *Handbook of self-regulation* (2nd ed., pp. 300–320). Guilford Press.

Brophy, J., & Alleman, J. (2007). *Powerful social studies for elementary students.* Wadsworth.

Brunzell, T., Stokes, H., & Waters, L. (2016). Trauma-informed flexible learning: Classrooms that strengthen regulatory abilities. *International Journal of Child, Youth & Family Studies, 7*(2), 218–239. https://doi.org/10.18357/ijcyfs72201615719

Costa, A. L., & Kallick, B. (2009). *Habits of mind across the curriculum: Practical and creative strategies for teachers.* Association for Supervision and Curriculum Development.

deLara, E. (2009). Peer predictability: An adolescent strategy for increasing a sense of personal safety at school. *Journal of School Violence, 1*(3), 31–56. https://doi.org/10.1300/J202v01n03_03

Delpit, L. (1995). *Other people's children: Cultural conflict in the classroom.* The New Press.

Diamond, A., & Lee, K. (2011). Interventions shown to aid executive function development in children 4 to 12 years old. *Science, 333*(6045), 959–964. https://doi.org/10.1126/science.1204529

Doucet, A., Netolicky, D., Timmers, K., & Tuscano, F. J. (2020). *Thinking about pedagogy in an unfolding pandemic: An independent report on approaches to distance learning during COVID-19 school closures.* Authors.

Dweck, C., Walton, G. M., & Cohen, G. L. (2011). *Academic tenacity: Mindsets and skills that promote long-term learning.* The Gates Foundation.

Elias, M. J., Zins, J. E., Graczyk, P. A., & Weissberg, R. P. (2003). Implementation, sustainability, and scaling up of social–emotional and academic innovations in public schools. *School Psychology Review, 32*(3), 303–319. https://doi.org/10.1080/02796015.2003.12086200

Farrington, C. A., Roderick, M., Allensworth, E. A., Nagaoka, J., Johnson, D. W., Keyes, T. S., & Beechum, N. (2012). *Teaching adolescents to become learners:*

The role of noncognitive factors in academic performance—a critical literature review. The University of Chicago Consortium on Chicago School Research.

Glew, S., Oto, R., & Mayo, J. B. (2020). With love: Attempting to instill the lasting value of humanity while teaching during a global pandemic. *Journal of International Social Studies, 10*(2), 60–66.

Goff, M., & Ackerman, P. (1992). Personality-intelligence relations: Assessment of typical intellectual engagement. *Journal of Educational Psychology, 84*(4), 537–552. https://doi.org/10.1037/0022-0663.84.4.537

Gonzalez, N., Moll, L. C., & Amanti, C. (2005). *Funds of knowledge: Theorizing practices in households, communities, and classrooms.* Lawrence Erlbaum Associates.

Goodman, R. D., & West-Olatunji, C. A. (2010). Educational hegemony, traumatic stress, and African American and Latino American students. *Journal of Multicultural Counseling and Development, 38*(3), 176–186. https://doi.org/10.1002/j.2161-1912.2010.tb00125.x

Grant, S. G., Swan, K., & Lee, J. (2017). *Inquiry-based practice in social studies education.* Routledge.

Higgins, M., Ishimaru, A., Holcombe, R., & Fowler, A. (2011). Examining organizational learning in schools: The role of psychological safety, experimentation, and leadership that reinforces learning. *Journal of Educational Change 13*(1), 67–94. https://doi.org/10.1007/s10833-011-9167-9

Jennings, P.A. (2018). *The trauma-sensitive classroom: Building resilience with compassionate teaching.* W.W. Norton.

Jewell, T., & Durand, A. (2020). *This book is anti-racist: 20 lessons on how to wake up, take action, and do the work.* Quarto.

Jones, S. M., & Kahn, J. (2017). *The evidence base for how we learn: Supporting students' social, emotional, and academic development.* The Aspen Institute.

Knowles, M. S. (1975). *Self-directed learning: A guide for learners and teachers.* Association Press.

Kraag, G., Zeegers, M. P., Kok, G., Hosman, C., & Abu-Saad, H. H. (2006). School programs targeting stress management in children and adolescents: A meta-analysis. *Journal of School Psychology, 44*(6), 449–472. https://doi.org/10.1016/j.jsp.2006.07.001

Larmer, J. (2018). Project-based learning in social studies. *Social Education, 82*(1), 20–23.

Larmer, J., Mergendoller, J., & Boss, S. (2015). *Setting the standard for project based learning: A proven approach to rigorous classroom instruction.* Buck Institute for Education.

Masten, A. S. (2007). Resilience in developing systems: Progress and promise as the fourth wave rises. *Development and Psychopathology, 19*(3), 921–930. https://doi.org/10.1017/s0954579407000442

Morris, T., McGuire, M., & Walker, B. (2017). Integrating social studies and social skills for students with emotional and behavioral disabilities: A mixed methods study. *Journal of Social Studies Research, 41*(4), 253–262. https://doi.org/10.1016/j.jssr.2017.04.001

Muetterties, C., & Swan, K. (2019). Be the change: Guiding students to take informed action. *Social Education, 83*(4), 232–237.

National Council for the Social Studies. (2013). *The college, career, and civic life (C3) framework for social studies state standards.* Author.

Pawlo, E., Lorenzo, A., Eichert, B., & Elias, M. J. (2019). All SEL should be trauma-informed. *Phi Delta Kappan, 101*(3), 37–41. https://doi.org/10.1177%2F0031721719885919

Payton, J., Weissberg, R. P., Durlak, J. A., Dymnicki, A. B., Taylor, R. D., Schellinger, K. B., & Pachan, M. (2008). *The positive impact of social and emotional learning for kindergarten to eighth-grade students: Findings from three scientific reviews.* Collaborative for Academic, Social, and Emotional Learning.

Reeve, J., & Tseng, C. (2011). Agency as a fourth aspect of students' engagement during learning activities. *Contemporary Educational Psychology, 36*(4), 257–267. https://doi.org/10.1016/j.cedpsych.2011.05.002

Reidel, M., & Salinas, C. (2011). The role of emotion in democratic dialogue: A self study. *Social Studies Research and Practice, 6*(1), 2–20.

Reisman, A., Enumah, L., & Jay, L. (2020). Interpretive frames for responding to racially stressful moments in history discussions. *Theory & Research in Social Education, 48*(3), 321–345. https://doi.org/10.1080/00933104.2020.1718569

Rosenberg, M. B. (2003). *Nonviolent communication: A language of life.* Puddle Dancer Press.

Sheppard, M., Katz, D., & Grosland, T. (2015). Conceptualizing emotions in social studies education. *Theory & Research in Social Education, 43*(2), 147–178. https://doi.org/10.1080/00933104.2015.1034391

Sondel, B., Baggett, H. C., & Dunn, A. H. (2018). "For millions of people, this is real trauma": A pedagogy of political trauma. *Teaching and Teacher Education, 70*, 175–185. https://doi.org/10.1016/j.tate.2017.11.017

Stafford-Brizard, K. B. (2016). *Building blocks for learning: A framework for comprehensive student development.* Turnaround for Children.

Swan, K., Lee, J., & Grant, S. G. (2018). *Inquiry design model: Building inquiries in social studies.* Routledge.

Sylwester, R. (1994). How emotions affect learning. *Educational Leadership, 52*(2), 60–65.

Tai, D. B. G., Shah, A., Doubeni, C. A., Sia, I. G., & Wieland, M. L. (2020). The disproportionate impact of COVID-19 on racial and ethnic minorities in the United States. *Clinical Infectious Diseases.* Advance online publication. https://doi.org/10.1093/cid/ciaa815

Toshalis, E., & Nakkula, M. J. (2012) Motivation, engagement, and student voice. *Students at the center: Teaching and learning in the era of the Common Core.* A Jobs for the Future Project.

Tversky, B. (2019). *Mind in motion: How action shapes thought.* Basic Books.

Yaver, M. [@mirandayaver]. (2020, May 31). *You know, I always wanted to know what it would be like to simultaneously experience the Spanish flu, Great Depression, and 1968 mass protests while Andrew Johnson was president.* [Tweet]. Twitter. https://twitter.com/mirandayaver/status/1267177527912480768

CHAPTER 4

Examining COVID-19 with Young Learners

An Interdisciplinary Inquiry Design Model Approach

Lisa Brown Buchanan, Cara Ward, Tracy Hargrove, Amy Taylor, Maggie Guggenheimer, and Lynn Sikma

When COVID-19 began to spread throughout communities, rapid changes took place in homes, schools, communities, and commerce in an effort to "flatten the curve" and stop the spread of the virus. No group of humans, however, was impacted quite like K–12 learners. As a group, children have shown the lowest rate of infection and death, yet young learners have faced their own challenges during COVID-19. Unlike their peers in secondary grades, children in grades K–8 were quickly relegated to online forms of schooling, experienced changes in childcare that happened overnight, and watched as the adults in their lives scrambled to secure basic provisions for weeks at a time to guide their families through sheltering in place.

In this chapter, we provide teachers with an interdisciplinary unit for the young learner that teaches foundational content in epidemiology, data analysis, and primary source analysis within the context of COVID-19. We build on that content by incorporating the Inquiry Design Model Blueprint to answer the following compelling questions: *What is a virus and how does it spread? How has COVID-19 impacted our lives, communities, and the world?*

This chapter offers two parts. The first is a brief review of scholarship on teaching public health emergencies with young learners, including an overview of how to situate COVID-19 in elementary content-area standards for social studies, math, and science. The second half of the chapter describes two interdisciplinary inquiries for teaching COVID-19 with young learners.

COVID-19 was and continues to be unprecedented. As such, instructional resources that can help young learners understand the pandemic and its effects are less available at the elementary and middle levels than in secondary grades. The resources we suggest here for teaching about COVID-19 help fill that gap and provide an opportunity to teach elementary social studies, science, and math content in a way that offers social-emotional benefits.

TEACHING PUBLIC HEALTH CRISIS WITH LEARNERS IN GRADES 3-8

While COVID-19 is the greatest public health crisis of our lifetime to date, prior health crisis situations are addressed in resources for grades 3–8 and can help us understand not only how we might teach about the coronavirus but also ways to teach public health issues and the impact on our lives and communities. We first recognize that teaching a public health crisis is important in children's homes, and organizations, such as the National Association for the Education of Young Children, provided resources on their websites with practical strategies for how to talk to children about COVID-19. While the coronavirus is certainly the most widely televised, documented, and recent pandemic, placing a classroom examination of it within the larger scope of epidemiology provides students with a stronger understanding of the local and international impact than teaching it as a stand-alone topic (Centers for Disease Control and Prevention [CDC], 2016). In this vein, organizations like the Public Broadcasting System (PBS, 2006) offer resources for teaching epidemics, including their *American Experience* episode on the 1918 flu, and the popular PBS Learning Media (2020a, 2020b) source sets that examine a number of epidemics, including polio and yellow fever. These sets include both digitized primary and secondary sources. On the classroom portion of their website, the CDC (2016) offers tangible suggestions on teaching epidemiology, including integrating it into math and science instruction.

Both national organizations for teaching math and teaching science have created resources for teachers to develop classroom instruction about epidemiology and the coronavirus specifically. The National Council for Teaching Mathematics' (2020) resources include a pandemic simulation app and resources for teaching modeling within the context of COVID-19. The National Science Teaching Association (2020) also offers a large collection of resources, including discussion strategies, epidemiology basics, and ready-to-use teaching resources. Both organizations have made resources for teaching elementary, middle, and secondary students available. The unit that follows adds an additional strand to this recommendation by including social studies among the content areas in which epidemiology can be taught.

THE INQUIRY DESIGN MODEL

In 2013, the National Council for the Social Studies published the *College, Career, and Civic Life (C3) Framework* to address the marginalization of social studies, increase student engagement, and encourage responsible citizenship. In response to the emphasis placed on inquiry in the *C3 Framework*, social studies scholars Kathy Swan, John Lee, and S. G. Grant (2015) developed the Inquiry Design Model (IDM). This model for instructional planning emphasizes a thorough examination of a compelling question through supporting questions, analysis of featured sources, and formative tasks; it also encourages learners to extend beyond the lesson by "taking informed action."

After selecting a compelling question to guide the inquiry, teachers break that overarching question down into several supporting questions, typically three. For each supporting question, teachers then select sources (photographs, data, video clips) that students analyze through a formative task. Through the process of source analysis guided by tasks and supporting questions, students are able to form evidence-based answers to the compelling question, thus developing a thorough understanding of a topic or concept. A summative performance task allows students to showcase the new knowledge they have gained, and teachers then encourage students to apply their learning through actions and conversations in the real world. Due to the flexible nature of this model, it can easily be adapted for use in other subject areas, making it an effective framework for an interdisciplinary unit such as the one we present here.

TEACHING ACADEMIC VOCABULARY FOR GRADES 3-8 IN AN INTERDISCIPLINARY STUDY OF COVID-19

Before engaging the IDM template and narrative that follows, we suggest that teachers think about the role of academic vocabulary in a study of COVID-19. Academic vocabulary refers to the Tier 2 or 3 words of our vocabulary that are often encountered by readers or within content area instruction; they can be both specialized and subject area–specific. Academic vocabulary words are directly related to navigating a content area. For example, a "beaker" in science is directly related to the process of scientific exploration, experimentation, and overall inquiry in science and would be considered academic vocabulary. As our understanding of a phenomenon like the coronavirus grows, so does the use of academic vocabulary. Table 4.1 serves as a resource for teachers as they consider the vocabulary students might use, see, or hear while they navigate the three tasks that follow.

Table 4.1. Academic Vocabulary by Compelling Question

Compelling Question 1		Compelling Question 2	
What is a virus and how does it spread?		How has COVID-19 impacted our lives, communities, and the world?	
Virus	Illness	CDC	World Health
Host	Symptoms	Shelter in place	Organization
Vectors	Presumptive case	Isolation	Antibodies
Epidemic	Capsid	Social distancing	Novel coronavirus
Pandemic	Infectious agent	Quarantine	Vaccine
Replicate	Epidemiology	Herd immunity	
Curve	Disease	Compromised	
Epicenter	COVID-19	Population	
Outbreak	Coronavirus	Ventilator	
Carrier	Immune system	Antiviral	
Asymptomatic	Immunity		
Fever			

INQUIRY DESIGN MODEL 1:
WHAT IS A VIRUS AND HOW DOES IT SPREAD?

Lately, viruses have been dominating our minds and reality. The news is a constant onslaught of COVID-19, lockdowns, social distancing, and vaccines. This information can be confusing and scary for children, but these feelings can be mitigated through instruction. The topic of viruses and their transmission naturally lends itself to an integrated unit that can be modified for various grade levels. The IDM Science and Math Connections Blueprint (Table 4.2) provides an overview of such a unit for classroom instruction.

Introduction to the Inquiry

In the first part of this inquiry, we suggest that teachers guide a class discussion to access students' prior knowledge about viruses by asking questions such as *What is a virus?* and *Are all viruses the same?* Depending on the grade level of the students, sharing a read-aloud is a strategy that can be used to engage students' thinking about microscopic germs that can make us sick. Possible book choices for this unit may include *Germs Make Me Sick!* (Berger, 1995), *Giant Germ* (Capeci & Cole, 2001), *It's Catching* (Gardy, 2014), or *Inside Your Insides* (Eamer, 2016).

Table 4.2. Inquiry Design Model (IDM) Blueprint™: Viruses and Spread

Compelling Question	What is a virus and how does it spread?

Standards and Practices	Next Generation Science Standards (NGSS Lead States, 2013)
	3-LS4-2. Use evidence to construct an explanation for how the variations in characteristics among individuals of the same species may provide advantages in surviving, finding mates, and reproducing.
	4-LS1-1. Construct an argument that plants and animals have internal and external structures that function to support survival, growth, behavior, and reproduction.
	5-LS2-1. Develop a model to describe the movement of matter among plants, animals, decomposers, and the environment.
	MS-LS2-1. Analyze and interpret data to provide evidence for the effects of resource availability on organisms and populations of organisms in an ecosystem.
	MS-ESS3-2. Analyze and interpret data on natural hazards to forecast future catastrophic events and inform the development of technologies to mitigate their effects.
	National Council of Teachers of Mathematics (NCTM) Standards (NCTM, 2000)
	Formulate questions that can be addressed with data and collect, organize, and display relevant data to answer them
	Grades 3–5 Expectations: design investigations to address a question and consider how data-collection methods affect the nature of the data set; collect data using observations, surveys, and experiments; represent data using tables and graphs such as line plots, bar graphs, and line graphs; recognize the differences in representing categorical and numerical data.
	Grades 6–8 Expectations: formulate questions, design studies, and collect data about a characteristic shared by two populations or different characteristics within one population.
	Select and use appropriate statistical methods to analyze data
	Grades 3–5 Expectations: describe the shape and important features of a set of data and compare related data sets, with an emphasis on how the data are distributed.
	Develop and evaluate inferences and predictions that are based on data
	Grades 3–5 Expectations: propose and justify conclusions and predictions that are based on data and design studies to further investigate the conclusions or predictions.
	Grades 6–8 Expectations: use observations about differences between two or more samples to make conjectures about the populations from which the samples were taken; use conjectures to formulate new questions and plan new studies to answer them.
	Understand numbers, ways of representing numbers, relationships among numbers, and number systems
	Grades 6–8 Expectations: develop an understanding of large numbers and recognize and appropriately use exponential, scientific, and calculator notation.

Table 4.2. Continued

Staging the Question	With so much on the news about COVID-19, what do we really know about a virus? What is a virus? Can we see a virus? How does it spread through our community?
	For younger students who may be frightened by a discussion of viruses, you could simulate the spread of a good idea instead. Other suggestions may include how a yawn and acts of kindness can be contagious.

Supporting Question 1	Supporting Question 2	Supporting Question 3
What is a virus? How big is a virus?	How does a virus spread through a population?	How do you stop the spread of a virus?

Formative Performance Task

Conduct research on viruses and modeling sizes	Viral spread simulation activities	Statistical analysis

Featured Sources

PBS's (2020) *How to talk to your kids about coronavirus.*	Data collected during the simulation activity (see narrative for details)	Table of Data: open-source data are available from the *Our World in Data* website
Britannica Kids's (2020) *Virus.*		
National Geographic Kids's (2020) *Factors about coronavirus.*		PBS's *It's Okay to Be Smart* (2020). What this chart actually means for COVID-19
Germs Make Me Sick! by Melvin Berger (Gr. PK–3)		
Giant Germ by Anne Capeci and Joanna Cole (Gr. 2–5)		National Council of Teachers of Mathematics. (2020). *Pandemics: How are viruses spread?*
It's Catching: The Infectious World of Germs and Microbes by Jennifer Gardy (Gr. 2–7)		
Inside Your Insides by Claire Eamer (Gr. 2–7)		

Summative Performance Task	Argument	Written task: Using data from the simulations, explain which mitigating strategy worked the best in preventing virus spread and why. How can we "flatten the curve" and what does that mean?
	Extension	How could a community be prepared for a pandemic in the future?
		How could each person help prevent the spread of current and upcoming viruses?
		Predict the outcome if we did the simulation with other classrooms in the building

Taking Informed Action	Design an information campaign to create awareness of how to actively control the spread of disease.

When discussing the term *germ,* it is important to remember to also distinguish between bacteria and viruses. Both of these microbes may cause sickness, but they differ in structure and function. Viruses are microscopic parasites that are nonliving, and bacteria are living single-celled organisms. The discussion and read-aloud provide an opportunity for students to begin thinking about the nature of germs and how they are spread, which naturally leads to additional questions that may be answered through data investigation. We recommend that teachers record student-generated questions, displaying them in a prominent place in the classroom. These questions can lead to future investigations that are more meaningful, as students have ownership of the ideas.

Supporting Question 1:
What is a virus? How big is a virus?

We cannot see bacteria or viruses with our eyes because they are microscopic; however, scientists have high-powered microscopes to capture images of them. Students are often fascinated by things that are very large or tiny, but those extreme scales make these things challenging to comprehend. In order to explore common viruses that cause sickness, we suggest having students carry out a mini-research project to answer questions such as: What disease does the virus cause? What does it look like under the microscope? Does a vaccine exist for it? How has this virus impacted humans over the course of history? When presenting the possible choices for students to research, it is important to note that some types of viruses may include content that is not appropriate for children. See Table 4.3, Virus Exploration, for a sample student guide for this research activity. A possible extension for the virus research is a sorting activity of the virus pictures and/or models derived from the student's research based on size. See Table 4.4 for a virus-sorting activity.

Supporting Question 2:
How does a virus spread through a population?

In order to answer Supporting Question 2, the following activities have been adapted from the NOVA Teachers (2017) *ScienceNOW* 1918 flu simulation, with the addition of a simulation of how social distancing impacts the spread of a virus. Before the simulation activity, a brainstorming session would be useful for students to think about ways viral diseases spread from person to person. This generated list could possibly include examples such as fluids, blood, surfaces, sneezing, coughing, and ingestion. For younger students, we suggest discussing other things that can be spread like smiles, yawns, ideas, and acts of kindness. Other supporting questions to assist the

Table 4.3. Virus Exploration

Name of virus: Choose from: Polio, Influenza, COVID-19 (coronaviruses), Common Cold (rhinoviruses), Measles, Chickenpox, Smallpox, Rubella, Mumps
What disease does this virus cause?
How does this virus spread?
Describe the disease in 1-3 sentences.
List 3 historical facts about this virus.
Does this virus have a vaccine? If yes, then describe it.
Include a link to a news article about this virus.
What does this virus look like under a microscope?   Draw a picture on the back of this sheet.
Extension: Make a model of your virus.

Table 4.4. Card Sort Activity: Sizes of Viruses

Name of virus	Size of virus	Include image here
Polio	30 nm	
Cold	30 nm	
Rubella	60-70 nm	
Flu	80-120 nm	
Mumps	100-600 nm	
Measles	120-250 nm	
COVID-19	125 nm	
Chickenpox	150-200 nm	
Smallpox	200 nm	

Table 4.5. Data Collection Table

	Round #1	Round #2
Simulation One: *Viral spread*		
How many people were infected?		
Simulation Two: *Social Distancing*		
How many people were infected?		
Simulation Three: *Vaccine*		
How many people were infected?		

class discussion about viruses before the simulation activity could include: Do all viruses spread the same way? What do we call a widespread occurrence of an infectious disease in a particular community? What is a pandemic? How can we prevent spreading viruses/germs?

This activity simulates how viruses spread from person to person and allows students to collect data over 1 to 3 days. As part of this task, the teacher should discuss the different ways to collect data (i.e., survey, experiment, simulation, and sampling) and explain how this activity is a simulation. As the simulations are implemented, Table 4.5 can be used to log data on chart paper, whiteboard, or science notebooks.

Simulation One: Viral Spread

To begin the first simulation, we recommend asking a student volunteer to be the virus-spreader. This volunteer will be given a set of red dot stickers. The spread of the virus will be represented by the distribution of those stickers. For one minute, the virus spreader will slowly circulate throughout the room and place stickers on the back of students' hands to represent viral spread. The class will be circulating around the room but should not try to move toward or away from the viral spreader. After 1 minute, the students should stop and raise their hands if they have a dot. The teacher then records the number of infected people.

For Round 2, another student should be asked to volunteer to be the virus spreader once again. The spread of the virus will be represented by the exponential distribution of red dots. The teacher should explain that the virus spreader will circulate throughout the room placing only one dot on the back of students' hands, but the first three students will also receive an entire sheet of dots for them to also start distributing. The timer for Round 2 (1 minute) can begin, and the teacher should ask the students to slowly start circulating around the room. At the end of Round 2, the students stop and raise their hands if they have a red dot. The number of infected people should be recorded on the data table. After Round 2, students should discuss: What do these data tell you about the differences in the two rounds for simulation one? Which round represents an epidemic and why?

Simulation Two: Social Distancing

For simulation two, students will be modeling the effects of social distancing on viral spread in a population. It is best if this simulation is completed outside (or in a large area such as a gym) where students can spread out at least six feet apart. For Round 1, students should stand at least six feet from one another. The timer for Round 1 (1 minute) can begin and students should slowly start circulating around, remaining six feet apart, as the viral spreader distributes the red dots. At the end of Round 1, the students stop and raise their hands if they have a red dot. The number of infected people should be recorded on the data table.

For Round 2, the class should be divided into groups of five to eight people standing within one foot of one another. The timer for Round 2 (1 minute) can begin and the students should slowly start circulating around the room in their groups. The viral spreader can then slowly start distributing the red dots. At the end of Round 2, the students stop and raise their hands if they have a red dot. The number of infected people should be recorded on the data table. Following Round 2, students should discuss: How did social distancing affect the number of infected persons? What do these data tell you about group gathering? Do you think it affects the number of infected persons?

Simulation Three: Vaccine

In this simulation, some of the students will be vaccinated for the viral disease. Using a different color dot, 10% of the students in the class will be "vaccinated." These students can receive a red dot, but they should not be counted in the tally since they will not get sick. The timer for Round 1 (1 minute) should begin and the students should slowly start circulating around the room. At the end of Round 1, the students stop and raise their hands if they have *only* a red dot. If they have a vaccine dot, they are not counted as infected persons. The number of infected people should be recorded on the data table.

For Round 2, 80% of the students in the class should be "vaccinated." These students can receive a red dot, but they should not be counted in the tally since they will not get sick. At the end of Round 2, the students stop and raise their hands if they have *only* a red dot. The number of infected people should be recorded on the data table. After Round 2, students should discuss: How do different levels of inoculation affect how a virus spreads through a community?

Supporting Question 3:
How do you stop the spread of a virus?

In the previous section, students explored how a virus spreads. Data were collected for three different simulations including no mitigating strategies (Simulation One), social distancing (Simulation Two), and use of a vaccine (Simulation Three). After each simulation, students record data for each trial in a table. These data can be compiled into a bar graph that can be used to compare the spread of the virus given the use of strategies for decreasing spread of the disease. While these graphs are useful for comparing mitigating strategies, they do not show the way in which a virus spreads rapidly in a population. Prior to this experience, students may have thought about data increasing in a linear way; however, infectious diseases spread exponentially. When graphed over time, the line for exponential growth looks different from linear phenomena that students are accustomed to graphing. Instead, students work with data where the line curves upward, modeling an almost immediate need for the use of large numbers.

In order to mitigate the sharp rise in cases, students explore mitigating strategies for helping to flatten the sharp curve. In order to more fully explore how viruses work, it is important that students understand the concept of exponential growth. Just as the COVID-19 virus was beginning to spread in the United States, PBS published an 8-minute video explaining this concept (It's Okay to Be Smart, 2020). The video begins with a graph comparing two sets of data displaying the number of people infected by a virus. While the number of people infected is the same for each data set, the first graph shows a sharp curve, and the second graph shows a flatter curve spread out over a longer period of time. The video explains exponential growth in a way that is developmentally appropriate for upper elementary and middle grade students and helps students understand why it is so important to identify mitigating strategies for controlling the spread of the virus. It is recommended that this video be shown to students after they have been given an opportunity to investigate the concept of exponential growth. Once students have simulated how a virus spreads and strategies for slowing the spread of a virus, we believe it is useful to examine actual data collected over time documenting a real virus as it spreads to a population. The following section provides a description of a statistical investigation that utilizes real-world, open-source COVID-19 data from *Our World in Data* (2020).

Extending Simulations to Real-World Data

In its *Principles to Actions: Ensuring Mathematical Success for All*, the National Council of Teachers of Mathematics (2014) emphasized the importance of "connect[ing] new learning with prior knowledge and informal reasoning" (p. 9). Building on the lived experience of COVID-19 that students now share, mathematics may be used to help students make sense of the pandemic. The COVID-19 pandemic presents a mathematical context for exploring real-world data and engaging in statistical processes.

After answering the listed supporting questions with students, using the PCAI Model of Statistical Investigation (Graham, 1987), students are provided a structure for engaging in statistical problem solving. Graham's model for the statistical investigation includes the following four components: pose the question, collect the data, analyze the data, and interpret the results. A description of the PCAI process with real-world COVID-19 data follows. Building on students' knowledge of earlier simulations modeling how the virus slows when various mitigating factors are introduced, we suggest engaging in a discussion of why scientists and mathematicians may use simulations in their work. Such a discussion should lead to the idea that simulations allow us to explore questions about real-world phenomena by engaging in experiments that model a real-life situation.

Because viruses cannot be contained in the real world, a simulation allows us to explore what the spread might look like in a larger population and the impact of mitigating factors on the spread. Once students understand that the data they have collected thus far has been through simulation and that these simulations help us predict how the virus will behave in the real world, we recommend having students explore real-world data for comparison. The following investigation using real-world COVID-19 data is described using the PCAI model as a framework:

(P) *Pose the Question*: How did the COVID-19 virus spread in the United States?

(C) *Collect the Data*: While there are multiple online sources for obtaining real-world data sets, we found the open-source data available from the Our World in Data (2020) website to be useful. It is helpful to navigate the website together at first, showing students that they can explore various countries and extract data points for the number of cases in the United States on select dates.

(A) *Analyze the Data*: Once students have recorded the number of cases on specific dates over time, it is helpful to discuss why the use of graphs can make the data easier to understand. Depending on students' age and experience with various graphical representations, students may select from a variety of graphs such as a bar graph, line plot, stem and leaf plot, box and whisker plot, line graph, or circle graph to help them better communicate what is happening with the data.

(I) *Interpret the Data*: Results should clearly show that the total number of people infected by the virus doubled every few days.

Having students make predictions on the number infected at various times (e.g., 1 month later, 2 months later) allow students to apply prior knowledge from simulations to a real-world context (e.g., if the virus continues to grow at this rate, how many people will be infected in a year?). Discussion may include reference to the measures of central tendency, different graphs, ways to look beyond the data, and making hypotheses about what the graphs do not tell us. Students should be encouraged to use their prior experience with simulations to draw plausible conclusions about what the results would be if mitigating measures were taken. Students may choose to explore the spread of the virus in other countries that used more or less restrictive measures to mitigate the disease and compare the growth of the virus in these countries to that in the United States.

Summative Performance Task: Written Task

At the conclusion of the simulations, students should complete a written task that answers the compelling question: Using data from the simulations, explain which mitigating strategy worked the best in preventing virus spread and why. How can we "flatten the curve" and what does that mean?

Extension Activity

As a written task and/or oral discussion, have students respond to the following: How could a community be prepared for a pandemic in the future? How could each person help with the spread of current and upcoming viruses? Predict what would happen if we did the simulation with other classrooms in the building. What can you do to actively control the spread of diseases?

INQUIRY DESIGN MODEL 2: HOW HAS COVID-19 IMPACTED OUR LIVES, COMMUNITIES, AND THE WORLD?

In the second inquiry, students explore the second compelling question, "How has COVID-19 impacted our lives, communities, and the world?" (See Table 4.6.) This inquiry is staged by using a PBS (2006) video resource on the flu of 1918. Prior to viewing the video clip, we suggest that students record the names, terms, and information that they predict will be included in the video clip and while viewing, record additional terms, names, and information included in the video. As a class, students will highlight the words that were heard or seen in the video to see if their predictions were correct. This video will prepare students to address the three supporting questions.

Table 4.6. Inquiry Design Model (IDM) Blueprint™: Impact of COVID-19

Compelling Question	How has COVID-19 impacted our lives, communities, and the world?	
Standards and Practices	NCSS Standard 2: Time, Continuity and Change NCSS Standard 3: People, Places, and Environment NCSS Standard 8: Science, Technology, and Society C3 Framework Dimension 2: Change, Continuity, and Context C3 Framework Dimension 3: Gathering and Evaluating Sources Teaching Tolerance Social Justice Anchor Standard 12: Students will recognize unfairness on the individual level and injustice at the institutional or systemic level.	
Staging the Question	PBS 1918 Flu Pandemic/American Experience Clip Predicting ABCs Strategy	

Supporting Question 1	Supporting Question 2	Supporting Question 3
(A) What is the impact of a pandemic on social behavior? (B) How have discrimination and biased speech been used during COVID-19 and other public health crises throughout U.S. history?	(A) How do communities respond to public health emergencies? (B) How does the coronavirus impact communities differently?	How do we identify and use reliable sources in the time of a pandemic?

Formative Performance Task		
Notice and Wonder (Question A) Time for Kids' McGrath (2020) *A Different Halloween* Jigsaw Teaching (Question B) Using the jigsaw teaching method, each group will teach their reading to peers; jigsaw teaching will focus on answering Question B.	Visual Mapping (Question A) Using the featured sources, students work in triads to create a visual map of local, state, and national responses to public health emergencies. Think-Pair-Share Discussion (Question B)	Understanding Misinformation Using the article, infographic, and quiz, create an original infographic that outlines the concept of misinformation and how to identify and use reliable sources."

Table 4.6. *Continued*

Featured Sources		
Source for Part A	Sources for Part A	Scholastic News's (2020) *Were you fooled?*
Time for Kids' McGrath (2020) *A Different Halloween*	CDC's (2013) *United States Public Health 101*	News Literacy Project's (2020a) *Five Types of Misinformation*
Sources for Part B	FEMA's (2020) *Coronavirus (Covid-19) Response*	News Literacy Project's (2020b) *Get Smart About Covid-19* quiz
National Geographic's (Strochlic, 2020) *America's Long History of Scapegoating Asian Americans*	Time for Kids' Joyce (2020) *Handwashing Helper*	News Literacy Project's (2020c) *Fighting Falsehoods on Social Media*
NBC News' (Yam, 2020) *Anti-Asian Bias Rose After Media, Officials Used "China Virus," Report Shows*	NCDHHS's (2020) *Do You Know Your 3 Ws?*	
Time Magazine's (Kambhampaty, 2020) *I Will Not Stand Silent*	NCOSHR's (2020) 3Ws Flyer	
	Sources for Part B	
	Facing History's (2020a) *Why is the Coronavirus Disproportionately Impacting Black Americans?*	
	CDC's (n.d.) *Covid-19 Hospitalization and Death Rates by Race/Ethnicity*	
	NBCNews' (Constante, 2020) *With Largest Share of Migrant Nurses, Entire U.S. Filipino Community Hit Hard by COVID-19*	

Summative Performance Task	Argument	Construct a written, oral, or digital response that answers the compelling question.
	Extension	Book Study
		Titles: *Fever Year: The Killer Flu of 1918* (Brown, 2019); *Blue* (Hostetter, 2010); and *Fever 1793* (Anderson, 2002)
		Task: Student journaling (Facing History, 2020b), Making choices for the common good (Facing History, 2020c)
		How is COVID-19 similar to and different from other epidemics?
		How are the modes of information sharing in *Fever Year*, *Blue* and *Fever 1793* different from the modes of communication used today in communicating about COVID-19?
		What are the differences in how the individuals in *Fever Year*, *Blue*, *Fever 1793*, and today have experienced the three diseases?
Taking Informed Action		Presentation: How has your understanding of COVID-19 developed through this inquiry?

Supporting Question 1:
What is the impact of a pandemic on social behavior? How have discrimination and biased speech been used during the COVID-19 pandemic and other public health crises throughout U.S. history?

Teachers model the notice-and-wonder strategy while the class reads *A Different Halloween* (McGrath, 2020). Students can then discuss examples of changes in social behavior identified in the article. Students are provided with a variety of images (photographs, posters, infographics) that communicate the social behaviors set forth in mandates and CDC recommendations. Images that address social gestures and interactions (e.g., hugs, handshakes), guidelines for quarantining in the home, and business policies are particularly helpful. Students consider the images and discuss what they notice and wonder about how COVID-19 has impacted social behavior in homes, communities, and larger communal spaces.

We suggest organizing students into three groups; each group will read one of the following resources that describes how Asian Americans have been discriminated against since the start of the COVID-19 pandemic: *America's Long History of Scapegoating Asian Americans* (Strochlic, 2020), *Anti-Asian Bias Rose after Media, Officials Used "China Virus," Report Shows* (Yam, 2020), or *I Will Not Stand Silent* (Kambhampaty, 2020). Students explore their online article and images, preparing for a jigsaw teaching seminar in which they teach their article to the other jigsaw groups.

Supporting Question 2
How do communities respond to public health emergencies? How does the coronavirus impact communities differently?

To answer the first question, students work in triads to first examine the featured sources in Part A of Figure 4.6 (CDC, 2013; Federal Emergency Management Assistance, 2020; Joyce, 2020; North Carolina Department of Health and Human Services, 2020; North Carolina Office of State Human Resources, 2020). Then they will create a visual map of their local, state, and national responses to public health emergencies. Their visual might compare and contrast the three levels of responses or display them individually. Identified responses might include: federal government versus state and local governments, vaccines, mandates on masks, reducing density of people, schools moved to remote learning, or securing personal protective equipment. If time allows, students can share the visual maps in small groups.

After creating a visual map, students consider the second question and accompanying sources using a Think-Pair-Share model. These three informational articles (CDC, n.d.; Constante, 2020; Facing History, 2020a) provide information about the disproportionate impact on various groups. Think-Pair-Share allows students to first think about the information individually, then discuss it with a partner, and then move into a small group to share their reactions to the sources. We encourage teachers to link this discussion back to the compelling question during a debriefing of this task.

Supporting Question 3
How do we identify and use reliable sources in the time of a pandemic?

Throughout the series of inquiries in this interdisciplinary unit, students are asked to use a variety of sources, varied by text type, complexity, and content. We know from our shared lived experiences during the COVID-19 global pandemic that we have to be deliberate consumers of media in our use of sources. We also know that the circulation of misinformation, including fake news, has increased during 2020, resulting in many individuals and families unsure of the integrity of sources related to COVID-19.

In this task, students are organized into small groups. Within these groups, students examine the Scholastic News (2020) article *Were You Fooled?* about the broom hoax to introduce the concept of misinformation. Teachers should encourage students to look carefully at the #HowToSpotA-Fake chart at the bottom of the article. This source introduces the idea of misinformation and will help students answer the supporting question. Building on the idea of misinformation, students will examine the News Literacy Project's (2020a) infographic on the *Five Types of Misinformation*; we encourage teachers to have students in small groups discuss practical examples of each type of misinformation that they have seen circulated around COVID-19. Finally, students should take the News Literacy Project's (2020b, 2020c) two featured quizzes, *Get Smart About COVID-19* and *Fighting Falsehoods on Social Media*. After answering each question, students see an explanation of the correct answer. At this point, students will be positioned to answer the compelling question and take informed action.

Extending the IDM and Taking Informed Action

Also noted in Figure 4.6 are two historical fiction chapter books, *Fever 1793* (Anderson, 2002) and *Blue* (Hostetter, 2010), and one nonfiction graphic novel title, *Fever Year: The Killer Flu of 1918* (Brown, 2019), to extend the study of COVID-19. In the extension activity, students self-select the title they would like to read. Both historical fiction titles center the experiences of individuals and communities directly impacted by an epidemic, and the graphic novel describes the flu of 1918 and explains what we know today about why this flu was so deadly. While each of the titles could be used exclusively as a whole-class read-aloud, we believe that using the titles in tandem provides students the opportunity to compare and contrast four public health crises—yellow fever, influenza, polio, and coronavirus—spanning over 227 years and identify how epidemiology has impacted the way humans exist over time.

We suggest running simultaneous book studies with the titles while also planning whole-class activities that allow the students to compare and contrast the four health crises. Parallel book studies can also provide space to facilitate students' bridging the historical fiction to today's world, an important skill for understanding the relevance of the past as it relates to the experiences of individuals and communities around the globe today. In the book study model, we suggest providing focused discussions or extension activities based on the following: communities' responses to public health crises, the development or use of isolation and quarantine, how modes of communication impacted the sharing of information, and how epidemiology has developed over time. The use of student journaling during the parallel book studies provides a place for individual formative and summative assessment and can be used as a discussion tool for students to hold student-facilitated seminars about the books. When used in conjunction with the three IDM tasks, the parallel book studies have the potential to extend and deepen students' engagement with the three supporting questions and overall understanding of the lasting impact of COVID-19. To encourage students to take informed action, we have included an inquiry from Facing History (2020c) that focuses on promoting the common good.

CONCLUSION

As COVID-19 continues to be unprecedented in its impact, we believe there is incredible opportunity for teachers to address the pandemic in ways that bring deeper learning in math, science, and social studies. This chapter offers a practical approach for young and adolescent learners to think about COVID-19 within the larger scope of epidemiology. This type of instructional planning at the elementary and middle level provides students a comprehensive opportunity to study complex and enduring issues of misinformation, public health, and social behavior through three disciplines.

The disciplines of science and social studies naturally overlap content, and math is used to expand learners' understanding of epidemiology and the far-reaching impacts of COVID-19. As elementary social studies is concerned with teaching learners how to make informed decisions and giving them the ability to analyze sources, this approach is a useful tool for reaching both aims. We argue that this work is especially important for this age group—elementary and middle grades—since laying the groundwork to promote an informed citizenry should not and cannot wait until the secondary years.

REFERENCES

Anderson, L. H. (2002). *Fever 1793*. Simon & Schuster Books for Young Readers.

Berger, M. (1995). *Germs make me sick!* Harper Collins.

Britannica Kids. (2020). *Virus*. Author. https://kids.britannica.com/kids/article/virus/390098

Brown, D. (2019). *Fever year: The killer flu of 1918*. HMH Books for Young Readers.

Capeci, A., & Cole, J. (2001). *Giant germ*. Scholastic.

Centers for Disease Control and Prevention. (2013). *United States Public Health 101*. Author. https://www.cdc.gov/publichealthgateway/docs/usph101.pdf

Centers for Disease Control and Prevention. (n.d.). *Covid-19 hospitalization and death rates by race/ethnicity*. Author. https://www.cdc.gov/coronavirus/2019-ncov/covid-data/investigations-discovery/hospitalization-death-by-race-ethnicity.html

Centers for Disease Control and Prevention. (2016). *Epidemiology in the classroom*. Author. https://www.cdc.gov/careerpaths/k12teacherroadmap/classroom/index.html

Constante, A. (2020, August 27). *With largest share of migrant nurses, entire U.S. Filipino community hit hard by Covid-19*. NBC News. https://www.nbcnews.com/news/asian-america/largest-share-migrant-nurses-entire-u-s-filipino-community-hit-n1237327

Eamer, C. (2016.) *Inside your insides*. Kids Can Press.

Facing History. (2020a, April 17). *Why is the coronavirus disproportionately impacting Black Americans?* https://www.facinghistory.org/educator-resources/current-events/why-coronavirus-disproportionately-impacting-black-americans

Facing History. (2020b, November 23). *Student learning during coronavirus*. https://www.facinghistory.org/educator-resources/current-events/student-journaling-during-coronavirus-pandemic

Facing History. (2020c, November 23). *How can we make choices that promote the common good?* https://www.facinghistory.org/educator-resources/current-events/covid-19-how-can-we-make-choices-promote-common-good

Federal Emergency Management Assistance. (2020). *Coronavirus (Covid-19) response*. https://www.fema.gov/disasters/coronavirus

Gardy, J. (2014). *It's catching: The infectious world of germs and microbes*. Owlkids.

Graham, A. (1987). *Statistical investigations in the secondary school*. Cambridge University Press.

Hostetter, J. M. (2010). *Blue*. Calkins Creek.

It's Okay to Be Smart. (2020, March 18). *What this chart actually means for Covid-19*. PBS. https://www.pbs.org/video/what-this-chart-actually-means-for-covid-19-ybsbtd/

Joyce, J. (2020a, September 24). Handwashing helper. *TIME for Kids*. https://www.timeforkids.com/g56/handwashing-helper-2/

Kambhampaty, A. (2020, June 25). I will not stand silent: 10 Asian Americans reflect on racism during the pandemic and the need for equality. *Time*. https://time.com/5858649/racism-coronavirus/

McGrath, B. (2020b, October 16). A different Halloween. *TIME for Kids*. https://www.timeforkids.com/g56/a-different-halloween-2/

National Council for the Social Studies. (2013). *College, career, and civic life (C3) framework for social studies state standards.* Author.

National Council of Teachers of Mathematics. (2000). *Principles and standards for school mathematics.* Author.

National Council of Teachers of Mathematics. (2014). *Principles to actions: Ensuring mathematical success for all.* Author.

National Council of Teachers of Mathematics. (2020). *Featured math resources: Covid-19, coronavirus, and pandemics.* Author. https://www.nctm.org/Corona-virus-and-Pandemics-Math-Resources/

National Geographic Kids. (2020). *Facts about coronavirus.* Author. https://kids.nationalgeographic.com/explore/science/facts-about-coronavirus/

National Science Teaching Association. (2020). *Why do we all have to stay home? Elementary version collection.* https://my.nsta.org/collection/ibqdc04FvYI_E

News Literacy Project. (2020a). *Five types of misinformation.* http://newslit.org/wp-content/uploads/2020/09/Misinformation-2020.pdf

News Literacy Project. (2020b). *Get smart about Covid-19.* https://newslit.org/educators/resources/get-smart-about-covid-19/

News Literacy Project. (2020c). *Fighting falsehoods on social media.* https://newslit.org/educators/resources/fighting-falsehoods-on-social-media/

NGSS Lead States. (2013). *Next generation science standards: For states, by states.* Author.

North Carolina Department of Health and Human Services. (2020). *Do you know your 3Ws?* YouTube. https://www.youtube.com/watch?v=JPb3lAMUfiQ&feature=youtu.be

North Carolina Office of State Human Resources. (2020). *Covid-19 safe return to work: Follow the three Ws.* Author. https://files.nc.gov/ncoshr/documents/files/20200603-COVID-19-Safe-Return-To-Work_Follow-the-Three-Ws-Quick-Reference.pdf

NOVA Teachers. (2017). *Nova science NOW: 1918 Flu.* PBS. https://www.pbs.org/wgbh/nova/teachers/activities/3318_02_nsn.html

Our World in Data. (2020). *Covid-19 data set for the US.* Author. https://ourworldindata.org/coronavirus/country/united-states?country=~USA

Public Broadcasting System. (2006). *American experience: Influenza 1918.* Author. https://www.pbs.org/wgbh/americanexperience/features/influenza-chapter-1/

Public Broadcasting System. (2020, March 6). *How to talk to your kids about coronavirus.* Author. https://www.pbs.org/parents/thrive/how-to-talk-to-your-kids-about-coronavirus

PBS Learning Media. (2020a). *Teaching guide: Exploring the polio epidemic and vaccine.* Author. https://unctv.pbslearningmedia.org/resource/dpla-tg-096/teaching-guide-exploring-the-polio-epidemic-and-vaccine/

PBS Learning Media. (2020b). *Teaching guide: Exploring the yellow fever epidemic of 1878.* Author. https://unctv.pbslearningmedia.org/resource/dpla-tg-095/teaching-guide-exploring-the-yellow-fever-epidemic-of-1878/

Scholastic News. (2020, March 30). *Were you fooled?* Author. https://sn56.scholastic.com/pages/promotion/033020/were-you-fooled.html

Strochlic, N. (2020, September 2). *America's long history of scapegoating Asian Americans.* National Geographic. https://www.nationalgeographic.com/history/2020/09/asian-american-racism-covid/

Swan, K., Lee, J., & Grant, S. G. (2015). The New York state toolkit and the inquiry design model: Anatomy of an inquiry. *Social Education, 79*(5), 316–322.

Yam, K. (2020, September 29). *Anti-Asian bias rose after media, officials used "China virus," report shows*. NBC News. https://www.nbcnews.com/news/asian-america/anti-asian-bias-rose-after-media-officials-used-china-virus-n1241364

CHAPTER 5

Ideology, Information, and Political Action Surrounding COVID-19

Christopher H. Clark

Our current president has failed in his most basic duty to this nation. He failed to protect us. He failed to protect America. And, my fellow Americans, that is unforgivable.

—Joe Biden, August 2020

I think we did a great job.

—Donald Trump, September 2020

The 2020 presidential campaign, as with much of life during 2020 and beyond, was shaped extensively by COVID-19. In addition to drastically altering what it means to campaign (digital conventions, socially distant interviews, superspreader campaign rallies, etc.), the government's handling of COVID-19 was a central issue. Both quotations above (the first from Mr. Biden's speech accepting his nomination [Stevens, 2020], the second from a town hall held by Mr. Trump [Cathey, 2020]) reference the government response to the disease, and it is noteworthy that their assessments are mutually exclusive. Whether one trusts the first or the second statement will largely depend on a person's ideology. While such a gap is unlikely to surprise followers of politics, the political stagnation resulting from these opposite assessments of government action/inaction has implications for both democracy and democratic education.

Civic reasoning is often centered on the question "What should we do?" in response to a given issue that impacts the common good (McAvoy & Hess, 2013; Parker, 2006; Parker & Hess, 2001). Depending on how issues are framed, however, individuals may provide different answers to that question. These differing conclusions are often rooted in differing identities,

experiences, and ways of viewing the world. The case of COVID-19 illustrates the larger necessity of moving beyond teaching about the structure
and powers of the government or ideal deliberative conditions (Knowles &
Clark, 2018) and toward helping students understand the oft-messy process
of governance in the United States today. In this chapter, I address how
students can understand actions taken by the government and individuals
during the COVID-19 crisis through one such lens: ideology.

IDEOLOGY AND POLITICAL THINKING

American politics is typically described in terms of a left–right spectrum,
with liberals occupying the left and conservatives occupying the right. Particular points on the spectrum are often given specific labels to add further
distinction, such as "democratic socialist" being used to describe policies
that are further to the left than those of the mainstream Democratic Party.
Many political scientists have argued for a multidimensional conceptualization of political ideology to better capture groups, such as libertarians, who
do not neatly fit on a single left–right spectrum. Political scientists Stanley
Feldman and Christopher Johnston (2014), for example, argued that individual issue positions should be classified on two axes, one for preferred
economic policies and another for preferred social policies.

For the purposes of this chapter, however, I rely on the simpler, one-di-
mensional definition of "liberal" or "left" to indicate a belief in active
government economically (e.g., robust regulations, well-funded social and
economic programs) and support for equal rights and social justice (e.g.,
laws protecting minority groups). By "conservative" or "right," I refer to
a more laissez-faire economic approach (e.g., low taxes and limited government regulation) and a belief in government promotion of "traditional
values" (e.g., defining marriage as between one man and one woman).

When teaching about ideology, teachers should note the distinction between political *ideology* and political *party*. While the correlation of Republicans with conservative ideology and Democrats with liberal ideology
generally holds true, the two major political parties in the United States are
coalitions and contain substantial ideological variance within their voting
blocs and among the politicians who caucus with the party. It is important
for students to understand these distinctions, as media accounts will often
frame stories in terms of political parties and not ideological positions.

It is also necessary to draw a distinction between ideology as a con-
stellation of political beliefs and ideology as an identity. In the former
case, it is arguable whether most people even have a consistent ideology,
as individuals' positions on particular issues may or may not coherently
align with conservatism or liberalism. In early research on ideology in the
American public, political scientist Philip Converse (1964/2006) found that

individuals' issue positions tended to shift over time and that only 3.5% of American voters held ideologically consistent views. The lack of ideological consistency may be a function of simple knowledge, as Americans tend to score low on measures of political knowledge or policy (Delli Carpini & Keeter, 1996). In other words, the average person may not know enough about political issues to have an ideology.

Many political scholars, however, challenge the notion that American voters are completely uninformed. Arthur Lupia (2016), for example, noted that standard measures of political knowledge are not aligned with information that individuals use in their everyday lives to make political judgments. For example, many measures of political knowledge ask the number of years a senator serves but do not ask about current issues that voters might use to make selections at the ballot box. Additionally, Stephen Goggin and colleagues found that most participants in their experiment were able to correctly associate issue positions and even candidate demographic characteristics (such as religious beliefs) with ideology. In other words, even relatively uniformed voters had a general sense of "what goes with what" in terms of ideologies (Goggin et al., 2020, p.992).

There is also evidence that different age cohorts in American society may have differing levels of ideological consistency and that consistency may have increased in recent years. A study by political scientists Laura Stoker and M. Kent Jennings (2008) found that younger generations tend to be more ideologically aligned on many issues than previous generations were at the same age. Thus, a young voter today is likely to exhibit more ideological consistency than a young voter in previous decades. Another political scientist, Matthew Levendusky (2009), has theorized that growing up in a polarized society may explain the increasing ideological alignment among young people.

Despite being debatably ideological in terms of issue positions, many Americans identify as liberals or conservatives (or Democrats and Republicans). Many political scientists suggest that these identifications substitute for issue knowledge when individuals are unaware of specific policies, resulting in voters simply following the lead of party leaders or political "elites" (Achen & Bartels, 2016; Lenz, 2012). While the influence of identification or party elites is not absolute (Lavine et al., 2012) and voters still weigh issue information alongside partisan or ideological cues when available (Bullock, 2011), ideological and partisan labels carry a lot of weight in determining which leaders and what types of information people trust.

Research in social sciences has illustrated the various ways in which ideological identities shape interpretations of information (Achen & Bartels, 2016; Haidt, 2012; Lodge & Taber, 2013; Lupia, 2016). Ideology, when it is a salient part of an individual's identity, pushes individuals to view information in ways that favor and reinforce that identity, a phenomenon called motivated reasoning. Political scientists Milton Lodge and Charles

Taber (2013) have linked motivated reasoning to association networks in human memory that connect information to emotions. For example, if an individual sees the name of a political party, they will also likely experience an emotional response (positive or negative) based on how they feel about that party in general.

When information is perceived as relevant to an individual's ideological identity, motivated reasoning is likely to occur, even if the individual believes they are being rational. In one experiment, psychologist Dan Kahan and colleagues found that individuals' numerical ability was a chief determinant of their interpretation of researcher-generated data about the effectiveness of a fictional rash cream, but that individuals' political ideology was more influential when that same fictional data were relabeled as the effectiveness of handgun bans in reducing violent crime (Kahan et al., 2017). In other words, making the data about gun control activated participants' politically motivated reasoning and made individuals more likely to interpret the data (often incorrectly) in favor of their political positions. Similar phenomena have been observed with real-world data. Using the October 2012 jobs report (during the Obama administration), public opinion scholars Brian Schaffner and Cameron Roche (2017) found that Republican participants in their study continued to state that the unemployment rate had increased during the time period covered by the report despite viewing data that showed a decrease in unemployment.

IDEOLOGY AND SCIENCE

In the case of COVID-19, there is a disconnect between the recommendations of scientists and the behaviors of politicians and citizens that is mostly confined to the political right. COVID-19 is still relatively new in terms of the time it takes to conduct and publish research, but many political scientists have studied the phenomenon of science denial (denying or disregarding scientific information) regarding topics such as climate change, and this research can inform how we understand ideological responses to the pandemic. Surveys of the U.S. public tend to find that conservatives are more skeptical about the existence and causes of climate change (Bolsen et al., 2015). Psychologists Stephan Lewandowsky and Klaus Oberauer (2016) argued that although the mechanisms that drive science denial are not specific to conservatives or Republicans (though these groups do show overall lower trust in scientists than the opposite end of the political spectrum), scientific consensus in recent years about issues such as climate change has tended to challenge conservative values (such as preference for economic nonintervention) more than it has liberal values. Science denial on issues such as climate change may also represent an intersection between conservatives' political and religious beliefs. Social studies scholar Jennifer Hauver James (2010), for example, documented instances of religious students considering climate change a closed issue (see Hess, 2009), viewing actions taken to mitigate or reverse the phenomenon as contradictory to divine will.

Cues from media and political leaders may influence the beliefs of individuals who identify with a given ideology on topics such as climate change. Political scientist Gabriel Lenz (2012) has argued that because individuals are generally not fully informed on all relevant political issues, they will trust cues from party leaders, even if the issue positions of party leaders shift over time. Often, these cues will be conveyed via news and other media. One study using data from 2000 to 2014 found that media coverage of climate change was a key correlate of perceived climate change threat among partisans (Carmichael et al., 2017). For example, perceived climate change threat rises among self-identified Democrats with increases in time devoted to the issue in outlets such as *The New York Times* or National Public Radio. Conversely, perceptions of climate change threat drop among Republicans during periods when the issue received more coverage on Rush Limbaugh's radio program.

While peer-reviewed research on public perception of COVID-19 is still limited as of this writing, early studies found correlations between ideology and perceptions of the virus (Calvillo et al., 2020; Shepherd et al., 2020). Similar to trends seen in climate change research, both a broad distrust of scientists and cues from political leaders and conservative media outlets shape conservative attitudes and beliefs about the virus. Conservatives are far less likely to trust information about COVID-19 coming from public health officials (Shepherd et al., 2020) and generally perceive the virus as less dangerous than liberals do. As with climate change, these perceptions may stem partially from a motivated rejection of the science based on conflicts with conservative values (such as viewing lockdowns as impinging on economic activity or personal liberty) or due to dismissals and minimizations of the virus threat from then-President Trump and members of the virus response team.

Additionally, conservatives also were more likely than liberals to think the virus was the product of a conspiracy and that the media were exaggerating the threat of the virus (Calvillo et al., 2020). Conservatives also seem more likely to amplify misinformation about the virus on social media platforms, tweeting positive sentiments about unproven treatments like hydroxychloroquine and voicing conspiratorial thoughts about Bill Gates's and China's role in the virus more often than liberals (Havey, 2020). Cues, whether through tweets from then-President Trump or messages from other prominent conservative leaders, are also likely influential in fostering this spread of misinformation.

In short, there is ample evidence that political ideology influences individuals' behavior and processing of information, and COVID-19 is no exception. Moreover, actions that might make sense within one's ideological frame of mind might make no sense to those outside of the frame. If students are to understand the widely divergent beliefs and actions taken by government and individual citizens, they will need to understand the role ideology plays. Below are ideas for lessons that have students examine these connections.

TEACHING ABOUT IDEOLOGY AND THE COVID-19 PANDEMIC

The COVID-19 pandemic represents a human tragedy on a scale rarely seen, and it will likely shape politics and discourse about the functions of government for years to come. COVID-19 highlighted differences in how politicians and various segments of the public in the United States view the rightful function of government, especially during a crisis. Further, the pandemic has highlighted lines of political and ideological division in the United States government and population. Even after the crisis has passed, these rifts in the United States will persist, and COVID-19 will be a valuable case study for educators who wish to study these divisions, and the mechanisms that drive them, with their students.

Teachers hoping to help students understand the significance of COVID-19, both as an illustration of politics and governance in action and as an event that will likely shape life in the United States going forward, can utilize ideology as a lens through which to inquire about the crisis. In this section, there are suggested questions and resources for two inquiries that teachers could conduct that illustrate the influence of ideology on responses to the pandemic.

Prior to inquiries into ideology, teachers can engage students with the myriad practical definitions of the terms "liberal" and "conservative." Students can define the terms in their own words and collect the definitions to compare them. Teachers may also use a political typology survey, such as the one offered by Pew Research (https://www.pewresearch.org/politics/quiz/political-typology/), for students to gauge their own political ideological label and how it compares to their own self-conception and other political "types." Once they have reflected on their own ideology, they should consider the ideological tendencies of common sources of news and information. There are multiple websites that classify the ideologies of news media. While such ratings are often subjective, AllSides (https://www.allsides.com) and Media Bias/Fact Check (https://mediabiasfactcheck.com) provide detailed descriptions of their rating methodologies that teachers and students can evaluate. These activities will lay the foundation for inquiry into the effects of ideology on political discourse and the public by providing clarity as to what is meant when the words "conservative" or "liberal" come up and illustrating what outlets tend to give voice to (and/or shape) the thoughts of each group.

Inquiring into Mask-Wearing

The first example encourages teachers and students to conduct inquiries about how ideological frames shape public behavior using the trove of public statements, polling data, and media accounts available on COVID-19. It is best to narrow students' focus to a specific question about the pandemic. In this case, the focus will be on *Why do some people refuse to wear masks to help prevent the spread of COVID-19?* To be clear, in such inquiries, whether wearing a mask helps prevent the spread of COVID-19 should be considered a closed question, as most medical experts and health organizations around the globe recommend it. Instead, teachers should focus on why individuals would choose to ignore sound medical advice about masks and, specifically, how ideology does or does not influence that choice.

A key resource for inquiring into mask-wearing is data about how many people are wearing masks, especially when it is broken down by demographics and party/ideological preference. Organizations such as Pew Research offer many polls that allow for tracking relative numbers of individuals who regularly wore masks at certain points during the COVID-19 crisis. For example, one report compared mask-wearing among members of the public in June and August of 2020 (Kramer, 2020). That survey noted that mask-wearing had increased for both Republican (53% in June, 76% in August) and Democratic-identifying respondents (76% in June, 92% in August). The report's authors note a persistent, albeit narrowed, gap between the parties in terms of reported mask-wearing.

Another analysis of Pew data analyzed open-ended responses to questions about how different life was during the crisis, noting substantial differences in the types of comments made about masks by individuals identifying with each major political party (Van Kessel & Quinn, 2020). Democrats who mentioned masks in their sample were more likely than Republicans to express concerns about people improperly wearing masks or not wearing them at all. Republicans, on the other hand, were more likely than Democrats to express skepticism about the efficacy of masks or view them as an infringement on individual liberties.

Another resource for an inquiry into ideology and mask-wearing could be the statements and examples set by leaders or elites. Perhaps the most dramatic examples are differences between the two presidential candidates in the 2020 election, in which COVID-19 was a major issue. Students can track the statements of each candidate about masks, as well as the frequency with which each candidate wore a mask in public. Further, media clips from major networks such as CNN and FOX News can show how the messages from leaders about masks were amplified to various audiences.

To begin the inquiry, students can employ quotations from individuals interviewed about mask-wearing to generate a list of underlying reasons why individuals choose not to wear masks. From there, students can classify those beliefs (e.g., impingement on civil liberties, belief that they are ineffective, mistrust of individuals and institutions that recommend them) and investigate how people might come by them. Most reasons for not wearing a mask are connected in some way to ideology or ideological identity. Using the resources described above, students can begin to recognize correlations between ideological identity and mask-wearing, as well as trace messages from leaders that are repeated by those who refuse to wear masks.

As the inquiry progresses, students will be able to see the various ways that ideology functions. Some of the reasons given by antimaskers will likely be connected to ideology as a belief system, such as when individuals express a belief that wearing a mask violates individual liberty. Other reasons could reflect ideology as an identity, such as when an individual expresses skepticism about certain leaders who put mask mandates in place or support for other leaders, like former President Trump, who eschewed and even mocked mask-wearing. As an informed action project, students could research ways to counteract these influences, such as framing messages to appeal to conservative values (Feinberg & Willer, 2015), and devise a campaign to promote public health measures in their community.

Inquiring into Government Action

A second example engages students with ideological beliefs about the role of government and how they shape actions deemed acceptable to address the crisis. Here, students draw upon congressional debates about financial stimulus, loans to businesses, and voting reform to compare politicians' priorities with given political ideologies. As an example, here I pursue the framing question *What is the role of government during a crisis?* Further guiding questions that will help students could include *What is the nature of the COVID-19 crisis?* and *What, if anything, should the government do about it?*

The first guiding question, about the nature of the COVID-19 crisis, is seemingly straightforward, though students will find that not everybody sees the crisis through the same lens. Because the main concern is the spread of a virus, COVID-19 is clearly a public health crisis. The novel coronavirus also represents an economic crisis, in that fears of spreading the virus and lockdowns or other actions taken to stop the spread (though they varied substantially among states, communities, and individuals) created hardships for individuals and businesses.

The degree to which individual politicians and government officials treated COVID-19 as either a health or economic crisis may reflect their priorities. Students could compare statements of various public officials throughout the crisis to examine the degree to which they use public-health–centered rhetoric (containing the virus, providing recommendations from public health experts) versus economic rhetoric (focusing on businesses and employment). Do the students see different rhetoric coming from liberal political figures than from conservatives, or do they observe no correlation between ideology and public statements? Does it vary at different points in the crisis? Teachers looking for resources to help pursue these questions can check the plethora of transcripts of coronavirus briefings given by the White House, government agencies such as the Centers for Disease Control and Prevention, or state and local governments, all of which are available via a quick Internet search. Depending on the exact questions or goals of the lesson, teachers may choose to compare transcripts from different points in the crisis or look at multiple transcripts from different individuals or agencies from the same point during the pandemic.

For the latter guiding question (what, if anything, should the government do?) students can examine debates at the national and state levels about issues such as economic relief. As a starting point in evaluating economic stimulus, students can examine the initial action taken by the government in March 2020 as businesses were shuttering and jobs were being lost at a high rate. Numerous news outlets provided accessible summaries of the emergency relief bill, known as the CARES Act (e.g., Snell, 2020). Students can research these summaries, as well as highlights from the debate over the bill in Congress. A second stimulus, smaller than the first, was passed in December 2020. During the negotiations for the latter stimulus, many Republicans deemed the various proposals too spendy, while Democrats argued they did not go far enough. Debates about further stimulus packages are ongoing as of the beginning of 2021.

By looking at the statements in support of or against each of the stimulus packages, students can evaluate the way that ideology frames what each group considers plausible answers to the guiding inquiry questions. Liberals and conservatives have different conceptions of how much the government should intervene in the economy and how much the government should render direct assistance to individuals (with liberals favoring more intervention and assistance and conservatives favoring less). Students can explore how these ideological positions shape what is included in each proposed plan and how ideology frames what each side views as acceptable solutions to the crisis.

Here again it is useful to remind students that the ideological positions do not necessarily parallel political party allegiance. Even within political parties, differing ideological groups disagree on how to evaluate the proposals. For example, Alexandria Ocasio-Cortez, a representative who identifies as a Democratic Socialist and typically takes positions more liberal than those of the mainstream Democratic Party, stated in September 2020 that her party should hold out for bigger stimulus measures than those for which they were currently advocating (Zeballos-Roig, 2020). Early in the pandemic, Bernie Sanders, another self-identified Democratic Socialist, advocated for recurring stimulus checks rather than the one-time check provided as part of the CARES act. Both positions are in line with Democratic Socialist ideology but not necessarily the positions of mainstream liberals.

It is also useful to remind students that not every proposal or action taken by politicians is driven solely by ideology. The COVID-19 crisis also coincided with the 2020 presidential election. The desire to win that election may have shaped what each party considered an acceptable action and whose interests they favored when responding to the crisis. For example, politicians facing reelection in competitive states may have moderated their views or put forward policy proposals more as signals to a voting base rather than as realistic solutions with a chance of becoming law.

Further, not all politicians base their actions on accurate information. Through ignorance, motivated reasoning, or bad-faith misrepresentations of science for political gain, numerous politicians have contributed to the spread of misinformation about COVID-19 and have likely contributed to the severity of the crisis. Inquiry into how government should handle a crisis like COVID-19 should also examine such actions, whether they are in service of an ideological agenda or other political goal.

GOVERNANCE ON PAPER VS. GOVERNANCE IN ACTION

State standards for civics and government courses typically highlight structures, key documents, and individuals when discussing how the United States functions politically. While necessary as a foundation, focusing exclusively on these relatively basic elements presents an incomplete picture of the messiness of the American political system. Students should understand how the government operates in the real world and how that operation impacts the lives of citizens directly or indirectly. For example, simply knowing that the House and Senate must each pass a bill for it to go to the President does not help them fully grasp the complexities of negotiations surrounding COVID-19 relief bills.

As previously mentioned, students should also understand the distinction between ideological belief systems and ideological identities. Individuals can act consciously to pursue ideological agendas, but ideological identity can impact behavior in subtler or even subconscious ways (Lodge & Taber, 2013). This distinction can help demystify behavior among the public that may be confusing on the surface, such as resistance to wearing masks despite overwhelming scientific consensus about their efficacy in slowing the spread of the virus. In addition, awareness of ideological frames can help students understand difficulties politicians have in coming to agreements, even on issues that theoretically should prompt widespread agreement, such as relief to citizens and businesses during a pandemic.

Much of governance and civic life falls outside of civics standards, and indeed even outside the conscious awareness of citizens. Ideological identity, while not the only force with subtle workings and profound consequences impacting U.S. politics, is key to understanding how the political world works. Moreover, using an ideological lens to evaluate critical moments in governance, such as the COVID-19 crisis, can help students understand why the country they see on paper in their civics classes is not the country they see on the news.

REFERENCES

Achen, C. H., & Bartels, L. M. (2016). *Democracy for realists: Why elections do not produce responsive government*. Princeton University Press.

Bolsen, T., Druckman, J. N., & Cook, F. L. (2015). Citizens', scientists', and policy advisors' beliefs about global warming. *Annals of the American Academy of Political and Social Science, 658*(1), 271–295. https://doi.org/10.1177/0002716214558393

Bullock, J. G. (2011). Elite influence on public opinion in an informed electorate. *American Political Science Review, 105*(3), 496–515. https://doi.org/10.1017/S0003055411000165

Calvillo, D. P., Ross, B. J., Garcia, R. J. B., Smelter, T. J., & Rutchick, A. M. (2020). Political ideology predicts perceptions of the threat of COVID-19 (and susceptibility to fake news about it). *Social Psychological and Personality Science, 11*(8), 1119–1128. https://doi.org/10.1177/1948550620940539

Carmichael, J. T., Brulle, R. J., & Huxster, J. K. (2017). The great divide: Understanding the role of media and other drivers of the partisan divide in public concern over climate change in the USA, 2001–2014. *Climatic Change, 141*(4), 599–612. https://doi.org/10.1007/s10584-017-1908-1

Cathey, L. (2020, September 15). Trump's ABC town hall: President faces tough questions. *ABC News*. https://abcnews.go.com/Politics/trump-questions-uncommitted-voters-abc-news-town-hall/story?id=73005086

Converse, P. E. (2006). The nature of belief systems in mass publics. *Critical Review, 18*(1), 1–74. (Original work published 1964) https://doi.org/10.1080/08913810608443650

Delli Carpini, M. X., & Keeter, S. (1996). *What Americans know about politics and why it matters*. Yale University Press.

Feinberg, M., & Willer, R. (2015). From gulf to bridge: When do moral arguments facilitate political influence? *Personality and Social Psychology Bulletin, 41*(12), 1665–1681. https://doi.org/10.1177/0146167215607842

Feldman, S., & Johnston, C. (2014). Understanding the determinants of political ideology: Implications of structural complexity. *Political Psychology, 35*(3), 337–358. https://doi.org/10.1111/pops.12055

Goggin, S. N., Henderson, J. A., & Theodoridis, A. G. (2020). What goes with red and blue? Mapping partisan and ideological associations in the minds of voters. *Political Behavior, 42*, 985–1013. https://doi.org/10.1007/s11109-018-09525-6

Haidt, J. (2012). *The righteous mind: Why good people are divided by politics and religion*. Vintage Books.

Havey, N. F. (2020). Partisan public health: How does political ideology influence support for COVID19 related misinformation? *Journal of Computational Social Science, 3,* 319–342. https://doi.org/10.1007/s42001-020-00089-2

Hess, D. E. (2009). *Controversy in the classroom: The democratic power of discussion.* Routledge.

James, J. H. (2010). "Democracy is the devil's snare": Theological certainty in teacher education. *Theory & Research in Social Education, 38*(4), 618–639. https://doi.org/10.1080/00933104.2010.10473441

Kahan, D. M., Peters, E., Dawson, E. C., & Slovic, P. (2017). Motivated numeracy and enlightened self-government. *Behavioural Public Policy, 1*(1), 54–86.

Knowles, R. T., & Clark, C. H. (2018). How common is the common good? Moving beyond idealistic notions of deliberative democracy in education. *Teaching and Teacher Education, 71,* 12–23. https://doi.org/10.1016/j.tate.2017.12.002

Kramer, S. (2020, August 27). *More Americans say they are regularly wearing masks in stores and other businesses.* Pew Research Center. https://www.pewresearch.org/fact-tank/2020/08/27/more-americans-say-they-are-regularly-wearing-masks-in-stores-and-other-businesses/

Lavine, H. G., Johnston, C. D., & Steenbergen, M. R. (2012). *The ambivalent partisan: How critical loyalty promotes democracy.* Oxford University Press.

Lenz, G. (2012). *Follow the leader: How voters respond to politicians' policies and performance.* University of Chicago Press.

Levandusky, M. (2009). *The partisan sort: How liberals became Democrats and conservatives became Republicans.* University of Chicago Press.

Lewandowsky, S., & Oberauer, K. (2016). Motivated rejection of science. *Current Directions in Psychological Science, 25*(4), 217–222. https://doi.org/10.1177/0963721416654436

Lodge, M., & Taber, C. (2013). *The rationalizing voter.* Cambridge University Press.

Lupia, A. (2016). *Uninformed: Why people seem to know so little about politics and what we can do about it.* Oxford University Press.

McAvoy, P., & Hess, D. (2013). Classroom deliberation in an era of political polarization. *Curriculum Inquiry, 43*(1), 14–47. https://doi.org/10.1111/curi.12000

Parker, W. C. (2006). Public discourses in schools: Purposes, problems, possibilities. *Educational Researcher, 35*(8), 11–18. https://doi.org/10.3102/0013189X035008011

Parker, W. C., & Hess, D. (2001). Teaching with and for discussion. *Teaching and Teacher Education, 17*(3), 273–289. https://doi.org/10.1016/S0742-051X(00)00057-3

Schaffner, B. F., & Roche, C. (2017). Misinformation and motivated reasoning: Responses to economic news in a politicized environment. *Public Opinion Quarterly, 81*(1), 86–110.

Shepherd, H., MacKendrick, N., & Mora, G. C. (2020). Pandemic politics: Political worldviews and COVID-19 beliefs and practices in an unsettled time. *Socius, 6,* 1–18. https://doi.org/10.1177/2378023120972575

Snell, K. (2020, March 26). *What's inside the Senate's $2 trillion coronavirus aid package.* National Public Radio. https://www.npr.org/2020/03/26/821457551/whats-inside-the-senate-s-2-trillion-coronavirus-aid-package

Stevens, M. (2020, August 20). Joe Biden accepts presidential nomination: Full transcript. *New York Times.* https://www.nytimes.com/2020/08/20/us/politics/biden-presidential-nomination-dnc.html

Stoker, L., & Jennings, M. K. (2008). Of time and the development of partisan polarization. *American Journal of Political Science, 52*(3), 619–635.

Van Kessel, P., & Quinn, D. (2020). *Both Republicans and Democrats cite masks as a negative effect of COVID-19, but for very different reasons.* Pew Research Center. https://www.pewresearch.org/fact-tank/2020/10/29/both-republicans-and-democrats-cite-masks-as-a-negative-effect-of-covid-19-but-for-very-different-reasons/

Zeballos-Roig, J. (2020, September 16). Alexandria Ocasio-Cortez says Democrats should look past the 'sugar high' of another $1,200 stimulus check—and urges them to hold out for a bigger package that includes state aid and health funding. *Business Insider.* https://www.businessinsider.com/aoc-democrats-bigger-coronavirus-aid-deal-stimulus-checks-unemployment-2020-9

CHAPTER 6

The Spatiality of a Pandemic

Deconstructing Social Inequality
Through Social Inquiry

Sandra J. Schmidt

Historically, pandemics have forced humans to break with the past and imagine their world anew. This one is no different. It is a portal, a gateway between
one world and the next. We can choose to walk through it, dragging the
carcasses of our prejudice and hatred, our avarice, our data banks and dead
ideas, our dead rivers and smoky skies behind us. Or we can walk through
lightly, with little luggage, ready to imagine another world.

—Arundhati Roy, 2020

I take inspiration from this call by Indian activist Arundhati Roy. The pandemic has exposed broken systems. Limited global infrastructure has meant
a lack of coordinated problem solving, exacerbating global poverty and inequitable access to vaccines and protections. Racial and economic disparities
in the United States have led to disproportionate deaths, long-term illnesses,
less access to quality healthcare, and intensified poverty and housing vulnerability among Black, Indigenous, and People of Color (BIPOC) populations,
as well as poor families who serve as frontline/essential workers.

Stories of struggle do not merely belong to individuals; they are systemic. Thus, it is not surprising that Black Lives Matter protests and platforms
gained traction during the pandemic. People most harmed by inequities have
long understood the implications of racial oppression and class suppression.
The rest of us rely on social scientists and media to expose social inequities.

After glimpsing this brokenness and (re)posting our outrage on social
media, do we return to our familiar lives, or do we accelerate the work of
social change? Have we finally encountered a moment that reveals enough
to commit us to education that abolishes racist, classist, and patriarchal
structures? This chapter explores how social inquiry can navigate young

learners into critical encounters with their communities and media sources to pursue understanding for social change.

As a social studies educator, I am drawn to education as a site that embodies social inequities but simultaneously contains possibility for remedy. Dewey (1938/2003) argued that social inquiry would transform mere observation into social understanding. In my courses, we emphasize the *process* of ongoing inquiry and deemphasize the *product*. As we analyze sources, students are prompted to continue posing questions and to further examine the root structures that shape the visible symptoms/observations behind our initial questions. Social inquiry is ultimately an engagement with inequity, as it demands critical consideration of why certain stories are available, what sources are privileged, and how social structures differentially shape lives (Dickens & Fontana, 2015). If social inquiry is offered as an alternative to traditional teaching in the wake of the coronavirus pandemic and Black Lives Matter protests, then concerns about racism, class suppression, and patriarchy need to be central to how teachers frame inquiry.

In hiding behind discourses of progress, reducing geography to naming places on maps, and ignoring the exclusionary practices of civics, the field of social studies can be a technology of unequal social reproduction. Contrarily, we can use practices like social inquiry to make disparities visible and help young learners act on this knowledge. As a geographer, I use spatial observations to begin an inquiry that will lead my students to a better understanding of the world around them. This chapter takes up three COVID-19-inspired inquiries that are adaptable to K–12 classrooms. Each inquiry begins with a conceptual discussion that situates the inquiry in a social studies issue, demonstrates a method/tool of inquiry, and culminates with a "next thinking" section that offers ways K–12 teachers could pursue further inquiry for learners and teachers.

INQUIRY 1: IS THE COVID-19 PANDEMIC A GLOBAL ISSUE?

Framing "Global"

The query of the pandemic as a global issue is situated within global citizenship education. Philosopher Peter Singer (2002) argued that we need a global ethic wherein we have greater obligation to foreigners than our countrymates. He explored problems that float across the world, like climate change and a pandemic. In the face of a lack of global institutions for remedy, Singer argued that addressing global issues rests upon individuals developing globally oriented ethics that they put into action. Singer's ideas are shared by global educators who have argued that most contemporary dilemmas do not comply with national borders and that we need new structures for problem-solving.

Borders are political and social constructions that impact lives. The borders between countries and around development communities contain people and distinguish people on either side of the border. Individuals are identified through the bounded places to which they claim membership/citizenship. Citizens are afforded protections and rights that others are denied. People are increasingly migratory and disconnect themselves from the singularity of national belonging. They find some borders more permeable than others, depending on a hierarchy of nations, races, and geopolitical powers. I can move easily between Malawi and Mozambique at many points along the border, but a Malawian must present extensive documentation to enter the United States. Borders are not merely lines on maps, but lines of consequence.

Concepts like "global" and "borders" are part of an array of spatial ideas that we can use to examine a disease that has crossed borders to cover the globe, a *pandemic*. From Singer's (2002) perspective, we may finally have a global issue around which we can align ourselves with foreigners. How do the flow of the virus and its remedies teach us about globalization and how we position ourselves in relation to others?

Inquiry: Discourse Analysis

My wondering/wandering into this inquiry arose while teaching Global Citizenship Education in Spring 2020. My students were preparing essays defending a claim about a global issue when the university suddenly became virtual. By the time I read their essays, my students were scattered across the globe. What was briefly a virus disrupting China and South Korea was suddenly a global pandemic. Within my course, it seemed important to watch whether we might transcend self-interests (Singer, 2002) to globally tackle a threat more immediate than climate change. To query this issue, students downloaded news articles from English-speaking sources into a class folder. We then read and shared our analysis of the discourse related to people racing to get "home," where home might be a country of birth, a preferred place to live, or where college students find their families. This section offers a sampling of the themes we found about a nationalistic response to this seemingly global issue.

As COVID-19 became global, media reported that countries were prioritizing the repatriation of citizens/residents. Repatriation was fueled by the closing of national borders, producing a sharp distinction of people based on citizenship. When Morocco and Peru closed their borders, national governments sent in planes to rescue their stranded citizens (Finnegan, 2020).

Repatriation distinguished citizens from foreign nationals who sought to return to the United States. In a quick motion, the U.S. president signed a measure shutting the borders to travelers from Europe (McAuley, 2020). As U.S. citizens/residents and people with reason to be in the United States rushed to European airports to rebook flights, clarification was made that the travel ban did not affect U.S. citizens or travelers from the United Kingdom, Ireland, and non-Schengen countries (BBC News, 2020). The policies distinguished between certain Europeans and U.S. citizens/residents, as earlier policies did with China. At the border, the distinction was less clear. Sources reported that at Chicago's O'Hare Airport all travelers were corralled into one hall with no medical screening for anyone (McAuley, 2020). European and U.S. travelers from Europe were differentiated even though they traveled from the same locales and presumably presented the same risk; one was (re)presented as dangerous and the other was not.

The discourse of "foreign" produced a strange rhetoric of safety for a virus that did not discern nationality/borders. Evacuations presumed an obligation to citizens, but the corresponding travel orders attached safety to "domestic" and danger to "foreign." The naming of COVID-19 reflected a similar distancing effort. The U.S. government consistently referred to COVID-19 as the "foreign virus," "China virus," and "Wuhan virus," linking the virus/problem to Other places. As Wuhan reopened and COVID-19 began to threaten other Asian countries, the Chinese embassy referred to it as the "Japanese coronavirus" (Campbell, 2020).

The U.S. government was one of the last to evacuate people, claiming it was not their responsibility to evacuate citizens (Finnegan, 2020). Their response did not reflect the desire of travelers and expats to return home, nor the desire of places to expel "foreigners." Perhaps U.S. citizens desired to return home because they were secure in the belief that the medical technologies in their country would protect them if they fell ill, suggesting that the world was not working together to offer care for all. The self-identified "stranded" citizens reported ill treatment in Nepal, Morocco, and elsewhere, where locals feared these "foreigners" who had resided alongside them for weeks or months suddenly posed a health risk to locals (Schultz & Sharma, 2020).

Next Thinking

From shared interest to securing borders, this brief discussion of themes identified in our discourse analysis exemplifies inquiry exploring language around globalization and borders. By engaging a set of articles, students were positioned to carry out further inquiry about globalization, global inequalities, and interconnectedness, all designed to interrogate the "global" in a "global pandemic." From this inquiry, we found that national borders were stronger than global citizenship rhetoric.

A next inquiry that would be applicable to K–12 classrooms might explore what, when, and how transnational structures like the World Health Organization and Doctors Without Borders can react to a global pandemic. Why have these structures not been called upon more extensively to assist in COVID-19 treatment and to find and distribute vaccines, and (how) can they be re-formed to be global institutions? A line of inquiry that both teachers and students can further examine about global inequalities might consider why some countries were better equipped to handle the pandemic. What previous experiences, living arrangements, environments, and health issues prevented devastation in Africa so far? What types of government systems were better equipped to contain COVID-19? How will access to vaccines change travel and national health systems going forward?

Finally, this global issue offers questions about interconnectedness. We might pursue the interconnectedness of viruses, animals, humans, and technology, as well as how such connectedness can fuel or eradicate future pandemics. We can also ask why closing national borders was so important. It scattered people across the globe while countries were issuing stay-at-home orders domestically. If we have interconnected senses of belonging and economics, what did breaking those flows do to economic and health structures?

The culmination of inquiry/learning can be a call to action. Young learners can look critically at their local context and rethink divisional language and policies. They can call on the distribution of personal protective equipment and vaccines to "foreigners" as well as themselves. Any resultant action begins with understanding what constitutes a global issue and how and when we might identify as global citizens.

INQUIRY 2:
WHAT RIGHTS DO PEOPLE HAVE IN PUBLIC AND PRIVATE SPACES?

Framing Space

Can we mandate that people wear masks in public spaces? In privately owned stores? Many local governments and businesses require people to don masks when entering. Other ordinances regulate crowd sizes in outdoor and private spaces. Some of these mandates have met with resistance. The struggle to surveil behavior in public and private space is of long interest to social scientists.

Geographers trouble the social implications of distinguishing between these intersecting and/or relational spaces. Public spaces have never lived up to their aspirational potential. If the extension of political rights is supposed to open public spaces, then the United States has failed in physical and discursive manners (Mitchell, 2003). Public spaces have continuously used physical space and representation to control access to and use of space. Furthermore, public spaces are not necessarily specific physical areas; public space can be anywhere citizens claim space and engage in protest (Mitchell, 2003; Schmidt & Babits, 2014).

Urban planners Evelyn Blumenberg and Renia Ehrenfeucht (2008) have explored the encroachment of neoliberalism into public spaces. They specifically observe how people are regulated on sidewalks. New regulations privilege businesses over the ease of civilian movement. Some regulations are designed to displace homeless people—the placement of lights, gardens, and types of bench seating—even as they are otherwise experienced as physical upgrades that invite people to enjoy the space. Changes that invite pedestrians are often driven by economic rather than civic agendas. How people move in public and private spaces like sidewalks was increasingly important as the pandemic sought to control and limit social interaction. While some countries managed movement during lockdown, the United States was less stringent but still changed how people engaged with space. How did masks, the outdoor dining on sidewalks, and changes to indoor and outdoor space contribute to our thinking about public space and its regulations?

Inquiry: Sensory Walks

Space is curricular. It teaches us about the world, how people are invited to participate, and how we are supposed to move and interact. Too often, space is a curriculum through which we move passively. Sensory walks are a means of actively and reflexively using our senses and affective responses to critically examine our surroundings (Pink, 2008). My geography students were asked to take a sensory tour—see, smell, taste, hear, feel—of their neighborhood to think about access, movement, and equity during the pandemic. I modeled the activity for them, walking through Morningside Heights in New York City, and produced the following summary as an example of the description and inquiry produced from a sensory walk.

> It is summer and the air is hot and thick. It is a Friday, which means trash day, and the remnants of garbage heaps leave an acrid smell/taste in the air. I leave my mask up as a barrier to the taste. I walk a sidewalk adjacent to Morningside Park. The trees are tall and dark green and cast cool shade over the sidewalk. This street is lined with benches where people are sitting alone with a book or sharing with friends in conversation from opposite ends of the bench. I walk to the right so I can dangle my mask and keep distance from the benches, where many people are maskless. As I cross 116th Street, flowers come into view. The purple and red in the garden invite me to step closer. I hear the playful shouts of children. I look down and see families gathering for a BBQ. There are tables full of food. I smell meat being grilled and hear the laughter of adults. People are gathered in their clusters of 20–30, most of them Black in this park, contrasting with the White bodies on the edge of the park where I stand . . .

. . . I choose to take this street because on Google Maps it is designated as pedestrian only. The city has closed two blocks to cars to invite pedestrians and bikes to exercise in the road. As someone who exercises, I am not sure about the effectiveness of closing only two blocks. I notice that the blue police barricade that is supposed to warn cars is lying in three pieces on the sidewalk . . .

. . . This stretch of 13 blocks is the longest in the city that is closed on weekends for outdoor dining. Restaurants have quickly adapted to outdoor dining. They built platforms and set up tables in loading zones, parking, and fire lanes. Some are creative in how they enclose their space and separate diners from cars. The student bar has set up an outdoor garden. Most days, I walk on the sidewalk, being sure to wear my mask as I squeeze around diners. Sometimes, the smell of Thai food makes me hungry. Tonight, the street is closed, and no cars pass. Each restaurant extends into a full lane of road, and pedestrians walk in the middle lane. The restaurants are busy. One bar seems to have more space outside than it did inside, and Friday night happy hour is raucous. Delivery bikes are sharing the pedestrian space in the middle because the bike lane is busy with masked waitstaffs getting food and drinks to maskless customers. It is surprisingly quiet; the manner of people talking is dull in contrast to the usual roar of traffic. The restaurants are full, the homeless have been removed, and people are gathered with friends.

My notes from this 1-hour walk are extensive. As I walk, my goal is to observe. The *next thinking* examines the kinds of questions and further research teachers and students can take up once they have closely noticed their world.

Next Thinking

The sensory walk is designed to produce questions and analysis. Obviously, the questions generated will be specific to the communities in which teachers and students live. As I reread my description of walking through New York City, I think about the decision to wear or not wear a mask. I recall the looks that we send one another during other walks. People tend to wear masks when walking in areas with others but not when seated. I live in a place where people do not protest the use of masks. We surveil one another through looks and gesture, even though masks are not required in parks or on sidewalks. The regulations in restaurants convenience costumers but do not protect waitstaffs. In other places, the pressure lies on those who choose to mask. How has mask-wearing become a political marker? How might students living in a politically conservative community observe mask-wearing in their neighborhoods?

New York City prioritized restaurants over the opening of other civic and cultural spaces. Restaurants may set up tables in loading zones, forcing trucks to unload in lanes of traffic. They shut more streets for commerce than for exercise. Moving along sidewalks or bike lanes in areas dense with restaurants is difficult because of tables and waitstaff. Restaurants remain open, but outdoor performance spaces remain closed. Why this priority? Homeless people were relocated so they were not a threat to businesses and customers. Of course, other communities may have taken different measures, which is why it is important for students to be attuned not only to what is occurring nationally or globally, but also what is taking place within their own neighborhoods.

This inquiry attends to how we used, surveilled, and regulated space during the pandemic. We have had to rethink space and who, what, and where the private is surveilled and the public remains. The attentions to COVID-19 also extend beyond as we continue to ponder the changing relationships between public and private space. The final inquiry discussed in this chapter looks at how space can be used to better understand structural inequities within society.

INQUIRY 3: WHAT DO RACIAL DISPARITIES IN COVID-19 INFECTIONS AND DEATH REVEAL ABOUT UNDERLYING RACIAL/RACIST STRUCTURES IN THE UNITED STATES?

Two months into the pandemic, the United States was again forced to confront the murders of Black people at the hands of law enforcement. The murders of George Floyd, Breonna Taylor, and Ahmaud Arbery sparked a month of nationwide protests demanding racial justice. The deaths came amid a pandemic disproportionately infecting, hospitalizing, and killing BIPOC populations. Boston University's Center for Antiracist Research (2021) set up a website to track COVID-19 racial disparities. According to this website, in New York State, the epicenter of the first wave of COVID-19 in the United States, Black people accounted for 25% of deaths while comprising 14% of the population. It concluded, "In New York, Black/African American people were most likely to have died from COVID-19."

Social studies education has a history of teaching Master narratives that center White men and decenter racism (Brown & Au, 2014). Studies of curricula and textbooks record the troubling absence of BIPOC. Furthermore, the manners of including more individuals or positing civil rights movements into the trajectory of progress in the United States do little to disrupt the racist infrastructure in the country (Schmidt, 2014). Textbook questions that ask students to deliberate whether slavery was good or bad reproduce racist dispositions; they fail to account for the ideologies and practices of power that maintain racial oppression (Kendi, 2017). The lived experiences of BIPOC do not make their way into contemplations on justice that would contest narratives of progress based on racial inequality (King, 2015).

The pandemic's exposure of the disregard for Black lives creates an interest convergence for social studies teachers to engage critically with racism. Critical Race Theory (CRT) (Ladson-Billings, 2009) and spatial theory (Schmidt, 2013; Soja, 2010) provide lenses through which young learners can conduct antiracist inquiry into the pandemic. Social geography begins with a recognition of racial unevenness (Soja, 2010). Spatial justice research explores the social-spatial dynamics that produce uneven access to resources. The placement of hospitals, distances between work and home, population density, and proximity to outdoor spaces are a few of the social-spatial indicators linking race, class, and geography during the pandemic. It encourages the study of the experiences of BIPOC communities too often made invisible by White narratives.

CRT argues that we need to center racism and the (counter)narratives of Black people (Ladson-Billings, 2009). CRT is also intersectional. It asks whether a story is the account of Black people or whether these experiences are reflected more broadly among social systems. The practice of retelling stories of past and present should serve as catalyst for radical change. This inquiry thinks with CRT about spatial data to explore how the pandemic has affected BIPOC communities.

Inquiry: Racial Analysis of Spatial Data

This inquiry introduces five online resources that contain spatial data about racial inequity. Using these sources, this section explores one county as a model of the insight and questions these sites can provoke. The COVID-19 Racial Data Tracker (Center for Antiracist Research, 2021) updates daily with numbers of infections, hospitalizations, and deaths at the state level. It disaggregates data by census categories and provides per capita data. It also provides some county-level data. University of California, Los Angeles's COVID-19 Behind Bars Data Project (UCLA Law, 2020) examines cases of COVID-19 among inmates and staff at federal and state prisons, county jails, and U.S. Immigrations and Customs Enforcement (ICE) detention centers. It uses mapping and tables to visualize data. The Opportunity Insights Economic Tracker (Chetty et al., 2020), maintained by Harvard University, Brown University, and the Bill and Melinda Gates Foundation, has a variety of tools to search economic impacts of the pandemic at the national, state, county, and metropolitan level. The U.S. Census Bureau (2020) provides state- and county-level data about demographic and economic indicators and compares them to the national average. Princeton's Eviction Lab (2018) features multilevel eviction tracking data, policy information, and people's stories.

Using these resources, I selected Hancock County, Georgia, for this analysis because it appeared in November 2020 as a county with one of

Table 6.1. Per Capita Infections and Deaths in Hancock County, GA, by Race and Ethnicity

	Cases per 100,000 people	Deaths per 100,000
Native Hawaiian/Pacific Islander	9,508	116
Hispanic/Latino	6,094	57
Black/African American	4,239	111
White	3,512	92
Asian	2,414	41
American Indian	1,621	52

the highest death rates in the country and with Blacks as the group with the highest death rate. Table 6.1 summarizes the COVID-19 data for this county.

The county is 71% Black, and 5% of the total population is veterans. They have a high occupant owner rate in housing and average two people per household. Hancock County has a very low eviction rate, just a fraction of the state's rate. The U.S. Census Bureau reports high school completion at 74% but college completion at 8%, both below national averages. These statistics may help explain why 31% of the residents live in poverty. Hancock County has a state prison that has had 90 infections among incarcerated people and 15 cases on staff. In ICE facilities across the state of Georgia, there are 531 cases and three deaths. The economic tracker offers limited data for Hancock County. In April 2020, the number of unemployment claims per 100 people spiked to 7.16; it has continuously fallen since but has still not returned to the pre-pandemic levels. For other indicators, we can look across the state and see that the economic picture is not strong. Things were far from pre-pandemic rates in November 2020. For example, the number of businesses open in November was 73% of the number in January—better than in April, when only 58% were open. Small business revenue dropped sharply in April, made some recovery in June, and has trended downward since. The population of Hancock is on the decline, and it has an older population.

These brief descriptors of Hancock County share some basic pandemic data that expose race and class realities in the county. Continuing this inquiry will have students make comparisons between counties or states to look for race and class patterns in the health and economic effects of the pandemic. Within Hancock County, or a locale that is familiar and accessible to students, teachers can ask students about the lives behind these numbers: How far do people travel to get to work, what are their means of transportation, what are the major jobs, what local safety measures have been enacted, and how many doctors and ventilators do nearby hospitals have? The specific goal is to examine the lives of BIPOC people during the COVID-19 pandemic, too often left out of the policy discussions and missing in the economic profiles that focus on business owners and feature those we are surprised to be stricken.

Next Thinking

The next thinking for this inquiry is focused on student action rather than new questions because CRT and antiracist educators argue that social action is central to abolitionist work (Kendi, 2019; Love, 2019). This work demands transforming knowledge into social change. Love (2019) argued that youth of color need curricula that validate their experience. Particularly in classrooms with large numbers of BIPOC students, engaging racial realness allows youth to see themselves and their families. Youth who have parents or grandparents who passed or suffered severe cases of COVID-19 can humanize the quantitative data.

Talking about how the pandemic has exposed racist ideologies and institutions makes this a dominant narrative of the pandemic. Youth can examine their local institutions that are implicated in these data and organize for change. Framing the pandemic around inequality gives power to these movements and demands for change. Finally, exploring national efforts like Black Lives Matter allows young people to think about federal policies while also examining how national movements require local transformations.

The pandemic is yet another moment for CRT to document the centrality of race in social theory, renew attention to racist institutions, and examine possibilities for change. Any inquiry teachers take up that poses questions about economic shutdowns, the classification and exposure of "frontline" workers, the failures of mass incarceration, and who is more likely to die, will implicate racism. There is not a singular story about the pandemic; the uneven spatiality of people's access to resources and power mean that BIPOC communities need to share theirs.

CONCLUSION

Social studies is/should be a study of the social. The assignments we give young people direct them in forming social wonderings. Our instruction offers the theoretical frames that orient young people as we send them to examine data about their social worlds. The examples of the inquiry process provided in this chapter engage socio-spatial thinking. They each diverge from traditional approaches in social studies in that they begin from a presumption that racist ideologies privilege and exclude full participation of people in society.

The first inquiry engages with the struggles of global citizenship. If these forms are supposed to offer a collective and humanistic remedy to global issues, then the strict regulation of borders to control access, protect ourselves from foreigners, and compete for access to the knowledge and materials that cure the virus reflect a massive failure of global citizenship. People in an uneven and interdependent world are left to fend for themselves.

The second inquiry engages with space. The promise of fully public, accessible space has never been actualized, and people often find themselves left out. During this inquiry, questions of neoliberalism and the privilege of capital over public use, the erasure of people from space (in my example, homeless people), and how we use and behave in public and private space make us think about spatial unevenness, political rights, and the tension between liberalism and communalism.

The final inquiry asks about the economic, health, and resource disparities that create the disparate impact of this virus on certain communities. These inequalities, the structures that facilitate them, and the actions of resistance people take against them should be the foundational material of inquiry in social studies.

Each inquiry thinks through a different type of data, all readily available to teachers and young learners. The first uses media, even though young people may prefer to use social media. It attends to a discursive study about how we frame society. The second introduces the curricular and pedagogical influences of space. We may walk or send ourselves into our communities to look for evidence of social structures. The final inquiry engages with social data. Each form of data initiates socio-spatial observation from which we can extend our inquiry to search for patterns across place, interrogate deep structures, and evaluate possible explanations of our observations.

This work is that of the social scientist—to acquire, explore, and theorize social data. We live in a world rich with social data, but we too often walk through accepting other people's stories about what our experiences should be. Inquiry invites our active accounting, values the multitude of stories, and challenges us to study what are the systems/sources of power that facilitate these experiences. Master narratives have too often limited our worldview. Good social inquiry, oriented from investigations of unevenness and power, may help us find how systems and structures act on us and how we connect with others in space and time.

REFERENCES

BBC News. (2020, March 12). *Coronavirus: Trump suspends travel from Europe to U.S.* Author. https://www.bbc.com/news/world-us-canada-51846923

Blumenberg, E., & Ehrenfeucht, R. (2008). Civil liberties and the regulation of public space: The case of sidewalks in Las Vegas. *Environment and Planning, 40(2)*, 303–322. https://doi.org/10.1068%2Fa37429

Brown, A. L., & Au, W. (2014). Race, memory, and master narratives: A critical essay on U.S. curriculum history. *Curriculum Inquiry, 44(3)*, 358–389. https://doi.org/10.1111/curi.12049

Campbell, C. (2020, March 12). "What is he afraid of?" Trump's European travel ban prompts scorn in China. *Time.* https://time.com/5801617/china-coronavirus-us-europe-travel-ban/

Center for Antiracist Research. (2021). *COVID racial data tracker.* The Atlantic Monthly Group. https://covidtracking.com/race

Chetty, R., Friedman, J. N., Hendren, N., Stepner, M., & the OI Team (2020-present). *Opportunity Insights economic tracker.* https://tracktherecovery.org/

Dewey, J. (2003). Social inquiry. In G. Delanty & P. Strydom (Eds.), *Philosophies of social science: The classic and contemporary readings* (pp. 290–297). Open University. (Original work published 1938)

Dickens, D. R., & Fontana, A. (2015). *Postmodernism and social inquiry.* Routledge.

Eviction Lab. (2018). *Eviction Lab.* Princeton University. https://evictionlab.org/.

Finnegan, C. (2020, March 20). *Americans evacuated from Morocco, Peru, as travel bans to block coronavirus strand thousands.* ABC News. https://abcnews.go.com/Politics/us-evacuating-americans-morocco-bans-block-virus-strand/story?id=69699997

Kendi, I. X. (2017). *Stamped from the beginning: The definitive history of racist ideas in America.* Random House.

Kendi, I. X. (2019). *How to be an antiracist.* One World.

King, L. J. (2015). Forward. In P. T. Chandler (Ed.), *Doing race in social studies: Critical perspectives* (pp. ix–xii). Information Age.

Ladson-Billings, G. (2009). Critical race theory in education. In M. W. Apple, W. Au, & L. A. Gandin (Eds.), *The Routledge international handbook of critical education* (pp. 110–122). Routledge.

Love, B. L. (2019). *We want to do more than survive: Abolitionist teaching and the pursuit of educational freedom.* Beacon.

McAuley, J. (2020, March 13). Chaos at European airports on eve of Trump's travel ban. *The Washington Post.* https://www.washingtonpost.com/world/chaos-at-european-airports-on-eve-of-trumps-travel-ban/2020/03/13/28ba7ef0-653e-11ea-845d-e35b0234b136_story.html

Mitchell, D. (2003). *The right to the city: Social justice and the fight for public space.* Guilford.

Pink, S. (2008). An urban tour: The sensory sociality of ethnographic place-making. *Ethnography, 9(2)*, 175–196. https://doi.org/10.1177%2F1466138108089467

Roy, A. (2020, April 3). The pandemic is a portal. *Financial Times.* https://www.ft.com/content/10d8f5e8-74eb-11ea-95fe-fcd274e920ca

Schmidt, S. J. (2013). Claiming our turf: Students' civic negotiation of the public space of school. *Theory & Research in Social Education, 41(4)*, 535–551. https://doi.org/10.1080/00933104.2013.840717

Schmidt, S. J. (2014). Civil rights continued: How history positions young people to contemplate sexuality (in)justice. *Equity & Excellence in Education, 47*(3), 353–369. https://doi.org/10.1080/10665684.2014.933068

Schmidt, S. J., & Babits, C. (2014). Occupy Wall Street as a curriculum of space. *Journal of Social Studies Research, 38*(2), 79–89. https://doi.org/10.1016/j.jssr.2013.08.004

Schultz, K., & Sharma, B. (2020, April 4). Stranded abroad, Americans ask: Why weren't we warned sooner? *The New York Times.* https://www.nytimes.com/2020/04/03/world/asia/coronavirus-state-department-tourists.html

Singer, P. (2002). *One world: The ethics of globalization.* Yale University Press.

Soja, E. W. (2010). *Seeking spatial justice.* University of Minnesota Press.

University of California, Los Angeles School of Law. (2020). *COVID-19 behind bars data project.* Author. https://uclacovidbehindbars.org/

U.S. Census Bureau (2020). *United States Census Bureau quick facts.* U.S. Department of Commerce. https://www.census.gov/quickfacts/

PART II

COVID-19 AND A CRITICAL EXAMINATION OF SOCIAL STUDIES TEACHING AND LEARNING

CHAPTER 7

A Hill Made of Sand

COVID-19 and the Myth of American Exceptionalism

Wayne Journell

I've spoken of the shining city all my political life, but I don't know if I ever quite communicated what I saw when I said it. But in my mind it was a tall, proud city built on rocks stronger than oceans, wind-swept, God-blessed, and teeming with people of all kinds living in harmony and peace; a city with free ports that hummed with commerce and creativity. And if there had to be city walls, the walls had doors and the doors were open to anyone with the will and the heart to get here. That's how I saw it, and see it still.

—Ronald Reagan, 1989

In a sermon delivered in 1630, John Winthrop issued a warning to his fellow Puritans that their new Massachusetts Bay settlement would be a "city upon a hill" that would be visible to the rest of the world. Winthrop adapted the phrase from Jesus's Sermon on the Mount, and it was intended to be a warning that if the Massachusetts Bay colony failed to uphold the moral standards it had set for itself, then their sins would be exposed for all to see. If, however, the Puritans could remain steadfast in their devotion to God, then they would have created a society that would cause others to exclaim, "May the Lord make [subsequent settlements] like that of New England" (Winthrop, 1630/1838, p. 47).

In the centuries since, Winthrop's imagery has been evoked by scores of politicians from John F. Kennedy to Barack Obama. But the meaning has changed over time. Where Winthrop used the phrase to challenge his fellow settlers to aspire to greatness, the modern use of the phrase has been to describe a nation that has already achieved greatness and is the envy of the rest of the world. The politician who most famously embraced this message was Ronald Reagan, who regularly spoke of the United States as a shining city upon a hill. This imagery was the cornerstone of the "resurgence of national pride" that Reagan sought to instill during his 8 years in office (1989, para. 27). As the quotation from his farewell address that prefaces this chapter shows, Reagan viewed the United States as an exceptional nation divinely positioned to be a permanent beacon of hope in an otherwise dangerous world.

Reagan's vision of the United States is one that has been promoted since the nation's founding and still persists today. Although critics have argued that American exceptionalism is a myth not grounded in reality (e.g., Coates, 2015; Hodgson, 2009; Noble, 2002; Zinn, 2005), that image of the United States as a shining city upon a hill has withstood chattel slavery, a civil war, multiple unpopular military engagements overseas, economic recessions/depressions, one presidential resignation and four presidential impeachments, and too many civil rights violations and international scandals to name. Yet, as others have argued (e.g., Friedman, 2020; Haiphong, 2020), the nation's response to the COVID-19 pandemic may have finally dealt a fatal blow to the idea of American exceptionalism. While it is too soon to determine whether the national ethos will indeed change in substantive ways post–COVID-19, social studies educators can use lessons from the pandemic to combat the belief in American exceptionalism that is pervasive within the formal curriculum.

AMERICAN EXCEPTIONALISM AND SOCIAL STUDIES EDUCATION

At the outset of this discussion, it is important to acknowledge that the United States has been, and remains, exceptional in many ways. As Alexis de Tocqueville (1840/2000) noted in his analysis of American society in the early 1800s, the U.S. democratic experiment stood in stark contrast to the rest of the developed world that was largely still ruled by monarchs, and through the early part of the 21st century the American democratic process remained the envy of many nations throughout the world. Similarly, the freedom and prosperity enjoyed by most Americans has earned the United States the moniker "the land of opportunity" and is the reason why over a million people immigrate to the United States every year.

Critics of American exceptionalism often get accused of failing to acknowledge these facts or of always seeking to find fault in the face of progress. Such accusations, however, are too simplistic. Most Americans of all political stripes recognize that living in the United States, broadly speaking, affords more privileges than in most nations around the world where abject poverty, poor sanitation, legal oppression, and genocide lead to higher mortality rates and an overall lower quality of life.

American exceptionalism becomes problematic when it is applied uncritically and with broad strokes. It is difficult, for example, to frame the

United States as a beacon of freedom when one understands that for much of U.S. history an entire race of people was first enslaved, then treated as second-class citizens, and still today is disproportionately the victim of systemic violence and incarceration by the state. Similarly, photographs of children locked in cages at the U.S.–Mexico border troubles the idea that the United States is a land of opportunity. In short, the imagery of the United States as a shining city upon a hill may be the reality for some or even most, but it is certainly not true for all.

The question then becomes: How does an ethos of exceptionalism become so engrained within a society when contradictory examples are so prevalent? One reason is that American exceptionalism has always been intertwined with morality, as illustrated by Reagan's description of his shining city as "God-blessed." When people believe that they have been chosen for success by a higher power, it helps justify atrocities that occurred on that path to prosperity as being part of a larger, divine plan. Moreover, proponents of American exceptionalism do not necessarily make the case that the United States has always been perfect; rather, they argue that this moral superiority has allowed us to right injustices when they occur, and as a result, our failings are minimal in comparison with those that have occurred in other nations.

Perhaps the most fundamental reason why American exceptionalism exists is the same reason that the false story of George Washington cutting down a cherry tree has survived for over two centuries. If a myth caters to the majority of a population and is repeated enough, it becomes accepted regardless of whether it is true. This repetition occurs in a variety of settings—family conversations, popular media, places of worship—but one of the most influential is public education. Schools are apparatuses of security for the state (Foucault, 1991); those in power have a vested interest in ensuring that what students learn in school reinforces the American exceptionalism narrative.

Again, Reagan's 1989 farewell address is instructive to understanding this relationship between American exceptionalism and schooling. At the end of his speech, Reagan issued a warning to the nation about what he believed was a declining sense of patriotism among the American public:

And are we doing a good enough job teaching our children what America is and what she represents in the long history of the world? Those of us who are over 35 or so years of age grew up in a different America. We were taught, very directly, what it means to be an American. And we absorbed, almost in the air, a love of country and an appreciation of its institutions. If you didn't get those things from your family you got them from the neighborhood, from the father down the street who fought in Korea or the family who lost someone at Anzio. Or you could get a sense of patriotism from school. And if all else failed you could get a sense of patriotism from the popular culture. The movies celebrated democratic values and implicitly reinforced the idea that America was special. TV was like that, too, through the mid-sixties.

But now, we're about to enter the nineties, and some things have changed. Younger parents aren't sure that an unambivalent appreciation of America is the right thing to teach modern children. And as for those who create the popular culture, well-grounded patriotism is no longer the style. Our spirit is back, but we haven't reinstitutionalized it. We've got to do a better job of getting across that America is freedom—freedom of speech, freedom of religion, freedom of enterprise. And freedom is special and rare. It's fragile; it needs [protection].

So, we've got to teach history based not on what's in fashion but what's important—why the Pilgrims came here, who Jimmy Doolittle was, and what those 30 seconds over Tokyo meant . . . I'm warning of an eradication of the American memory that could result, ultimately, in an erosion of the American spirit. Let's start with some basics: More attention to American history and a greater emphasis on civic ritual. (paras. 28–30)

Of course, there is nothing wrong with having pride in one's country, but what Reagan is advocating more closely resembles what scholars have termed "authoritarian patriotism" (Westheimer, 2007) or "belligerent patriotism" (Ben-Porath, 2006), which demands unquestioned loyalty to the nation. When apparatuses of security, such as schools, deviate from that stance and take a more critical approach to the curriculum, those in power begin to lose control of the narrative. As a result, those in power often take steps to mandate adherence to the majoritarian narrative, as evidenced by President Trump's establishment of a "1776 Commission" in response to growing interest in the *1619 Project* (The New York Times, 2019), a curriculum that directly challenges American exceptionalism by reframing the study of U.S. history around the legacy of slavery (The National Review, 2020). In his remarks announcing the commission, Trump accused schools of teaching "hateful lies about [the] country" and called the framing of U.S. History around the concept of race/racism "a form of child abuse" (Pettypiece, 2020, paras. 1 & 4). That President Biden dissolved the 1776 Commission on his first day in office matters little; the cultural fear that prompted its creation still remains.

Despite Trump's handwringing, history suggests that the *1619 Project* will likely join previous attempts over the past century to take a critical perspective to the social studies curriculum that failed to have a lasting impact on the way social studies is taught in the United States (Evans, 2004). Although there exists a near-collective agreement among social studies scholars that a curriculum taking a critical approach offers a more dynamic, realistic, and culturally sustaining (Paris & Alim, 2017) social studies education, the social studies curriculum in the United States has remained entrenched in what Miller-Lane et al. (2007) described as a "non critical–unity" perspective.

Their analysis along the crossed axes of critical/non critical and unity/diversity perspectives situates U.S. social studies largely in the quadrant valuing national unity over diversity and non critical presentation of information over critiques of U.S. actions and policy.

This non critical–unity perspective not only fails to address diversity and systemic inequalities within U.S. society, but it also exudes American exceptionalism. Under a non critical–unity perspective, American misdeeds are minimized or ignored, and any injustices that are acknowledged are spun into a storyline of achievement and inclusion. To quote the example offered by Miller-Lane et al. (2007), a non critical–unity version of U.S. history would frame "the fact that the nation was formed only when African Americans were considered 3/5 of a human [as] less significant than the Fourteenth Amendment 150 years later and the Voting Rights Act of 1965" (p. 560).

One reason why this type of spin works is that it caters to what the majority of Americans believe, or at least what they want to believe. Those who object to the storyline of achievement and inclusion are often at the margins of American society, and those in the majority can either ignore or discount societal injustices and systemic failures because they have not been personally affected by them. American exceptionalism is closely aligned with the myth of people pulling themselves up by their bootstraps and achieving success purely through hard work and perseverance. If the United States is the land of opportunity and the envy of the rest of the world, it is easy for those in the majority to view those who have not been successful as deficient in some way, instead of being the victims of systemically oppressive systems.

The COVID-19 pandemic presents a unique opportunity to challenge that narrative given that it has affected all aspects of U.S. society, albeit not equally, and thus it is impossible to ignore. Moreover, in this age of cable news and social media, Americans can look beyond our borders to compare the U.S. response to the coronavirus with that of the rest of the developed world. The remainder of this chapter will discuss the ways in which the pandemic has exposed the myth of American exceptionalism and argue that teachers should use the U.S. response to the pandemic to counter the non critical–unity perspective found in the formal curriculum.

COVID-19 AND THE MYTH OF AMERICAN EXCEPTIONALISM

A remarkable aspect of American exceptionalism is that it has been commonly acknowledged even beyond our borders. From afar, the imagery of the United States as a city upon a hill has resonated even as the Internet and cable news have given the world greater access to American society. The COVID-19 pandemic, however, has altered this perception; whereas other nations once looked at us with admiration, they now view us with a sense of pity.

A quotation from an Italian journalist, speaking to the Associated Press (2020), illustrates this change in perception: "We Italians always saw America as a model . . . but with this virus we've discovered a country that is very fragile, with bad infrastructure and a public health system that is nonexistent" (para. 7). This sentiment aligns with polling data showing that international opinions about the United States have reached their lowest point in the past 20 years. Although these data show that the reputation of the United States suffered throughout the Trump presidency, there was a sharp decline during the pandemic, even among nations that consider themselves allies of the United States. On average, only 15% of respondents in these other nations believed the United States did a good job in dealing with the pandemic, whereas 74%, on average, believed that their own nation had effectively responded to the pandemic (Wike et al., 2020).

It is, of course, not difficult to explain this perception. By the numbers alone, it is hard to make the case that the United States has succeeded in mitigating the devastating effects of the coronavirus, particularly when compared to other developed nations around the world. As of this writing, over 700,000 Americans have died from COVID-19, which is, by far, the greatest number of COVID-19 deaths anywhere in the world. That number constitutes over 90,000 more deaths than the next nation on the list (Brazil) and over 200,000 more deaths than India, which has a population of over a billion people (Johns Hopkins Coronavirus Resource Center, n.d.). To put these numbers into context, an analysis in early September 2020 found that despite only constituting 4% of the world's population, the United States had 22% of the world's COVID-19 reported deaths (Leonhardt, 2020). Moreover, despite having a fairly low case fatality rate, the United States has one of the worst per capita death rates from COVID-19 in the world (Craig, 2020; Johns Hopkins Coronavirus Resource Center, n.d.).

Numbers, of course, only tell part of the story. China, Italy, and Spain have relatively high death tolls, but those numbers are largely due to the fact that those nations were among the first to be ravaged by the coronavirus when the world had little knowledge of the disease or how it spread. The United States, in contrast, had the benefit of seeing what was occurring in those nations; yet the federal government did little to mount a national response to the virus. President Trump repeatedly dismissed the threat posed by the virus, stating in late January and early February that his administration had the situation under control even though it was clear the virus was spreading rapidly in pockets of the country. Even as states began issuing lockdown orders, Trump remained defiant and failed to develop a national response to the pandemic. In the weeks that followed, he repeatedly claimed that the virus would "just disappear" on its own and sought to downplay the severity of COVID-19, stating on numerous occasions that it was a hoax and no more lethal than the common flu, even though recorded interviews with journalist Bob Woodward that were made public months later revealed that Trump was aware of the health risks posed by the virus (Forgey & Choi, 2020; Paz, 2020; Woodward, 2020).

The lack of a coordinated national response was somewhat mitigated by governors, both Democrat and Republican, who took it upon themselves to shut down their states. Yet these measures were only marginally effective due to the refusal of a large segment of the American population to adhere to public health guidelines, such as mask mandates and social distancing requirements. While COVID-19 led citizens in other nations around the world to band together, the virus only exacerbated existing political and cultural divides in the United States. "Reopening rallies" were held in state capitals with protesters claiming that they should have the freedom to decide how to live their lives, including whether to risk contracting COVID-19. Mask-wearing became a divisive political issue, with conservatives claiming that it was unnecessary and an affront to their personal freedoms.

Trump regularly sought to stoke these cultural divides, famously stating that he would not be wearing a mask even after the Centers for Disease Control and Prevention recommended that all Americans wear one in public (Victor et al., 2020). As the election season began to heat up, Trump regularly held large, in-person rallies full of maskless supporters that openly defied state and local social distancing mandates. In the first presidential debate, Trump famously mocked Biden by saying, "I don't wear masks like [Biden]. Every time you see him, he's got a mask. He could be speaking 200 feet away from them and he shows up with the biggest mask I've ever seen" (Cillizza, 2020, para. 10). Trump's cavalier attitude toward the virus finally caught up with him 2 days later when an outbreak ravaged the White House, resulting in the supposed leader of the free world testing positive for COVID-19 and requiring hospitalization.

Trump makes for an easy, albeit well-deserving, scapegoat for the nation's poor response to the virus, and his failure to take COVID-19 seriously likely contributed to him losing his bid for reelection. Yet laying the blame solely on Trump and assuming that the United States would be faring similarly to other developed nations under a different president is likely shortsighted, as was the belief that the nation would immediately get the virus under control once Biden took office. Trump was always a symptom, not a cause; the anti-intellectual, antiscience, individualistic, distrust of authority mindset that propelled Trump into office will continue to hinder our ability to combat the virus. Even with mask mandates and calls for lockdowns, people will continue to view mask-wearing and other sensible measures to curb the virus as violations of their individual liberties without any regard for how those liberties might detract from the collective good. The deleterious effect of American individualism may be most aptly illustrated by the fact that despite the development of safe and effective vaccines that appear to offer a pathway for the world to soon move past COVID-19, public health officials in the United States remain concerned that the nation will be unable to achieve herd immunity because too many Americans will choose not to be vaccinated due to either a distrust of government or unfounded misconceptions about the safety of vaccines (Tyson et al., 2020).

COVID-19, of course, has illuminated more than contemporary U.S. political divides and general ignorance among large swaths of the American public. Many of the vaunted elements of the "city upon a hill" myth have been exposed as fraudulent, and cracks have been made in the veneer of exceptionality that the United States has projected to the rest of the world for centuries. Consider, for example, the belief that the United States is a land of opportunity. From the famous assertion in the Declaration of Independence that all men are created equal to the inscription on the Statue of Liberty that projects the United States as a nation offering sanctuary to the tired and poor, the United States has framed itself as a place where all can achieve the "American dream," a term that writer James Truslow Adams (1931) coined and described as "a land in which life should be better and richer and fuller for everyone . . . regardless of the fortuitous circumstances of birth or position" (p. 404).

Yet COVID-19 has clearly delineated the fault lines in American society with respect to race and socioeconomic class. Black, Indigenous, and People of Color (BIPOC), particularly those from low socioeconomic households living in urban areas, have disproportionately borne the brunt of the virus in the United States (Centers for Disease Control and Prevention, 2020). These individuals are not genetically predisposed to adverse reactions to COVID-19; rather, the virus has exposed systemic inequalities with respect to blue- versus white-collar work and access to quality healthcare, nutritious food, and secure housing.

Many people in these communities work low-wage hourly positions that were deemed "essential" in the early stages of the pandemic, putting them increasingly in harm's way while many white-collar workers had the luxury of being able to work from home. Yet many of these "essential" jobs do not provide workers with health care benefits or paid time off, meaning that these workers are more likely to continue showing up for work even when sick and to receive substandard care if they require hospitalization. Moreover, the chances of hospitalization due to COVID-19 in these communities is higher than in more affluent, White communities because of a greater prevalence of obesity and diabetes, two morbidities that have been found to be predictors of COVID-19 mortality (Cheng et al., 2019; Peterson et al., 2019; Zhou et al., 2020). These morbidities are not always the result of poor dietary choices; rather, many low socioeconomic households cannot afford healthy food options, leaving them to regularly consume cheaper, processed food that is detrimental to their overall health and leaves them more susceptible to disease.

The statistics detailing the deaths of BIPOC and those from impoverished areas of the country stand in stark comparison with the large number of politicians and celebrities who have received priority treatment upon contracting COVID-19. President Trump, for example, was given every drug that had been approved to fight the virus at the time he was hospitalized (i.e., remdesivir, dexamethasone), as well as an experimental cocktail of monoclonal antibodies that had not been approved for use with the general population (Bateman-House et al., 2020; Gallagher, 2020). At roughly the same time, Trump ally Chris Christie was able to check himself into a hospital upon being diagnosed with COVID-19 despite displaying only mild symptoms, and he also received monoclonal antibodies that had been approved for emergency use only (Chiu, 2020; Young, 2020). A month later, Secretary of Housing and Urban Development Ben Carson reported that Trump had "cleared" him to receive monoclonal antibody therapy after he was hospitalized during his own bout with COVID-19 (Goldberg, 2020). Then, amid a surge of the virus that was pushing the health care system to its breaking point, Trump's personal lawyer, Rudy Giuliani, was hospitalized for COVID-19 and procured the same treatments that Trump had received, including the monoclonal antibody cocktail. Upon his discharge, Giuliani noted that he had received the "celebrity" treatment and admitted, "I think if it wasn't me I wouldn't have been put in the hospital" (Gittleson & Phelps, 2020, para. 3). In short, the pandemic has shown that even the basics of the American dream—one's ability to live and receive care when needed—is only a reality for those with means and stature.

COVID-19 also exposed cracks in another ballyhooed aspect of American exceptionalism—the American democratic process. Even prior to the pandemic, American democracy seldom has lived up to its reputation. In every election, a large percentage of the electorate chooses not to participate, and many others are excluded from the process through voter suppression tactics such as photo identification requirements, few opportunities for early voting, and overcrowded polling places.

The pandemic, however, exacerbated the fragile nature of American democracy. The first warning came in April 2020 during the Democratic presidential primary. As most states either postponed their primary elections or conducted them via mail-in ballots only, the state of Wisconsin's Supreme Court blocked an attempt by Governor Tony Evers to delay the primary until June, and then the U.S. Supreme Court further promoted in-person voting by reversing a lower court ruling that gave voters 6 extra days to return absentee ballots (Bradner & Sullivan, 2020). As a result, many Wisconsinites were forced to choose between exercising their democratic rights and protecting their personal health. Roughly 400,000 people voted in that April 7th primary, and contract tracing suggests that crowded polling places led to a moderate spike in COVID-19 cases in subsequent weeks (Cotti et al., 2020; McCaskill, 2020).

As the pandemic persisted through summer, it became clear that it would impact the presidential election in November. Most states learned from the lessons of Wisconsin and made voting by mail easier, with some even choosing to mail ballots to all eligible voters. Yet some states, such as Texas, only allowed voters to submit ballots via mail if they were older than 65 years old or if they could prove that they had a morbidity that made them more susceptible to serious complications from COVID-19 (Ura, 2020).

While overall turnout for the 2020 presidential election shattered records, the increased number of mail-in ballots raised concerns in some political circles about the validity of the results. Given that more Democrats were inclined to vote by mail based on attitudes toward the coronavirus outlined above, mail-in ballots became a target for President Trump and his Republican allies. Trump sought to sow seeds of doubt about the election result in the months leading up to the election, and then, following his defeat, he refused to concede, arguing that the mail-in ballots constituted widespread fraud (Collinson, 2020; Schneider, 2020).

Although such allegations have been debunked (Kiely & Rieder, 2020), they had the intended effect; a large percentage of Trump supporters believe that widespread voter fraud occurred due to the prevalence of mail-in voting and that Biden was illegitimately elected (Kim, 2020). Moreover, Trump's unwillingness to concede and his insistence on doubling down on his unfounded claims that Biden's victory was fraudulent put the peaceful transfer of power, a hallmark of American democracy since the nation's founding, in peril. On the day Congress was set to certify the Electoral College results, a mob of Trump supporters stormed the U.S. Capitol in an unprecedented assault on our democratic process. Although democracy prevailed, Americans' confidence in U.S. elections was already shaky following reports of foreign interference in the 2016 contest, and it is likely that the pandemic may have cemented those concerns for a considerable portion of the electorate—not the best look for a democracy that is supposedly the envy of the rest of the world.

These are only a few examples of how COVID-19 has eroded the myth of American exceptionalism, and it is far from an exhaustive list. As the pandemic moved beyond the summer and the second wave of the virus swept across the country, additional examples of the nation failing to meet the lofty image it projects onto the world were plentiful (e.g., an inability or unwillingness to protect our most vulnerable members of society, prioritizing bars and movie theaters over children attending schools, the richest nation on Earth demonstrating an unwillingness to give monetary support to help people pay for basic necessities). Ultimately, COVID-19 exposed the United States for what it is and has always been: a shining city, but one built upon an unsteady hill of sand never too far away from collapsing.

CONCLUSION

Although COVID-19 has done more to shatter the myth of American excep-tionalism than any event in recent memory, pushing back against that myth remains difficult. Americans have been conditioned to avoid looking inward and assigning self-blame, as evidenced by over 70 million Americans voting to reelect Trump despite the coronavirus spreading exponentially under his watch. Moreover, as the world becomes further removed from COVID-19, the collective memory of the nation's failures will likely fade once we are able to reengage in the distractions that many of us enjoyed prior to the start of the pandemic.

Yet the pandemic provides teachers with a tangible event, one that students have experienced and will remember for the foreseeable future, that can be used to combat the American exceptionalism narrative found in text-books and state standards. It is rare to have such a profound "teachable moment" at one's disposal, particularly one that can easily be incorporated into all facets of the social studies curriculum. One can easily envision how the pandemic could be incorporated in a history or civics class to push back on repeated attempts to describe the United States as the "leader of the free world" or "guardians of democracy," or in an economics class when state curriculum standards hail the tenets of the U.S. capitalist system.

Again, the point of evoking the lessons of the pandemic is not to foster an anti-American sentiment; rather, it is to present a realistic assessment of the United States' strengths and limitations that can serve to balance the blind nationalism advocated by the likes of Reagan that are promoted in our textbooks and state standards. In short, the COVID-19 pandemic invites critical inquiry into many of the longstanding post-Cold War assumptions about the United States' reputation and stature as a world "superpower." It appears clear that COVID-19 has led the rest of the world to question the image of the United States as a city upon a hill, but it remains to be seen whether this (hopefully) once-in-a-lifetime event can lead to the type of col-lective self-reflection that the nation needs in order to reckon with the cracks in the veneer of American exceptionalism that the pandemic has exposed. Broaching these conversations in K–12 education can serve as a much-need-ed starting point for this process.

REFERENCES

Adams, J. T. (1931). *The epic of America* (2nd ed.). Greenwood Press.

Associated Press. (2020, August 10). *Europe watches in alarm as U.S. tops 5 million COVID-19 cases*. NBC News. https://www.nbcnews.com/health/health-news/europe-watches-alarm-u-s-tops-5-million-covid-19-n1236261

Bateman-House, A., Gustafson, M. S., & Caplan, A. (2020, October 8). Trump's regeneron treatment is a tangled ethical mess. *Barron's*. https://www.barrons.com/articles/trumps-regeneron-treatment-is-a-tangled-ethical-mess-51602188920

Ben-Porath, S. R. (2006). *Citizenship under fire: Democratic education in times of conflict*. Princeton University Press.

Bradner, E., & Sullivan, K. (2020, April 6). *Wisconsin primary set to go ahead on Tuesday after courts block attempts to delay voting due to coronavirus*. WRAL.com. https://www.wral.com/wisconsin-governor-orders-delay-of-primary-election-until-june/19044482/

Centers for Disease Control and Prevention. (2020, July 24). *Health equity considerations and racial and ethnic minority groups*. Author. https://www.cdc.gov/coronavirus/2019-ncov/community/health-equity/race-ethnicity.html

Cheng, Y. J., Kanaya, A. M., Araneta, M. R. G., Saydah, S. H., Kahn, H. S., Gregg, E. W., Fujimoto, W. Y., & Imperatore, G. (2019). Prevalence of diabetes by race and ethnicity, 2011–2016. *Journal of the American Medical Association, 322*(24), 2389–2398. doi:10.1001/jama.2019.19365

Chiu, A. (2020, October 6). Most covid-19 patients don't check themselves into hospitals. This is how experts say it usually works. *The Washington Post*. https://www.washingtonpost.com/lifestyle/wellness/hospital-chris-christie-covid-checkin/2020/10/06/4a6ce194-072a-11eb-a166-dc429b380d10_story.html

Cillizza, C. (2020, October 1). *How Donald Trump completely whiffed on his debate mask answer*. CNN. https://www.cnn.com/2020/10/01/politics/trump-masks-debate/index.html

Coates, T-N. (2015). *Between the world and me*. Random House.

Collinson, S. (2020, August 6). *Trump's mail-in voting falsehoods are part of a wide campaign to discredit the election*. CNN. https://www.cnn.com/2020/08/06/politics/donald-trump-mail-in-voting-election/index.html

Cotti, C. D., Engelhardt, B., Foster, J., Nesson, E. T., & Niekamp, P. S. (2020). *The relationship between in-person voting and Covid-19: Evidence from the Wisconsin primary*. National Bureau of Economic Research Working Paper Series (Working paper 27187).

Craig, J. (2020, August 5). *Charts: How the U.S. ranks on COVID-19 deaths per capita—and by case count*. National Public Radio. https://www.npr.org/sections/goatsandsoda/2020/08/05/899365887/charts-how-the-u-s-ranks-on-covid-19-deaths-per-capita-and-by-case-count

de Tocqueville, A. (2000). *Democracy in America* (H. C. Mansfield & D. Winthrop, Eds.). University of Chicago Press. (Original work published 1840)

Evans, R. W. (2004). *The social studies wars: What should we teach the children?* Teachers College Press.

Forgey, Q., & Choi, M. (2020, September 9). *'This is deadly stuff': Tapes show Trump acknowledging virus threat in February*. Politico. https://www.politico.com/news/2020/09/09/trump-coronavirus-deadly-downplayed-risk-410796

Foucault, M. (1991). Governmentality. In G. Burchell, C. Gordon, & P. Miller (Eds.), *The Foucault effect: Studies in governmentality* (pp. 87–104). University of Chicago Press.

Friedman, U. (2020, May 14). Why America resists learning from other countries. *The Atlantic*. https://www.theatlantic.com/politics/archive/2020/05/coronavirus-could-end-american-exceptionalism/611605/

Gallagher, J. (2020, October 9). *Dexamethasone, remdesivir, regeneron: Trump's Covid treatment explained.* BBC. https://www.bbc.com/news/health-54418464

Gittleson, B., & Phelps, J. (2020, December 10). *Rudy Giuliani says he got 'celebrity' coronavirus treatment, advice from president's doctor.* ABC News. https://abcnews.go.com/Politics/rudy-giuliani-celebrity-coronavirus-treatment-advice-presidents-doctor/story?id=74648914

Goldberg, M. (2020, December 10). Covid meds are scarce, but not for Trump's cronies. *The New York Times.* https://www.nytimes.com/2020/12/10/opinion/coronavirus-giuliani-regeneron.html

Haiphong, D. (2020). The great unmasking: American exceptionalism in the age of COVID-19. *International Critical Thought, 10*(2), 200–213. https://doi.org/10.1080/21598282.2020.1779527

Hodgson, G. (2009). *The myth of American exceptionalism.* Yale University Press.

Johns Hopkins Coronavirus Resource Center. (n.d.). *Mortality analyses.* Author. https://coronavirus.jhu.edu/data/mortality

Kiely, E., & Rieder, R. (2020, September 25). *Trump's repeated false attacks on mail-in ballots.* FactCheck.org. https://www.factcheck.org/2020/09/trumps-repeated-false-attacks-on-mail-in-ballots/

Kim, C. (2020, November 9). *Poll: 70 percent of Republicans don't think the election was fair.* Politico. https://www.politico.com/news/2020/11/09/republicans-free-fair-elections-435488

Leonhardt, D. (2020, September 1). America's death gap. *The New York Times.* https://www.nytimes.com/2020/09/01/briefing/coronavirus-kenosha-massachusetts-your-tuesday-briefing.html

McCaskill, N. D. (2020, April 27). *Wisconsin health department: 36 people positive for coronavirus after primary vote.* Politico. https://www.politico.com/news/2020/04/27/wisconsin-tested-positive-coronavirus-election-211495

Miller-Lane, J., Howard, T. C., & Halagao, P. E. (2007). Civic multicultural competence: Searching for common ground in democratic education. *Theory & Research in Social Education, 35*(4), 551–573. https://doi.org/10.1080/00933104.2007.10473350

The National Review. (2020, September 21). *President Trump's '1776 commission' on patriotic education is an overdue effort.* Author. https://www.nationalreview.com/2020/09/trump-1776-commission-patriotic-education-worthy-cause/

The New York Times. (2019). *The 1619 project.* Author. https://www.nytimes.com/interactive/2019/08/14/magazine/1619-america-slavery.html

Noble, D. W. (2002). *Death of a nation: American culture and the end of exceptionalism.* University of Minnesota Press.

Paris, D., & Alim, H. S. (Eds.). (2017). *Culturally sustaining pedagogies: Teaching and learning for justice in a changing world.* Teachers College Press.

Paz, C. (2020, October 1). All the president's lies about the coronavirus. *The Atlantic.* https://www.theatlantic.com/politics/archive/2020/10/trumps-lies-about-coronavirus/608647/

Peterson, R., Pan, L., & Blanck, H. M. (2019, April 11). *Racial and ethnic disparities in adult obesity in the United States: CDC's tracking to inform state and local action.* Centers for Disease Control and Prevention. https://www.cdc.gov/pcd/issues/2019/18_0579.htm

Pettypiece, S. (2020, September 17). *Trump calls for 'patriotic education,' says anti-racism teachings are 'child abuse.'* NBC News. https://www.nbcnews.com/politics/white-house/trump-calls-patriotic-education-says-anti-racism-teachings-are-child-n1240372

Reagan, R. (1989). *Farewell address to the nation.* Ronald Reagan Presidential Library and Museum. https://www.reaganlibrary.gov/archives/speech/farewell-address-nation

Schneider, C. (2020, November 11). Republicans set America up for their 'vote fraud' hoax. *USA Today.* https://www.usatoday.com/story/opinion/2020/11/11/trump-refuses-concede-and-keeps-pushing-cases-voter-fraud-column/6234793002/

Tyson, A., Johnson, C., & Funk, C. (2020, September 17). *U.S. public now divided over whether to get COVID-19 vaccine.* Pew Research Center. https://www.pewresearch.org/science/2020/09/17/u-s-public-now-divided-over-whether-to-get-covid-19-vaccine/

Ura, A. (2020, August 21). Here's how to vote by mail in Texas. *The Texas Tribune.* https://www.texastribune.org/2020/08/21/vote-by-mail-texas/

Victor, D., Serviss, L., & Paybarah, A. (2020, October 2). In his own words, Trump on the coronavirus and masks. *The New York Times.* https://www.nytimes.com/2020/10/02/us/politics/donald-trump-masks.html

Westheimer, J. (2007). Politics and patriotism in education. In J. Westheimer (Ed.), *Pledging allegiance: The politics of patriotism in America's schools* (pp. 171–188). Teachers College Press.

Wike, R., Fetterolf, J., & Mordecai, M. (2020, September 15). *U.S. image plummets internationally as most say country has handled coronavirus badly.* Pew Research Center. https://www.pewresearch.org/global/2020/09/15/us-image-plummets-internationally-as-most-say-country-has-handled-coronavirus-badly/

Winthrop, J. (1838). *A modell of Christian charity.* Massachusetts Historical Society. (Original work published 1630)

Woodward, B. (2020). *Rage.* Simon & Schuster.

Young, D. (2020, October 16). *Trump ally Chris Christie among the few to get Lilly COVID-19 antibody drug.* S&P Global. https://www.spglobal.com/marketintelligence/en/news-insights/latest-news-headlines/trump-ally-chris-christie-among-the-few-to-get-lilly-covid-19-antibody-drug-60757764

Zhou, Y., Chi, J., Lv, W., & Wang, Y. (2020). Obesity and diabetes as high-risk factors for severe coronavirus disease 2019 (Covid-19). *Diabetes Metabolism Research and Reviews.* Advance online publication. https://doi.org/10.1002/dmrr.3377

Zinn, H. (2005). The power and the glory: Myths of American exceptionalism. *Boston Review.* https://bostonreview.net/zinn-power-glory

CHAPTER 8

COVID-19 as a Symptom of Another Disease

Cathryn van Kessel

How we define a problem affects how we deal with our struggles at the time as well as how we imagine possible futures unfolding. COVID-19 is indeed a problem in itself as a virus, but its exacerbated impact on specific communities in the United States (and elsewhere) lays bare a different disease: intersecting (Crenshaw, 1991) forms of systemic violence such as ableism, ageism, classism, racism, sexism, and xenophobia (Hankivsky & Kapilashrami, 2020). Examples of this situation are disproportionate deaths of those in Latinx and Black communities, exacerbated economic precarity of Black communities, anti-Chinese racism and xenophobia, and inattention to emergency situations within Indigenous communities.

Social studies scholar Avner Segall (1999) aptly noted that "It is not the repetitive past we ought to fear (for the past never repeats itself) but, rather, the legacy of the past in our present" (p. 366). Furthermore, as educators explore these legacies, there can be a sense of "frozen futurism" where the assumption is that "the future will always be more of this, a perpetual unfolding of more and more of this," and it feels like the future "has *already happened*" (Smith, 2000, p. 17, emphasis in original). The COVID-19 pandemic has illuminated some of the legacies left by the interlocking systems of violence that persist in countries like (but not limited to) the United States and Canada (Solnit, 2020). How might educators teach this situation in a way that can "recover a future that truly is a future; that is, a condition that is actually open" (Smith, 2000, p. 17)?

With those considerations in mind, this chapter will consider the interlocking systemic violence highlighted by the current pandemic, as well as how the concepts of *heroification* (e.g., Loewen, 2007) and *villainification* (van Kessel & Crowley, 2017) are helpful in relation to engaging students in thinking about the underlying causes of these avoidable deaths. Such an approach is paired with explicit futures thinking and scenario reasoning (i.e., considering possible, probable, and preferable future scenarios) to encourage students to feel that they have agency to demand urgent institutional and social change (den Heyer, 2017).

FIGHTING SYSTEMIC VIOLENCE

As will be explored in other chapters of this book, systemic violence comes in many intersecting forms that reveal how power is distributed unequally and how its permutations and combinations have far-reaching material and psychological consequences for many. In the case of COVID-19, the crisis of the pandemic has highlighted serious, intertwined structural problems related to identity in combination with situational factors such as geography, immigration status, health, and whether or not a community benefits from intergenerational capital accumulation. As an example, health equity researcher Rachel Hardeman and colleagues made this statement in *The New England Journal of Medicine*:

> In Minnesota, where [B]lack Americans account for 6% of the population but 14% of Covid-19 cases and 33% of Covid-19 deaths, George Floyd died at the hands of police. . . . In the wake of his public execution, uprisings have ignited in cities throughout the United States and the world, many of them led by young black people. The truth is black people cannot breathe because the legacies of segregation and white flight, practices of gentrification and environmental racism, and local zoning ordinances combine to confine us in residential areas where we are disproportionately exposed to toxins and pollutants. As a result, black populations have higher rates of asthma and cancer. And recent data suggest that chronic exposures to particulate matter in the air may contribute to a risk of death from Covid-19 as much as 15% higher for black Americans than that faced by white Americans. (Hardeman et al., 2020, pp. 197–198)

Although "COVID-19 doesn't discriminate" is a popular saying (e.g., Moore, 2020)—and, sure, the virus itself is not diabolically targeting certain groups—it is folly to think that this pandemic affects everyone in the same way. As an example, nurses are put at great risk during a pandemic because of their close and continual contact with patients (Gupta, 2020). In Canada (and elsewhere), most nurses are female (roughly 90%); almost a quarter of nursing staff are racialized immigrants, particularly in the lower echelons, due to the implicit and explicit racism in the credentialing process; and in some contexts (e.g., long-term care homes in Alberta), immigrants comprise 55% of the nursing staff (Salami, 2020). As social psychologist Lisa Bowleg (2020) aptly stated: "We are not all in this together . . . adroitly deadly viruses spotlight fissures of structural inequality" (p. 917).

HEROIFICATION, VILLAINIFICATION, AND AGENCY

In order to fight the variety of forms of structural violence linked in inequity, we (as interconnected humans in communities) need to understand that people not unlike ourselves can both help and hinder efforts to create a more just society. Teaching for activism involves facilitating students' understanding of how everyday individuals have formed communities to improve society (Martell & Stevens, 2021). Two impediments to such learning are *heroification* and *villainification* narratives—parallel but opposite processes that divorce ordinary humans from their roles in making change.

Heroification creates larger-than-life, perfect heroes in history (Loewen, 2007), and villainification shifts our perspective from systemic (or structural) harms to the individual evildoer (van Kessel & Crowley, 2017). Heroification and villainification narratives trick students into inaccurately learning that social change occurs through the intentions and deeds of extraordinary individuals instead of by sustained collective assertions of values, rights, and a collective better way through interconnected communities and systems.

In Western worldviews, there is a tendency to consider agency as personal and disconnected from others in history (e.g., McKay, 2000). Consequently, students often see positive social and political change as the product of heroic individuals unlike themselves (den Heyer, 2003, 2018). In this way, collectives and collective action are reduced to an individual (Peck et al., 2011). To that end, students and teachers can wonder if "somebody already has to be famous to help motivate change or whether it is their job in making things change that makes them famous" (den Heyer, 2012, p. 313), and believe that they cannot effect change because they are not famous: "It just wouldn't work for me; I'm a nobody" (van Kessel, 2017, p. 592).

Although in many cases it is the opposite of the teacher's intent, heroification narratives can stifle students' feelings of civic agency and self-efficacy (Epstein, 1994). This unfortunate situation occurs by minimizing the importance of communities that mobilize to create social change (e.g., Woodson, 2016), as was the case for Ruth Bader Ginsburg, a Supreme Court Justice who was dangerously heroified as the last bastion of hope for U.S. democracy (Journell, 2020). Heroifying Ginsburg runs the risk of denying the role her legal team played in landmark rulings and suppressing discussions of anything that tarnishes her positive image (e.g., her stance in Indigenous legal cases). Furthermore, prior to her death, this heroification created much anxiety about her health, and seeing her as the sole guardian of democracy diverted attention from efforts to remedy "broader national dysfunction and division" (Jerkins, 2019, para. 6). In short, heroifying individuals does a disservice to both that individual and to society. Some students can express narratives of social progress that are more nuanced and take collective action into account (e.g., Epstein, 1998). Therefore, the task for educators is not necessarily to correct a deficit, but rather to provide time and space for such contemplations and not foreclose the possibility of students contemplating the varied nature of social change through time.

Although we may craft heroification narratives to provide inspiration, ironically these narratives can also cause disengagement by turning "flesh-and-blood individuals into pious, perfect creatures without conflicts, pain, credibility, or human interest" (Loewen, 2007, p. 11). Conversely, people seem to be fascinated by the aesthetic of evil and thus can even be more drawn to villains than to the heroes (Forbes, 2011). The dark side, however, is that then we (as ordinary humans) are discouraged from considering "our own complicity in parallel contemporary processes" (van Kessel & Plots, 2019, p. 22).

Villainification narratives harm us all by oversimplifying and obscuring our understanding of how we perpetuate evil through our daily actions. As author and journalist Ta-Nehisi Coates (2013) noted in the context of racism, people tend to interpret the cause as ill intent "in the heart of particularly evil individuals" instead of in the heart of society (para. 6), which is evident, for example, in how Texan history textbooks portray racially motivated violence (Brown & Brown, 2010). There is a need for both students and teachers to examine the broader system, as well as the individuals working within that system, in order to avoid absolving those who comprise this system of their responsibility, regardless of whether or not they are aware of their complicity.

Individuals can make a difference—for good or evil—but their actions are always entwined with a broader milieu. Thus, as social studies educators, we need to tread carefully to avoid heroification and villainification narratives while not diffusing agency into a completely amorphous entity like "society" (which, on its own, has no agency). Naming that tension with students is part of the solution, but preparing nuanced examples is also important. To that end, when discussing COVID-19, educators could consider examining potential heroes and villains in a more nuanced context.

Heroes and Villains of COVID-19

Individuals like Dr. Anthony Fauci, the Director of the National Institute of Allergy and Infectious Diseases, have become folk heroes worthy of some admiration (e.g., for his comments about how the pandemic is highlighting the unacceptable, disproportionate suffering faced by the African American community). Nonetheless, assigning Fauci sole responsibility for saving us from a pandemic (and racism) is dangerous. A significant collective effort is needed to keep COVID-19 cases at bay (e.g., wearing masks, avoiding large indoor gatherings, etc.), as well as for much-needed educational reform in many jurisdictions, such as smaller class sizes and more humane policies about teacher, student, and family illness. Many of us will need to take active roles for these urgent actions to occur, and our hopes should not be contingent upon one lone individual.

Compounding these issues is the fact that heroifying such individuals entails that they will inevitably disappoint us, because—like any human—they are flawed. In Alberta, Canada, for example, Dr. Deena Hinshaw, the Chief Medical Officer of Health, was initially lauded a hero. There was even merchandise in her honor (e.g., t-shirts) that instilled comfort and hope (and usually raised money for charity). A Facebook fan club of more than 12,000 Albertans was created early on in the pandemic, but as weeks turned into months, more comments became "abusive and aggressive" toward Dr. Hinshaw and the group's administrators, who had to remove over 100 group members (Stillger, 2020).

Public despair, bubbled up from the ongoing pandemic, combined with frustrations over provincial government policies, such as cuts to municipalities, the public sector, public schools, and postsecondary institutions; reversals of recent K–12 curriculum development; changes to the fee structure for doctors; and the decision to keep schools open during the pandemic. In such a situation, it can be tempting to blame an individual instead of sitting in the frustration of a complicated nexus of factors and responsibility. To be sure, it is fair to critique policies (e.g., it is reprehensible that there were group limits of 15, and later 10, for the general public, and yet there were many schools with over 30 students in a classroom), but setting up medical officers like Hinshaw as solely responsible for those policies is inaccurate and does not encourage collective action to fight the issue of large class sizes during a pandemic (as well as under more normal circumstances).

Similar to how it is easy to heroify people like Fauci and Hinshaw, it is also convenient (and also not entirely incorrect) to blame former President Trump for the racism that has led to a disproportionate death toll for those who are part of communities identified as Black and/or African American, Indigenous, and/or as People of Color, as well as increased racism and xenophobia toward those perceived to be Chinese (e.g., Chandra, 2020). Trump's policies and dog whistles to White supremacist groups have exacerbated the problem, as these groups feel empowered (Simon & Sidner, 2020), and allowances for (and encouragement of) racist words and actions trickle down into schools and other everyday contexts (Southern Poverty Law Center, 2016).

To be sure, citizens of the United States (and humans everywhere) should hold individuals accountable for their racist words and actions in any context, COVID-19 or otherwise. The problem lies when individuals like Trump are given sole responsibility instead of *also* holding others accountable, including the structural aspects. When teachers (or anyone) flatten a structural issue by blaming a singular villain, it "obscures our understanding of how we perpetuate evil through our daily actions" (van Kessel & Crowley, 2017, p. 429).

Racism is pervasive in U.S. (and other) institutions, including those that are key to surviving a pandemic, such as health care systems. But focusing on wide-reaching and daunting structural aspects without emphasizing ordinary individuals like ourselves can diffuse responsibility too much and/or dissuade from necessary action, thus leaving students feeling disempowered to effect change. Consequently, teachers need to educate in the messy space that examines the roles that both individual responsibility and systemic injustices play in perpetuating inequities. Part of the task includes reminding students that ordinary, interconnected people, not only "leaders," make positive social change (Woodson, 2016). To do that, educators can consider specific strategies with students, such as conceptualizing possible future scenarios.

FUTURES THINKING AND SCENARIO REASONING

To encourage a sense of the capacity for ordinary people to effect change, social studies educators can teach students to use scenario reasoning to strategize how communities can create both problems and solutions. As education scholar Neil Gough (1990) insightfully pointed out, in educational contexts (and beyond), the future is often *tacit* (i.e., implied and vague), *token* (i.e., clichés that are relatively meaningless), or *taken for granted* (i.e., one possibility of many is *the* future). In these ways, the COVID-19 pandemic can be thought of tacitly (e.g., "we'll get through this together!"), in a tokenized way (e.g., "finding a new normal"), or be taken for granted (e.g., "the only way to boost the economy is to open up"). Tacit and tokenized ways of talking about the pandemic are glib and also potentially hurtful. Such approaches deny the experiences of those harmed during the pandemic and provide no helpful guidance as to how we, collectively, might get through the situation. The taken-for-granted approach colonizes the future with the baggage of the present, foreclosing the possibility of creating a system in which individuals and their families are not as vulnerable to comparable situations that might occur in the future. Tacit, tokenized, and taken-for-granted approaches reveal a lack of imagination as well as an insidious (and arguably cynical) affinity for the inadequate status quo. As educators, we can do better, which is where explicit futures thinking can assist.

In a 1996 study, educational researcher Francis Hutchinson found it helpful to ask students to differentiate between *possible*, *probable*, and *preferable* futures, and Kent den Heyer (2017) has used these concepts to work with social studies students and preservice teachers in classroom settings. Such a method is easily applied to the context of COVID-19. As described in the following five steps, educators can shift the conversation with students from tacit, taken-for-granted, or tokenized futures into a tangible and potentially meaningful encounter with ideas in the context of communities.

Step 1: Present the Situation

Students would begin with a particular situation (e.g., how and why there are disproportionate deaths within communities that are subject to interlocking structural violence, such as the community of racialized immigrant women). The teacher could provide a news article or simply explain the situation briefly. For the purposes of this chapter, I will use the situation of Indigenous peoples being unaccounted for by U.S. COVID-19 data collection as an example (see Nagel, 2020).

Together, the class needs to examine (what are perceived to be) driving forces of that situation. In this case, the driving force is the ongoing legacies of settler colonialism (e.g., power dynamics, access to and conceptualizations of land, cultural genocide, etc.) in relation to why Indigenous folks might be overlooked and/or actively denied attention and services. During this time, the teacher may have to remind students about avoiding heroification and villainification. Engaging with this situation would lead toward discussions about settler colonialism and its cascading effects, the issue of flattening anti-Black and anti-Indigenous racism, and the role of data collection and media attention (or lack thereof) in shaping public opinion, among other topics.

Step 2: Explore Possible Futures

Next, students would identify all the *possible* ways that situation could play out—how it might stay the same as well as ways it might change. Returning to Nagel (2020), sample questions the teacher might pose to their students to prompt *possible* ways could be: What might unfold if those data were collected? Under what circumstances might those data change the situation (or not), such as actions taken (or not) by health departments and human rights groups? Again, teachers should ensure that anti-heroification and anti-villainification prompts are used as needed.

In this scenario, there is a possibility that the present situation continues (i.e., Indigenous communities continue to be ignored). Another possibility is that attention is brought to the situation of disproportionate infections and deaths, and yet government action is not taken to remedy the situation, in which case Indigenous groups and/or their allies may take action, which in itself can take multiple forms (e.g., various forms of dissent and civil disobedience, or even violent uprisings). Or perhaps attention is brought to the situation and something is done about it (although the possibility exists for that action to be inadequate, particularly if it is done without a partnership with Indigenous communities).

Step 3: Analyze the Probable Future(s)

After exhausting all the possibilities students can brainstorm, students would then explain which situation they interpret to be more *probable* given what they have learned already in class about social change, the particular situation itself, articles assigned for reading, and so on. If students have been primarily focusing on tragic stories of settler colonialism, they may find it likely that the present, unacceptable situation continues (or another bleak scenario). If, however, students have also been exposed to stories of resilience, resistance, and refusal (Madden, 2019), then they might see more of a probability of Indigenous dissent and political advocacy.

There is no one "right" answer (i.e., no one has a crystal ball to know what will happen), but it is helpful to discuss with students about why they picked their scenario as the most probable. If an educator wishes to assess this activity, they could, for example, consider students' argumentation and judicious use of evidence. Alternatively, or in tandem, this stage could also form the basis of a small research project into comparable situations or (better still, in my opinion) current collective efforts to change the situation.

Step 4: Imagine Preferred Futures

The next stage is the most important: teachers will ask students: Which outcome is preferred? Why? What are the preconditions for your preferred outcome to become the more probable one? The goal of such an approach is to move beyond "What if?" to "What ought I to do ethically alongside my community?" Such ponderings are in the service of radical hope (Gannon, 2020) rather than glib optimism. Thinking in groups about how such a pivot can occur can be one of many ways to name the problematic situation at hand while also considering where we, as interconnected humans in communities, might go from this juncture. For the situation described in this section, my preferred future, for example, is that attention is brought to the issue without the need for violence, the government (at multiple levels— municipal, state/provincial, and federal) chooses to take action about both the immediate problem and the underlying causes, and this action is done in partnership with Indigenous communities.

Step 5: Take Informed Action

Students formulate a plan regarding what they can do to help create the conditions for their preferred future. With the preferred situation mentioned above, this plan would likely include partnering with local organizations with a similar goal, developing reciprocal relationships with local Indigenous communities, and communicating with political representatives.

CONCLUDING THOUGHTS AND A CALL TO TAKE ACTION

Social studies educators can engage with the curricular context of COVID-19 to illuminate the nexus of individual and collective responsibility for interlocking structural violence to foster a sense of personal (and yet interconnected) responsibility to make the fundamental changes necessary for a society to hurt less from such violence. Key to many aspects of social studies education are explorations of and queries about:

> way[s] of living Now that could address the futility of frozen futurism while honoring the truth of human aspiration and dreaming; a way of living Now that makes possible a radical new acceptance of things, of one another, in the Now, without giving up on the possibility of continual regeneration through our mutual encounter. (Smith, 2000, pp. 18–19)

Inhabiting this space—living Now—invites us to consider how we are identifying "the problem," which, in turn, affects how we are imagining possible ways the situation might unfold. As aptly noted by den Heyer (2018), "Any 'problem' is but a powerful story around which researchers identify, stories themselves entangled and conveyed within larger stories . . . [that] convey particular understandings of people, their motivations, and a common good toward which we should strive" (p. 227). Although den Heyer (2018) is examining this situation in a different context (vis-à-vis the "nation"), this wisdom permeates a host of situations educators might consider in social studies, including the COVID-19 pandemic.

Teaching about the pandemic can help unmask systemic injustices in its many intersecting forms while also emphasizing the urgent need to work within communities to make change. To this end, part of this task is being mindful of how heroification and villainification narratives write "us" out of the story. However, the absence (or at least the troubling) of such narratives is perhaps insufficient on its own as pedagogical practice. Educators also can invite students to consider possible futures as fluid, including how they and others might be living Now and shaping the probability of each future scenario, perhaps without even knowing their role in those probabilities.

During the COVID-19 pandemic, people in the United States and elsewhere have witnessed not only the horrors of the structural violence laid bare, but also the "cascading effect" of protests against anti-Black racism (Hannah-Jones, 2020, para. 4). This situation, however, does not guarantee a preferred future of equality and justice. As activist and scholar Angela Davis noted, "After many moments of dramatic awareness and possibilities of change, the kinds of reforms instituted in the aftermath have prevented the radical potential from being realised" (Bakare, 2020, para. 3). Together, humans need to dream of the changes we seek to make and then work collectively to effect those changes: "If we are truly at the precipice of a transformative moment, the most tragic of outcomes would be that the demand be too timid and the resolution too small" (Hannah-Jones, 2020, para. 19). According to Davis, the most important task, then, is "to begin to give expression to ideas about what we can do next" (Bakare, 2020, para. 10). Considering the nexus of individual and collective responsibility in tandem with explicit futures thinking is one method in service of that task.

REFERENCES

Bakare, L. (2020, June 15). Angela Davis: 'We knew that the role of the police was to protect white supremacy.' *The Guardian.* https://www.theguardian.com/us-news/2020/jun/15/angela-davis-on-george-floyd-as-long-as-the-violence-of-racism-remains-no-one-is-safe

Bowleg, L. (2020, June 10). We're not all in this together: On COVID-19, intersectionality, and structural inequality. *American Journal of Public Health, 110*(7), 917. https://doi.org/10.2105/AJPH.2020.305766

Brown, A. L., & Brown, K. D. (2010). Strange fruit indeed: Interrogating contemporary textbook representations of racial violence toward African Americans. *Teachers College Record, 112*(1), 31–67.

Chandra, R. (2020, March 18). Calling COVID-19 a "Chinese virus" or "Kung Flu" is racist. *Psychology Today.* https://www.psychologytoday.com/ca/blog/the-pacific-heart/202003/calling-covid-19-chinese-virus-or-kung-flu-is-racist

Coates, T-N. (2013). The good, racist people. *The New York Times.* http://www.nytimes.com/2013/03/07/opinion/coates-the-good-racist-people.html

Crenshaw, K. (1991). Mapping the margins: Intersectionality, identity politics, and violence against women of color. *Stanford Law Review, 43*(6), 1241–1299.

den Heyer, K. (2003). Between every "now" and "then": A role for the study of historical agency in history and citizenship education. *Theory & Research in Social Education, 31*(4), 411–434. https://www.doi.org/10.1080/00933104.2003.10473232

den Heyer, K. (2012). Mapping the shadow: Bringing scholarship and teachers together to explore agency's shape and content in social change. *Theory & Research in Social Education, 40*(3), 292–323. https://www.doi.org/10.1080/00933104.2012.705680

den Heyer, K. (2017). Doing better than just falling forward: Linking subject matter with explicit futures thinking. *One World in Dialogue, 4*(1), 5–10.

den Heyer, K. (2018). Historical agency: Stories of choice, action, and social change. In S. A. Metzger & L. McArthur Harris (Eds.), *The Wiley international handbook of teaching and learning* (pp. 227–251). John Wiley & Sons.

Epstein, T. L. (1994). Tales from two textbooks: A comparison of the Civil Rights Movement in two secondary history textbooks. *The Social Studies, 85*(3), 121–126. https://doi.org/10.1080/00377996.1994.9956289

Epstein, T. (1998). Deconstructing differences in African American and European American adolescents' perspectives on United States history. *Curriculum Inquiry, 28*(4), 397–423. https://www.doi.org/10.1111/0362-6784.00100

Forbes, D. A. (2011). The aesthetic of evil. In J. Heit (Ed.), *Vader, Voldemort and other villains: Essays on evil in popular media* (pp. 13–27). McFarland & Company.

Gannon, K. M. (2020). *Radical hope: A teaching manifesto*. West Virginia University Press.

Gough, N. (1990). Futures in Australian education: Tacit, token, and taken for granted. *Futures, 22*(3), 298–310. https://doi.org/10.1016/0016-3287(90)90149-C

Gupta, A. H. (2020, March 12). Why women may face a greater risk of catching coronavirus. *The New York Times*. https://nyti.ms/33g2qAE

Hankivsky, O., & Kapilashrami, A. (2020). *Beyond sex and gender analysis: An intersectional view of the COVID-19 pandemic outbreak and response*. Melbourne School of Population and Global Health. https://mspgh.unimelb.edu.au/__data/assets/pdf_file/0011/3334889/Policy-brief_v3.pdf

Hannah-Jones, N. (2020, June 30). What is owed? *The New York Times*. https://www.nytimes.com/interactive/2020/06/24/magazine/reparations-slavery.html

Hardeman, R. R., Medina, E. M., Boyd, R. W. (2020). Stolen breaths. *The New England Journal of Medicine, 383*(3), 197–199. https://doi.org/10.1056/NEJMp2021072

Hutchinson, F. P. (1996). *Educating beyond violent futures*. Routledge.

Jerkins, M. (2019, January 13). Obsessing over Ruth Bader Ginsburg's health is bad for her, bad for us and bad for democracy. *The Washington Post*. https://www.washingtonpost.com/opinions/obsessing-over-ruth-bader-ginsburgs-health-is-bad-for-her-bad-for-us-and-bad-for-democracy/2019/01/13/94065d9a-15ae-11e9-803c-4ef28312c8b9_story.html

Journell, W. (2020). *Vice, On the Basis of Sex*, and the liberal imagination: Villainification and heroification in popular political film. *Educational Studies, 56*(1), 66–82. https://doi.org/10.1080/00131946.2019.1692021

Loewen, J. W. (2007). *Lies my teacher told me: Everything your American history textbook got wrong*. Simon & Schuster.

Madden, B. (2019). *Indigenous counter-stories in Truth and Reconciliation education*. EdCan. https://www.edcan.ca/articles/trc-education/

Martell, C. C., & Stevens, K. M. (2021). *Teaching history for justice: Centering activism in students' study of the past*. Teachers College Press.

McKay, I. (2000). The liberal order framework: A prospectus for a reconnaissance of Canadian history. *Canadian Historical Review, 81*(4), 617–645.

Moore, R. (2020, April 8). *If COVID-19 doesn't discriminate, then why are Black people dying at higher rates?* American Civil Liberties Union. https://www.aclu.org/news/racial-justice/if-covid-19-doesnt-discriminate-then-why-are-black-people-dying-at-higher-rates/

Nagel, R. (2020, April 24). Native Americans being left out of US coronavirus data and labelled as 'other'. *The Guardian*. https://www.theguardian.com/us-news/2020/apr/24/us-native-americans-left-out-coronavirus-data

Peck, C., Poyntz, S., & Seixas, P. (2011). Agency in students' narratives of Canadian history. In L. Perikleous & D. Shemilt (Eds.), *The future of the past: Why history education matters* (pp. 253–282). Association for Historical Dialogue and Research.

Salami, B. (2020, June 24). *Intersectionality, COVID-19 and healthcare workers* [Invited presentation]. Intersections of Gender in Conversation. https://www.ualberta.ca/intersections-gender/news-events/news2020/conversation-bukola-salami.html

Segall, A. (1999) Critical history: Implications for history/social studies education. *Theory & Research in Social Education,* 27(3), 358–374. http://dx.doi.org/10.1080/00933104.1999.10505885

Simon, M., & Sidner, S. (2020, July 16). *Trump says he's not a racist. That's not how white nationalists see it.* CNN. https://www.cnn.com/2018/11/12/politics/white-supremacists-cheer-midterms-trump/index.html

Smith, D. G. (2000). The specific challenges of globalization for teaching and vice versa. *Alberta Journal of Educational Research,* 46(1), 7–25.

Solnit, R. (2020, April 17). Coronavirus does discriminate, because that's what humans do. *The Guardian.* https://www.theguardian.com/commentisfree/2020/apr/17/coronavirus-discriminate-humans-racism-sexism-inequality

Southern Poverty Law Center. (2016). *The Trump effect: The impact of the 2016 election on the nation's schools.* Author. https://www.splcenter.org/sites/default/files/trump_effect_final_comments_2.pdf

Stillger, N. (2020, September 4). *COVID-19 may be further fraying Albertans' nerves 6 months into pandemic.* Global News. https://globalnews.ca/news/7315293/coronavirus-alberta-anxiety-deena-hinshaw/

van Kessel, C. (2017). A phenomenographic study of youth conceptualizations of evil: Order-words and the politics of evil. *Canadian Journal of Education,* 40(1), 576–602. https://journals.sfu.ca/cje/index.php/cje-rce/article/view/3105

van Kessel, C., & Crowley, R. M. (2017). Villainification and evil in social studies education. *Theory & Research in Social Education,* 95(4), 427–455. https://doi.org/10.1080/00933104.2017.1285734

van Kessel, C., & Plots, R. (2019). A textbook study in villainification: The need to renovate our depictions of villains. *One World in Dialogue,* 5(1), 21–31.

Woodson, A. N. (2016). We're just ordinary people: Messianic master narratives and Black youths' civic agency. *Theory & Research in Social Education,* 44(2), 184–211. https://doi.org/10.1080/00933104.2016.1170645

The Inclusion of Economic Inequality in the Social Studies Curriculum

Toward an Education for Participatory Readiness

Leonel Pérez Expósito and Varenka Servín Arcos

A rural community in Vermont has a great library. It is Sunday, and the parking lot is full. There is only one issue: The library is closed on Sundays. Some of those cars function as personal mobile offices, while others also carry kids doing their homework. Both grown-ups and children use "the wireless connectivity spilling out of the empty building" because "their rural homes lacked high-speed broadband" (Friedman, 2020, para. 2).

That scenario occurred in Vermont in the United States, during the COVID-19 pandemic, a country where high-speed Internet was available through terrestrial technologies to 93.5% of the total population in 2017, including 73.6% of those living in rural areas (Federal Communications Commission, 2019). However, these official figures are contested. Other sources estimate that probably less than half of the population accesses the Internet at that speed and that 69% of U.S. households have terrestrial broadband (Microsoft, 2018).

In Mexico, more than 43% of households lack any kind of internet connectivity. Only 22% of the rural population above 6 years old was declared to be a computer user in 2018, in contrast to 49% of those living in an urban zone (Instituto Nacional de Estadística y Geografía, 2020). While estimates suggest that in Latin America and the Caribbean, 51% of students had some kind of access to the Internet for school activities during 2020, only 6% of students in Eastern and Southern Africa could say the same (United Nations Children's Fund [UNICEF], 2020). These statistics are only a small part of the global digital divide that marks dramatically unequal access to the Internet not only among world regions and countries, but also within each of them. During the pandemic, these gaps threatened to deepen education inequalities (UNICEF, 2020).

In the wake of COVID-19, the project of democratic education for a democratic society cannot survive without addressing economic inequality as a fundamental issue. This chapter develops an argument for its inclusion into the social studies curriculum and outlines a general framework for defining its content. It is divided into three sections. First, we note that while a pedagogical emphasis prevails in previous research related to teaching about inequality, a scant literature focuses on what to teach about it. It parallels an exiguous content about inequality in official curriculum initiatives and standards.

In the second section, we argue for the inclusion of economic inequality in the curriculum based on its civic, political, and educational relevance. We locate that curriculum within a project of education for "participatory readiness" (Allen, 2016) and in relation to the development of its core capacities. From it, the third section offers a general framework for curricular content about economic inequality in the wake of COVID-19.

TEACHING INEQUALITY: FROM PEDAGOGY TO CURRICULUM

Spanish educational psychologist Cesar Coll (1987) distinguished between curriculum design and development. The first process refers to the planning, design, and composition of an educational project that broadly provides information on "what to teach, when to teach, how to teach, and what, how, and when to assess [what is meant to be taught]" (p. 32). This project is open to discussion and multiple permutations or developments by different situations as it is put into practice (curriculum development). In its final stretch, every single teacher unavoidably transforms—to different degrees—the curricular content that they aim to teach according to its pedagogy and didactics, as well as their scientific, social, political, educational, and cultural standpoint.

Based on a representative sample of 685 public high school social studies teachers in 293 schools in the United States, civic education scholars Joel Westheimer and John Rogers (2017) indicated that a vast majority (97%) reported that they discuss issues of economic inequality with their students. Almost 50% of their sample said that they do it at least once a week. These figures contrast with the fact that most U.S. states do not include content addressing economic inequality in their curriculum standards (Rogers & Westheimer, 2015, 2017).

This tension suggests that while a lack of attention to economic inequality prevails in the process of *curriculum design*, inequality has gained relevance through teachers' work of *curriculum development*. Rogers and Westheimer (2017) put forward that instead of addressing inequality as a central topic in their lessons, teachers mostly draw connections between it and "a wide variety of historical and contemporary social issues" or assume that inequality is somehow implied in their lessons about "poverty, stratification or exploitation" (p. 1051). The differential value of economic inequality in the processes of curriculum design and development corresponds to the pedagogical emphasis in the existing literature related to teaching inequality. The majority of work related to teaching inequality addresses the question of how to teach it rather than focusing on what to teach about it.

Since there is a long tradition of using simulation games or exercises to learn about inequality and social stratification, different works have critically analyzed this strategy or reported on its implementation in classrooms (e.g., Dorn, 1989). Other alternative strategies and approaches have been identified in the literature: cooperative learning groups, explicit discussions of prejudice and discrimination, role-playing and perspective-taking activities, and service learning (White et al., 2013). Other scholars have argued for the pedagogical efficacy of a wide range of teaching strategies to address inequality at the secondary level: interactive activities from popular education (Machum, 2018), participatory action research (Hormel et al., 2018), in-depth analysis of legal cases (Roisman, 2002), scaffolding (Bradley, 2018), quizzes and games (Kunkel, 2018), structured academic controversy (Journell et al., 2017), and critical quantitative analysis of government documents (Kersten, 2018).

While many of these works note specific content or topics related to economic inequality, less research focuses on what to teach about inequality and why. Some scholars have argued for the role that teaching and learning about inequality play to educate an efficacious and participatory citizenry for a democratic society, as well as its impact on democracy's legitimacy as a form of government (e.g., Pérez-Expósito, 2016). A few others outline general curricular goals within which specific contents about economic disparities can be arranged. For instance, Sober (2017) took the following students' needs as a standpoint to develop her *Teaching Economics as if People Mattered* curriculum:

(1) exposure to how moneyed interests operate behind the scenes of a democracy; (2) content knowledge that demystifies economic policies; (3) real-world examples of how the power of organized people has rivaled, and can continue to rival, organized money; and (4) a forum to explore their own beliefs about these topics. (p. 84)

Other scholars developed specific essential curricular content: civic capacities and skills (Allen, 2016), knowledge about the facts of economic inequality (Bowyer & Kahne, 2017), its historical causes (Bedolla & Andrade, 2017), the relationships between it and the political realm (Journell et al., 2017), and strategies for tackling economic inequality (Rogers & Westheimer, 2017).

It is still striking how the lack of content about economic disparities in official curriculum initiatives or standards parallels a scant literature centered on the question of *what to teach about inequality*. Of course, we should keep thinking about how to teach it, but it is also vital to clarify and sustain what should be the curricular content about economic inequality.

WHY INCLUDE ECONOMIC INEQUALITY IN THE SOCIAL STUDIES CURRICULUM?

We live in a world where around 60 individuals in 2016 "owned as much private net wealth as the poorer half of humanity, more than 3.5 billion people" (Scheidel, 2017, p. 1). Each year, this group of super-billionaires shrinks as its wealth grows. Similar conspicuous disparities exist within countries. The wealthiest 20 people in the United States "currently own as much as the bottom half of the country's households taken together" (p. 1). In Mexico, the richest 1% concentrated 43% of the total national wealth in 2013 (WealthInsight, 2013).

These inequalities are not a mechanical outcome of market forces. They are better understood as consequences of historical processes of oppression (I. M. Young, 1990) and political decisions that have favored a minority, not only economically, but also politically. As they become wealthier, their capacity to influence politics and policies also increases. In turn, this political power translates to more opportunities for wealth concentration.

For those lacking such resources, political participation in a democratic polity looks like an uneven field where the egalitarian spirit of democracy gradually disappears. In the last 25 years, the share of persons that are dissatisfied with democracy in North America, Latin America, Europe, Middle East, Asia, and Australasia has risen 10%. In the United States, less than 25% of adults were dissatisfied with democracy in 1995; by 2020, this figure reached 55%, with a sharp increase since the 2008 economic crisis (Foa et al., 2020). In Mexico, only 16% of adults are satisfied with the functioning of democracy, and 88% say that the country is governed by a few who act for their own benefit (Latinobarómetro, 2018).

The question becomes, then, how to disrupt this vicious circle of economic and political inequality. Tracing the global history of inequality from the Stone Age to the present, Scheidel (2017) argued that mass violence and catastrophes are the only forces that can seriously decrease economic inequality. Unfortunately, these are not the interventions that most of us desire.

Looking at more positive and desirable ways of reducing inequality, many have argued for education as the main equalizer (e.g., Greenstein & Merisotis, 2015). People with higher educational attainment obtain more market rewards than those with less education. If educational gaps narrow, disparities in the distribution of those returns should contract too. As Piketty (2014) stated: "historical experience suggests that the principal mechanism for convergence [. . .] is the diffusion of knowledge. [. . .] the poor catch up with the rich to the extent that they achieve the same level of technological know-how, skill, and education" (p. 71).

Other economists are not that enthusiastic about seeing education as the prime equalizer. Inequality in the 21st century is a problem of regulation. As such, it has to be faced through labor, taxation, trade, and social security policies in which redistribution and equality prevail over stimulus for profit to those who already amass a disproportionate amount of wealth (Atkinson, 2015; Reich, 2010; Stiglitz, 2013).

This line of reasoning does not overlook education, which becomes relevant not for its mere economic value, but for its civic and political meaning. Through education, students can learn and develop knowledge, capacities, and skills that prepare them to participate effectively in an unequal political arena and influence the decisions from which those regulations and policies become real (Pérez-Expósito, 2016). As Allen (2016) argued:

> An education that prepares students for civic and political engagement brings into play the prospect of political contestation around issues of economic fairness. [. . .] Education can affect income inequality not merely by spreading technical skills and compressing the income distribution [. . .] [but] by increasing a society's political competitiveness and thereby impacting how technology evolves, how markets function, and how the gains from various economic arrangements are distributed. (p. 32)

The emphasis of an education for "college readiness"—preparing students to become competitive in an uncertain, mutable, and flexible knowledge-based economy—needs to be coupled with what Allen (2016) calls an education for "participatory readiness." It is vital to make young people ready to participate in a changing, complex, and uneven political scene in which decisions leading to a better distribution of wealth and economic gains, healthier regulation of markets, and a restoration of political equality can be made. Keeping the egalitarian spirit of democracy alive and restoring its legitimacy among citizens depends greatly on succeeding in this challenge.

According to Allen (2016), three main capacities constitute the core of an education for participatory readiness:

- Verbal empowerment: the capacity of diagnosing our current situation, not only by interpreting data but also through dialogue with others and being able to move from that diagnosis to a prescription of a response that can be publicly justified.

- Democratic knowledge: the art and science of association, which consist of what Allen called "cosmopolitan bonding skills, on the one hand, and bridging skills on the other." Bridging skills are "capacities by which a translator, a mediator, and an individual who can surmount social difference can convert a costly social relationship into one that is mutually beneficial to both parties. Cosmopolitan bonding skills, in contrast, relate to the precise nature of the bonds that we form with the people to whom we feel the most affinity." (p. 41)
- Tactical and strategical understanding of the mechanics of political action. To comprehend how effective political participation succeeds is not limited to traditional constitutional knowledge and the study of governmental structure and procedures. Children and young people need to know about how "civic agents can interact with corporations and nongovernmental organizations or as part of social movements. It requires understanding how cultural norms can be changed and how changes in cultural norms bring about broader political changes. It also requires understanding a new architecture of communication [. . .], to master the architecture and rhetorics of the Internet and social media." (p. 43)

Social studies curriculum that is explicitly related to economic inequality and its consequences is essential for developing these capacities in students, especially *verbal empowerment* and *tactical and strategical understanding of the mechanics of political action*. Knowing, for instance, the facts of economic inequality and their social and political effects is particularly relevant for students to develop an accurate diagnosis of their reality from which they are able to move forward in justifying a response. Likewise, understanding current interlocking connections between political and economic powers, and how social movements from working and middle classes have been able to undermine those networks, is necessary to comprehend the mechanics of contemporary effective and efficacious political action.

There are also pedagogical reasons for attending to participatory readiness. The official curriculum reflects the status that a particular body of knowledge has in society (M. Young, 1971). When a topic enters the curriculum, it becomes more visible to teachers, educational authorities, and families. It becomes legitimized and validated knowledge, and such attributes may counter hesitations in teachers about whether to talk about it.

Curricular status helps to diminish the *political* charge of a body of knowledge. It is no longer perceived as the result of a given ideological position but as the embodiment of a wider social agreement between different political perspectives. To a certain extent, this process of depoliticization can be enhanced through a relation between that knowledge and well-established disciplinary fields. The study of economic inequality presents this advantage because it feeds from economics, sociology, history, philosophy, and political philosophy.

In sum, the inclusion of economic inequality in the social studies curriculum is of civic and political relevance in so far as knowledge about it lies at the heart of an education for participatory readiness. It is reasonable to argue that this knowledge, in turn, offers possibilities to prepare citizens with the capacity of impacting decisions that lead to a more just distribution of economic goods and weaken the vicious feedback loop between economic and political inequality. It is on these decisions that the legitimate future of democracy depends greatly.

TEACHING ABOUT INEQUALITY IN THE WAKE OF COVID-19: TOWARD A CURRICULAR FRAMEWORK

We have argued for a social studies curriculum that includes a body of knowledge about economic inequality. In this section, we address what such a curriculum might look like. Our framework relates closely to the development of what Allen (2016) called *verbal empowerment* and *tactical and strategical understanding of the mechanics of political action*. We assemble a set of questions under each of these two capacities in order to outline potential content in regard to economic inequality that a curriculum of social studies should articulate. In the wake of COVID-19, we cannot wait any longer to tackle those questions in social studies education.

Verbal Empowerment

What is Inequality? While some tech giants saw their revenues grow in 2020, millions of Americans have been unemployed during the pandemic. COVID-19 has expanded wage inequality between different sectors and deepened poverty, especially among African American and Hispanics. Thousands of undocumented workers who have contributed for years to the U.S. economy were left unemployed without social security and with limited access to health care or excluded from it (Brown & Ravallion, 2020; Economic Commission for Latin America and the Caribbean, 2020).

COVID-19 has revealed a wide range of inequalities. Why do we see them as such, and not merely as differences? What is the distinction between human diversity and inequality? A social studies curriculum should include knowledge that helps students tackle these questions and address the problem of *inequality of what* (Sen, 1992). It is important that the curriculum enables them to differentiate between disparities of income and wealth, and inequality of opportunities, rights, and liberties (Sen, 1992, 2009) and to comprehend the historical and cultural variants of economic assets and conceptions of equality/inequality.

What is the Extent of Economic Inequality in Our Communities? As we noted at the beginning of this chapter, the pandemic has bluntly reminded us that inequality is not only a national problem, but also affects us globally and locally. It has clearly brought to the surface the unequal access to quality healthcare in a single city like Phoenix, AZ (Stockton & King, 2021), while also showing how an entire region like Latin America has added more than 45 million people to poverty (Organisation for Economic Co-operation and Development [OECD], 2021a).

Students should know how unequal their world, country, state, district, and even neighborhood is and what contributes to this inequality. They should be able to understand the facts of inequality (Bowyer & Kahne, 2017), from global to local levels, and use them properly in their rhetoric. To do so, they must address the question of how to measure inequality and face some of its challenges (Piketty, 2015). They should also understand some common measures of it, like gross domestic product per capita and the Gini coefficient.

What Kinds and Amount of Inequality are Ethically Wrong, and Why? By February 2021, 90% of COVID-19 vaccines around the world had been administered in 10 countries, while several poor countries have been unable to secure any (OECD, 2021b). What does that disparity say about our humanity and the human rights project initiated since the end of World War II? Are such disparities ethically justifiable? What forms and amount of inequality are morally problematic, and why? If different forms of inequality have characterized human groups and societies throughout history, what is wrong with it?

As students are able to define inequality and understand facts about it, the curriculum should provide knowledge that allows them to engage with such questions. The social studies curriculum can help students to recognize, comprehend, and critically assess the central points of key theories that enable them to sustain their standpoint toward inequality, from the Marxist critique of the idea of justice as a functional resource to maintain the structural inequality of capitalism (Wood, 1972) to the works of John Rawls (2001) and Amartya Sen (2009).

What Are the Effects of Inequality in Our Society? The World Bank has said that, based on previous epidemics, we can expect a steady increase in income inequality, both globally and within countries, during the next 5 years (Hill & Narayan, 2021); increased crime (Hsieh & Pugh, 1993), lessened social mobility (Corak, 2016), and undermining of social trust (Jordahl, 2009) will follow. Although some may see positive outcomes, such as fostering meritocratic beliefs and trajectories (Mijs, 2019), the deleterious social and political effects of economic disparities are wide and diverse. The curriculum should articulate knowledge that allows students to critically analyze these effects of economic inequality in order to sustain their ethical scrutiny of inequality and subsequent position taking.

How Does Economic Inequality Relate to Political Inequality? During 2020, when the world faced a pandemic with no precedent and many European nations witnessed the saturation of their intensive care units, five tech giants (the so-called Big Five) spent more than 19 million euros in Brussels, lobbying the political heart of the European Union (EU) (Transparency International, 2021). While millions of immigrants in the EU and United States lack the political resources to demand their human right to healthcare, these five American companies know very well how to use their economic resources to gain political power across borders, in order to protect their interests.

The curriculum should present reasons to students about why, in democratic regimes, political powers must rule economically powerful stakeholders. It should also offer a realistic approach to the dynamics of what we have called the vicious circle of economic and political disparities, which helps students to understand how economic inequality affects political participation and government responses to citizens' demands (American Political Science Assoc. Task Force, 2004).

Why Are We Such an Unequal Country and How Did We Reach This Point? In many countries, the pandemic has exposed serious flaws in healthcare systems and profound disparities in access to quality medical care. While this analysis is still contentious, some studies have estimated that in Mexico, the fatality rate is more than four times higher in the main public health subsystems than in private hospitals (Badillo, 2020). How did our healthcare systems become so unequal? How and why, through our history, have we not been able to unlink economic inequality from the guarantee of the human right to healthcare?

In countries with deep economic disparities, students need to understand how their country reached that point. In other words, the study of inequality in social studies curriculum should include its historical causes. Among other benefits, this knowledge is relevant for students to assess how likely it is that present decisions will lead their society to a more equal or unequal scenario.

How Does Economic and Political Inequality Affect Us? Why could some students' parents not help in online school activities at home? Why do some parents not have a home office? In Mexico, why did some students have to take classes through radio or television, while other schools taught their students online? As with other social problems, the study of economic inequality might be perceived by students as distant. Yet the pandemic has illuminated contrasting realities among children and young people in their school experiences. The curriculum should provide students with knowledge that encourages them to examine how inequality expresses itself in their daily contexts, like school and family, and its consequences.

Being able to recognize income inequality and how it affects society is important for students; however, awareness alone is not sufficient. As Allen (2016) noted, awareness should lead to a response. Thus, the next step social studies educators should take is helping students understand and navigate political action.

Tactical and Strategical Understanding of the Mechanics of Political Action

What Are the Characteristics of Past and Current Experiences of Effective Political Participation? Critical times tend to be perfect for the emergence of social solidarity, social movements, and political mobilization. The pandemic has been the scenario of different forms of civic and political participation aiming at reversing the effects of a wide range of inequalities (economic, racial, political, gender, and their interconnections) (Bringel & Pleyers, 2020).

As Sober (2017) stated, a key contribution from a curriculum concerned with economic inequality is to provide "real-world examples of how the power of organized people has rivaled, and can continue to rival, organized money" (p. 84). More broadly, the curriculum should open opportunities to students to analyze the dynamics and characteristics of organized political actions that have succeeded in the pursuit of their goals despite powerful economic or political adversaries.

What Kinds of Participatory Actions Have Succeeded in Overcoming Certain Inequalities in Students' Daily Contexts, and What Were Their Characteristics? To better understand successful tactics and strategies in actions of political participation, it is important that students realize that people like them, living in similar contexts, can make a change. To this end, the curriculum should include the analysis of participatory experiences carried out by young people or children that have succeeded in constructing a more equal and inclusive space in context like school, family, and local community.

Many students, due to their age, may not have the ability to fully engage in political activism. Yet it is still important for schools to provide a foundation for future activism. If schools can make students aware of what constitutes effective political participation—beyond just voting—they will be better prepared to engage in the political arena once they are older.

CONCLUSION

The current state of economic inequality in the world, of which we were reminded during the COVID-19 pandemic, is threatening the egalitarian spirit of democracy, as well as its legitimacy, throughout the world. Conscious about its centrality as a contemporary issue, many teachers currently discuss economic inequality in their classrooms. Yet economic inequality is not yet relevant content in the social studies curriculum. As a result, teaching about inequality depends on the decisions made by each teacher, which frequently leads to discussing economic disparities as a tangential or peripheral topic.

In the wake of COVID-19, as the arenas of political participation become increasingly unequal, we have argued that economic inequality can no longer be peripheral; rather, it must be central to civic education. We have presented a broad curricular framework from which teachers and curriculum designers can draw to give prominence and viability to knowledge related to economic inequality in the social studies curriculum.

REFERENCES

Allen, D. S. (2016). *Education and equality*. University of Chicago Press.

American Political Science Association Task Force. (2004). American democracy in an age of rising inequality. *Perspectives on Politics, 2*(4), 651–666. http://dx.doi.org/10.1017/S153759270404040X

Atkinson, A. B. (2015). *Inequality: What can be done?* Harvard University Press.

Badillo, D. (2020, November 1). La tasa de letalidad por Covid-19 se cuatriplica en hospitales públicos que en los privados. *El Economista*. https://www.economista.com.mx/politica/La-tasa-de-letalidad-por-Covid-19-se-cuatriplica-en-hospitales-publicos-que-en-los-privados-20201101-0003.html

Bedolla, L. G., & Andrade, J. (2017). The invisible hand of history: Pluralism, power, and inequality. *PS: Political Science & Politics, 50*(4), 1062–1067. https://doi.org/10.1017/S1049096517001317

Bowyer, B., & Kahne, J. (2017). Facing facts in an era of political polarization: Young people's learning and knowledge about economic inequality. *PS: Political Science & Politics, 50*(4), 1056–1061. https://doi.org/10.1017/S1049096517001305

Bradley, S. L. (2018). Overcoming students' fear: Scaffolding to teach money and society. In K. Haltinner & L. Hormel (Eds.), *Teaching economic inequality and capitalism in contemporary America* (pp. 113–124). Springer.

Bringel, B., & Pleyers, G. (2020). *Alerta global. Políticas, movimientos sociales y futuros en disputa en tiempos de pandemia*. CLACSO.

Brown, C. S., & Ravallion, M. (2020). *Inequality and the coronavirus: Socioeconomic covariates of behavioral responses and viral outcomes across US counties*. National Bureau of Economic Research. https://nber.org/papers/w27549

Coll, C. (1987). *Psicología y currículum*. Paidós.

Corak, M. (2016). *Inequality from generation to generation: The United States in comparison*. IZA.

Dorn, D. S. (1989). Simulation games: One more tool on the pedagogical shelf. *Teaching Sociology, 17*(1), 1–18. https://doi.org/10.2307/1317920

Economic Commission for Latin America and the Caribbean. (2020). *Impact of*

COVID-19 on the United States economy and the policy response. Author. https://repositorio.cepal.org/bitstream/handle/11362/45984/S2000540_en.pdf?sequence=1&isAllowed=y

Federal Communications Commission. (2019). *2019 Broadband Deployment Report* [Report 19-44]. https://docs.fcc.gov/public/attachments/FCC-19-44A1.pdf

Foa, R. S., Claystone, A., Slade, M., Rand, A., & Williams, R. (2020). *The global satisfaction with democracy report 2020.* Bennett Institute for Public Policy, Centre for the Future of Democracy. https://www.bennettinstitute.cam.ac.uk/media/uploads/files/DemocracyReport2020_nYqqWi0.pdf

Friedman, T. L. (2020). Kamala Harris deserves a more important job. *The New York Times.* https://www.nytimes.com/2020/12/15/opinion/kamala-harris-rural-america.html

Greenstein, D., & Merisotis, J. (2015). Education does reduce inequality. *The Wall Street Journal.* https://www.wsj.com/articles/education-does-reduce-inequality-1428619552

Hill, R., & Narayan, A. (2021, January 07). *What COVID-19 can mean for long-term inequality in developing countries.* World Bank. https://blogs.worldbank.org/voices/what-covid-19-can-mean-long-term-inequality-developing-countries

Hormel, L., Ballesteros, C., & Brister, H. (2018). Participatory action research as problem-based learning: A course study of rural poverty, low-income housing, and environmental justice. In K. Haltinner & L. Hormel (Eds.), *Teaching economic inequality and capitalism in contemporary America* (pp. 169–182). Springer.

Hsieh, C.-C., & Pugh, M. D. (1993). Poverty, income inequality, and violent crime: A meta-analysis of recent aggregate data studies. *Criminal Justice Review, 18*(2), 182–202. https://doi.org/10.1177%2F073401689301800203

Instituto National de Estadística y Geografía. (2020). *Tabulados de la encuesta nacional sobre disponibilidad y uso de tecnologías de la información en los hogares 2019.* Author. https://www.inegi.org.mx/programas/dutih/2019/default.html#Tabulados

Jordahl, H. (2009). Economic inequality. In G. T. Svendsen & G. L. H. Svendsen (Eds.), *Handbook of social capital: The troika of sociology, political science and economics* (pp. 323–336). Edward Elgar.

Journell, W., Levy, B. L., & Hartwick, J. M. (2017). Helping students address the elephant in democracy's room: An interactive approach to teaching about campaign finance. In C. Wright-Maley & T. Davis (Eds.), *Teaching for democracy in an age of economic disparity* (pp. 103–118). Routledge.

Kersten, A. E. (2018). Teaching economic inequality and capitalism in contemporary America using resources from the federal government. In K. Haltinner & L. Hormel (Eds.), *Teaching economic inequality and capitalism in contemporary America* (pp. 145–156). Springer.

Kunkel, C. A. (2018). Capitalism in the classroom: Confronting the invisibility of class inequality. In K. Haltinner & L. Hormel (Eds.), *Teaching economic inequality and capitalism in contemporary America* (pp. 125–130). Springer.

Latinobarómetro. (2018). *Informe Latinobarómetro 2018.* Author. https://www.latinobarometro.org/lat.jsp

Machum, S. (2018). Experiencing the outcomes of economic inequality in the day-to-day workings of the classroom. In K. Haltinner & L. Hormel (Eds.),

Teaching economic inequality and capitalism in contemporary America (pp. 131–143). Springer.

Microsoft. (2018). *An update on connecting rural America: The 2018 Microsoft Airband Initiative.* Author. https://blogs.microsoft.com/uploads/prod/sites/5/2018/12/MSFT-Airband_InteractivePDF_Final_12.3.18.pdf

Mijs, J. J. B. (2019). The paradox of inequality: Income inequality and belief in meritocracy go hand in hand. *Socio-Economic Review, 19*(1), 7–35. https://doi.org/10.1093/ser/mwy051

Organisation for Economic Co-operation and Development. (2021a). *COVID-19 en América Latina y el Caribe: Consecuencias socioeconómicas y prioridades de política.* Author. https://read.oecd-ilibrary.org/view/?ref=134_134494-n1k-7ww92ro&title=COVID-19-en-America-Latina-y-el-Caribe-Consecuencias-socioeconomicas-y-prioridades-de-politica

Organisation for Economic Co-operation and Development. (2021b). *We must not fail humanity's greatest test.* Author. https://read.oecd-ilibrary.org/view/?ref=1060_1060309-xi2i240d24&title=We-must-not-fail-humanity-s-greatest-test

Pérez-Expósito, L. (2016). México: Educating citizens for social justice in a highly unequal country. In A. Peterson, R. Hattam, M. Zembylas, & J. Arthur (Eds.), *The Palgrave international handbook of education for citizenship and social justice* (pp. 485–507). Palgrave Macmillan.

Piketty, T. (2014). *Capital in the twenty-first century.* Belknap Press.

Piketty, T. (2015). *The economics of inequality.* Belknap Press.

Rawls, J. (2001). *Justice as fairness: A restatement* (E. Kelly, Ed.). Harvard University Press.

Reich, R. B. (2010). *Aftershock : The next economy and America's future.* Alfred A. Knopf.

Rogers, J., & Westheimer, J. (2015). *Learning inequality? A conceptual framework for examining how inequality is addressed in curricular frameworks* [Paper presentation]. American Educational Research Association Annual Meeting, Chicago, IL, United States.

Rogers, J., & Westheimer, J. (2017). Teaching about economic inequality in a diverse democracy: Politics, ideology, and difference. *PS: Political Science & Politics, 50*(4), 1049-1055. https://doi.org/10.1017/S1049096517001287

Roisman, F. W. (2002). Teaching about inequality, race, and property. *St. Louis University Law Journal, 46*(665), 1-26.

Scheidel, W. (2017). *The great leveler: Violence and the history of inequality from the Stone Age to the twenty-first century.* Princeton University Press.

Sen, A. (1992). *Inequality reexamined.* Russell Sage Foundation

Sen, A. (2009). *The idea of justice.* Belknap Press.

Sober, T. L. (2017). Teaching about economics and moneyed interests in twenty-first-century democracy. In C. Wright-Maley & T. Davis (Eds.), *Teaching for democracy in an age of economic disparity* (pp. 79-94). Routledge

Stiglitz, J. E. (2013). *The price of inequality.* W. W. Norton & Company.

Stockton, A., & King, L. (2021, February 24). Death, through a nurse's eyes. *The The New York Times.* https://www.nytimes.com/2021/02/24/opinion/covid-icu-nurses-arizona.html?action=click&module=Opinion&pgtype=Homepage

Transparency International EU. (2021). *Deep pockets, open doors: Big tech lobbying in Brussels*. Author. https://transparency.eu/wp-content/uploads/2021/02/Deep_pockets_open_doors_report.pdf

United Nations Children's Fund. (2020). *Covid-19: Are children able to continue learning during school closures?* Author. https://data.unicef.org/resources/remote-learning-reachability-factsheet/

WealthInsight. (2013). *Number of multi-millionaires in Mexico far exceeds global average*. Author. http://www.wealthinsight.com/pressrelease/number-of-multi-millionaires-in-mexico-far-exceeds-global-average

Westheimer, J., & Rogers, J. (2017). *Teaching about economic inequality is political, but not the way you think*. Brown Center Chalkboard. https://www.brookings.edu/blog/brown-center-chalkboard/2017/12/06/teaching-about-economic-inequality-is-political-but-not-the-way-you-think/

White, E. S., Mistry, R. S., & Chow, K. A. (2013). How do teachers talk about economic inequality? The complexity of teaching at a socioeconomically integrated elementary school. *Analyses of Social Issues and Public Policy, 13*(1), 370–394. https://doi.org/https://doi.org/10.1111/asap.12024

Wood, A. W. (1972). The Marxian critique of justice. *Philosophy & Public Affairs, 1*(3), 244–282.

Young, I. M. (1990). *Justice and the politics of difference*. Princeton University Press.

Young, M. (1971). *Knowledge and control: New directions for the sociology of education*. Collier-Macmillan.

CHAPTER 10

"Get Your Knee Off Our Neck!"

Historicizing Protests in the Wake of COVID-19

Kristen E. Duncan and Amber M. Neal

Although the COVID-19 pandemic has had a disastrous impact on the nation as a whole, its disparate impact on Black Americans was particularly damaging. Black Americans were more likely to contract COVID-19, require hospitalization, or die from the disease than White Americans (Gould & Wilson, 2020), and while the disease shortened the life expectancy for White Americans by 1 year, the life expectancy for Black Americans was reduced by 3 years (Arias et al., 2021). In addition to having damaging effects on the physical health of Black communities, the pandemic also had disparate impacts on the financial health of Black Americans, exposing structural and systemic racism in numerous facets of American life (Gould & Wilson, 2020).

While the disparate impact of COVID-19 on Black communities occasionally made news headlines at the beginning of the pandemic, White supremacy and racial terrorism took center stage as Americans learned to adjust to the "new normal" brought on by the pandemic. Although White vigilantes murdered Ahmaud Arbery before the pandemic began, it made national news headlines weeks later as Americans sheltered in place. Shortly thereafter, the death of Breonna Taylor, who was shot in her home by a police officer, made national news. Like Arbery's murder, Taylor's death became national news weeks after it occurred as the nation stayed home watching the news in hopes for more information about the novel coronavirus.

A few weeks later, George Floyd repeatedly declared, "I can't breathe!" while White police officer Derek Chauvin rested his knee on Floyd's neck. Three other police officers stood by and watched as Chauvin's body weight crushed the life out of Floyd's body for 8 minutes and 46 seconds. With no sports, live events, or other distractions because of the pandemic shutdowns, Americans had no choice but to watch the evocative video of this incident as it played repeatedly on national news and social media outlets. The image of Chauvin kneeling on Floyd's neck, along with the killings of Arbery and Taylor, mobilized resistance and large-scale protests across the country.

An estimated 15 to 26 million people (Buchanan et al., 2020), of every state, creed, age, and racial/ethnic background, poured into the streets, proclaiming #BlackLivesMatter as their battle cry. Amid the public health risks of mass congregation due to the potential spread of the coronavirus, nationwide protests erupted to showcase another fatal pandemic: the nation's egregious and unrelenting history of state-sanctioned violence, anti-Blackness, and White supremacy. Protestors called for accountability within the police force, staged die-ins, and highlighted the history of extrajudicial killings and police brutality in the Black community. Some demanded reinvestment in community-based projects such as civilian oversight boards and increased utilization of social and mental health services, while others radically imagined life outside of the police state with calls for abolition. The protests lasted for weeks. While this protest movement may be the largest in world history (Buchanan et al., 2020), it is merely the most recent in a strong historical legacy of Black-led resistance.

In this chapter, we answer Black studies scholar Christina Sharpe's (2016) impassioned question, "How do we memorialize an event that is still ongoing?" (p. 20). We do this by radically (re)membering vital moments in U.S. history that we have been seduced into forgetting (Dillard, 2012). We bridge the gap of past and present and situate the current rebellion within a historical legacy of Black-led resistance. Methods of refusal and resistance, we argue, have always emerged from a context of racial terror, displacement, and oppression in the United States.

Simultaneously, we position rebellions as being meaningful, transformational, and deeply grounded in freedom, love, joy, liberation, and hope. We critically examine the sociopolitical and historical backdrop of several Black-led rebellions throughout history, including slave insurrections of the 19th century, race riots of the 1960s, and contemporary movements against racial injustice. Finally, we argue the necessity of abolishing dangerous messianic master narratives (Alridge, 2006; Woodson, 2016) that pervade contemporary K–12 social studies curriculum and propose a move toward the teaching of radical, liberatory histories for transformational change. We argue that it is our (re)membering that has the power to fuel and sustain our contemporary movements for freedom and justice.

BLACK HISTORY IN SCHOOLS

Du Bois (1903/1989) noted that Black Americans had been implicitly labeled as "a problem" (p. 1) in the early 20th century, and one could argue that today, U.S. schools treat the teaching of Black history as a problem. Although state social studies curriculum standards provide an *illusion of inclusion* (Vasquez Heilig et al., 2012), they actually further marginalize issues of race and Black history. In U.S. history standards, the history of Black Americans is typically relegated to enslavement, Reconstruction, and the Civil Rights movement, as if these were the only historical eras in which Black Americans lived or made contributions to the nation.

If the dearth of Black history in U.S. history standards were not problematic enough, the ways in which Black history is presented in the few places it does appear is equally troubling. While Black Americans are afforded a sizeable presence during the historical periods of enslavement and Reconstruction, curriculum standards "trivialize the systemic institutional contexts of slavery and racial hierarchy" (C. B. Anderson & Metzger, 2011, p. 401), ultimately leaving students with superficial representations of Black experiences during these historical periods. The presentation of Black history in state curriculum standards covering the Civil Rights Movement is equally troubling, as collective movements of Black resistance are diluted to ascribe agency to only a few individual actors, many of whom are tokenized for breaking barriers (Smith, 2017), in the name of maintaining the grand narrative of American progress (Busey & Walker, 2017). As a result, Black history, as presented in state curriculum standards, is often additive and superficial (King, 2017).

The textbooks that teachers are assigned to use in the teaching of U.S. history are just as problematic as state curriculum standards because they provide students and teachers with oversimplified presentations of the racism that Black Americans face(d) both historically and contemporarily. Instead of helping students gain a greater understanding of how structural and systemic racism have affected the lives of Black Americans, textbooks tend to chalk racism and racial violence up to "bad men doing bad things" (Brown & Brown, 2010, p. 60). U.S. history textbooks also portray Black institutions, particularly schools, as sad and inferior, completely neglecting community bonds and the fact that Black Americans worked to bring quality education to their own communities (Pellegrino et al., 2013). Like state curriculum standards, these texts select a few extraordinary Black historical figures to valorize while simultaneously stripping other Black Americans of their agency (Alridge, 2006).

The presentation of Black history in both state curriculum standards and textbooks is particularly troubling when one juxtaposes this official history with the majoritarian narratives included in such textbooks and standards. In both textbooks and standards, one will find narratives of the nation's founding, victorious tales of war, and stories of White colonists' resistance to dominant power structures. Students learn all about resistance and rebellion through the Boston Tea Party, the American Revolution, and the Civil War, while Black-led rebellions and resistance are notably absent.

Collectively, this whitewashed curriculum supports social and political philosopher Charles Mills's (1998) argument that historical writing was a racial apparatus that perpetuated White supremacy and the inherent inferiority of Black people, as students are left with little opportunity to critically examine the ways Black people have resisted oppression in the United States for centuries.

It is imperative that all students, no matter their race or ethnicity, learn that Black people have not taken their subjugation and dehumanization lying down. Students need to be made aware that Black people have continually resisted their oppression throughout U.S. history, regularly pushing to get the oppressor's knee off Black Americans' metaphorical neck. In the next section, we provide examples of Black-led resistance that teachers can use as a guide to contextualize the racial uprising that took place in the summer of 2020.

HISTORICAL LEGACY OF BLACK-LED RESISTANCE

Since 1619, when the first enslaved Africans were brought to the Virginia colony, Black people in the United States have been fighting for their freedom. In what follows, we trace a brief history of Black-led protests and rebellion to highlight this long and enduring struggle.

1700S

There is little evidence of a systematic attack on the institution of slavery before the 18th century in the United States. However, captured Africans were the first to demonstrate active resistance to their enslavement, degradation, and subjugation. While still in Africa, men and women adopted defensive measures to elude capture by enslavers. In trading forts, castles, and dungeons along the African coast, they fought back and attempted to escape. Enslaved Africans refused the slave ships' hold by launching attacks, refusing to eat, and jumping overboard. Once ashore in the New World, early enslaved Africans agitated and disrupted the institution of slavery in a variety of ways; yet everyday resistance was the most common form of opposition. They self-mutilated to sabotage their purchase, feigned illness, staged slowdowns of their work in the fields, broke tools, and committed acts of truancy and arson (Aptheker, 1937).

The counternarrative produced through slave resistance disturbed the idea that enslaved people were docile, loyal, and happy in bondage (Sinha, 2016). It likewise demonstrates the means by which subjugated people sought wholeness, justice, and freedom in systems that perpetually dehumanize, oppress, and harm. In all their iterations, resistance and antislavery efforts signaled the inception of a long legacy of Black-led rebellions in the United States.

1800s

The 19th century is marred by the continuation of brutal chattel slavery, the building blocks of U.S. capitalism through slave labor, and pervasive ideals of Black inferiority and White supremacy. It is also defined by a revolutionary movement that addressed the entrenched problems of exploitation and disenfranchisement in a liberal democracy (Sinha, 2016). The abolitionist movement sought to alter the reality of enslavement in the United States (James, 2005). It grew out of the belief that Black people should be treated as humans and not property. While much of the history of abolition is written about the benevolent efforts of religious northern Whites to eradicate slavery, enslaved Africans were pioneers of the movement (Quarles, 1969). There was never one clear, linear path to freedom; resistance and activism were continuous and often grew in tandem. As such, the methods of Black abolitionists varied.

In 1829, David Walker, a Black abolitionist, writer, and antislavery activist, wrote his famous *Appeal to the Colored Citizens of the World*, defending slave rebellions and the use of violence in self-defense, inspiring a new wave of militant Black Americans. Insurrectionists contested the absence of freedom and rejected the (im)possibility of manumission or purchasing themselves and family from their captors (James, 2005). They carefully planned and enacted violent rebellions to immediately overturn the institution of slavery. Aptheker (1937) estimated that over 130 slave rebellions took place between 1670 and 1865 across the nation.

Militant Black abolitionists became frustrated with the persistent failure of reform, moral suasion, gradual abolition, and nonviolence to fully eradicate slavery. They believed that since chattel slavery was inherently violent, it would likewise have to be eradicated with violence (Carter-Jackson, 2019). As such, armed slave rebellions were constitutive of the abolitionist movement. Nat Turner led the bloodiest slave rebellion in the history of the United States on August 21, 1831. He and his followers rampaged from plantation to plantation, killing nearly 60 Whites (Aptheker, 1937). The inhumane conditions of enslavement coupled with the powerful desire for freedom inspired these insurrections; the actions illustrate the collective power of armed resistance, determination, and self-defense.

Another form of rebellion enacted by enslaved people during the 19th century was through *fugitivity*. With careful planning, enslaved men and women ran relatively short distances to temporarily withhold their labor. Other times, they organized a permanent escape. Fugitive slaves, as they were called, dared to imagine their lives without shackles. Humanities scholar Tina Campt argued that "the concept of fugitivity highlights the tension between the acts or flights of escape and creative practices of refusal, nimble and strategic practices that undermine the category of the dominant" (as cited in Sojoyner, 2017, p. 516).

The Underground Railroad was an expansive network of Black and White abolitionists who, between 1645 and the end of the Civil War, helped enslaved people escape to freedom. Notable people who gained freedom through this subversive system included politician Lewis Hayden, author Josiah Henson, women's rights activist Sojourner Truth, and renowned conductor Harriet Tubman, who helped hundreds escape through her efforts on the Combahee River. Particularly during the colonial period, enslaved Africans also formed runaway communities known as "maroon communities" (Blassingame, 1972). Located in swamps, mountains, woods, and other remote areas, some of these communities resisted capture for several decades, and some were never caught. According to Dunkley (2013), marronage was not exclusively resistance to enslavement or an attempt to escape but rather an assertion of the freedom that enslaved people always knew that they had, even in cases where they were truly enslaved. These communities served as sites of refuge for many enslaved people to fashion a new world all their own.

In addition to armed resistance, fugitivity, and the establishment of maroon communities, enslaved people also elected more imaginative means to refuse the institution of slavery. Henry "Box" Brown escaped to freedom by mailing himself in a wooden crate to abolitionists in Philadelphia in 1849 (Robbins, 2009). Similarly, 18-year-old Black girl Lear Green shipped herself in an old chest from Baltimore to Philadelphia. A married couple, Ellen and William Craft, escaped from Georgia by disguising themselves as a White female slave owner and enslaved personal servant (Berry & Gross, 2020). In 1862, Robert Smalls commandeered a Confederate ship, sailing it to a Union-controlled territory where he freed several enslaved families aboard (Gates, n.d.).

These tales illuminate the daring courage and ingenuity of freedom-seeking enslaved people who were determined to have liberty, even at the cost of life. Indeed, their actions of refusal, abandon, and fugitivity threatened the very foundation of U.S. chattel slavery. Historian Robin D. G. Kelley (2002) argued that these methods represented something deeper:

> Exodus provided black people with a language to critique America's racist state and build a new nation, for its central theme wasn't simply escape but a new beginning. Exodus represented dreams of black self-determination, of being on our own, under our own rules and beliefs, developing our own cultures, without interference . . . The impulse toward separatism, defined broadly, is rooted in maroonage and the desire to leave the place of oppression for either a new land or some kind of peaceful coexistence. (p. 17)

Through decades of struggle, antislavery activists and abolitionists remained steadfast in the face of violent opposition. Though obstacles threatened to dampen this racially inclusive movement, their labors would ultimately force the issue of slavery to the forefront of national politics, fuel the split between North and South that would lead the country into civil war, and endorse equal rights legislation for Black Americans in the subsequent century.

1900s

Just as in centuries past, the 20th century produced different kinds of Black resistance to meet new forms of oppression. Whereas resistance in the previous century was largely in pursuit of literal emancipation, much of the Black-led resistance of this century related to obtaining all of the rights and freedoms entailed in U.S. citizenship, including the right to vote and the right to equal protection under the law. This resistance includes the formation of the Brotherhood of Sleeping Car Porters, which was the first Black labor union; the Black Panther Party for Self-Defense; and the nearly 160 riots that took place during the "long, hot summer" of 1967 in response to police brutality, a lack of job opportunities, and other racial inequities in American cities. While Black Americans had acquired freedom from chattel slavery in the previous century, they knew that they had not acquired freedom in the truest sense until they were no longer oppressed and had acquired all of the rights and privileges associated with full U.S. citizenship.

One important aspect of Black resistance in the 20th century is that Black Americans began to find success in using the courts to resist oppression. Like nearly all aspects of life in the South in the early 20th century, schools were segregated until the *Brown v. Topeka Board of Education* decision was handed down by the U.S. Supreme Court in 1954. Until this point, Black teachers taught Black students and White teachers taught White students in schools that were required to be segregated by law. States created glaring disparities in the ways they funded these schools, providing Black students and teachers with only a minuscule portion of the funding provided to their White counterparts (J. Anderson, 1988). As these disproportionate expenditures supported teacher salaries, Black teachers earned much smaller salaries than White teachers did. In many states, Black teachers earned less than half of what White teachers did (Beezer, 1986).

In their efforts to resist this glaring disparity in the 1930s and 1940s, Black teachers throughout the South worked with Thurgood Marshall and the National Association for the Advancement of Colored People (NAACP) to raise funds and file suit against many of the school districts that perpetuated this inequity. Despite fear over the possibility of losing their jobs, many Black teachers and administrators joined the lawsuits and raised money to fund the NAACP lawyers. The plaintiffs included Viola Luis Duvall of Charleston, South Carolina, Thelma Paige of Dallas, Texas, and Mary White Blocker of Jacksonville, Florida, among others (Kirk, 2009). Ultimately, Black educators won lawsuits in 11 states, as the courts determined that these school districts violated the equal protection clause of the 14th Amendment (Beezer, 1986).

One of the most well-known instances of Black-led resistance is the Montgomery Bus Boycott. During the boycott, Black residents of Montgomery, Alabama, largely refused to ride the city's segregated buses for 381 days in protest of the treatment of Black bus riders. While the Montgomery Bus Boycott is often presented as an instantaneous reaction to Rosa Parks's arrest for not giving up her seat to a White passenger, this narrative is not only untrue, but also erases the agency of the Black women who had planned and waited for the most opportune moment to execute the boycott.

Jo Ann Robinson led the Women's Political Council (WPC), an organization for Black women to become politically active, in filing complaints about the treatment of Black bus riders, even sending a letter to the mayor that detailed the organization's demands for cultivating a bus system that was fair to the Black bus riders, who comprised the majority of bus ridership. After making no headway with city officials, Robinson and the WPC planned a boycott of the bus system. When Rosa Parks was arrested on December 1, 1955, Robinson seized the opportunity, mimeographing tens of thousands of flyers telling Black Montgomery residents to refuse to ride the bus the following Monday (Robinson, 1987). As the first day of the boycott ended, the Montgomery Improvement Association (MIA) was founded, and Dr. Martin Luther King Jr. was elected its president. While the boycott continued over a year under the watchful eye of the MIA, it was the agency of Jo Ann Robinson and the other Black women in the WPC who laid the groundwork for this massive act of resistance.

In the summer of 1964, the Student Nonviolent Coordinating Committee (SNCC), a group of young civil rights activists, coordinated a series of strategies that were to sow the seeds of resistance in Mississippi, a state where civil rights activists had been able to make little headway. This combined act of resistance was called Freedom Summer, and its focus was to register large numbers of Black voters and increase activism in local, state, and national politics (Chilcoat & Ligon, 1999). The Freedom Summer projects included the Mississippi Freedom Democratic Party and canvassing urban and rural neighborhoods. The young Black activists who coordinated Freedom Summer knew they needed not only to coordinate acts of resistance in Mississippi, but also to create an infrastructure that allowed Black Mississippians to continue this work long after the SNCC activists had left.

After learning of the horrendous disparities between Black and White schools in Mississippi, SNCC coordinators decided to add Mississippi Freedom Schools to their Freedom Summer projects. These freedom schools would "fill an intellectual and creative vacuum in the lives of young Negro Mississippians" (Cobb, 2011, p. 109) while helping the Black children of Mississippi develop the skills to question and critique. Black SNCC activists took on the work of designing the curriculum, but they assigned the teaching positions primarily to the White volunteers who traveled to Mississippi to participate in Freedom Summer. This decision was strategic, as SNCC leaders understood that the nation would not be attentive to the oppression of Black people in Mississippi unless they "[brought] the country's children down to help us, to face the kinds of risks we and the local people we were working with faced" (Cobb, 2011, p. 108). In the Mississippi Freedom Schools, Black Mississippi youth learned to question and critique their circumstances, and they also read the works of W. E. B. Du Bois, Carter G. Woodson, James Baldwin, and others. Through their carefully crafted design of the Mississippi Freedom Schools, the young Black leaders of SNCC enacted a resistance strategy that would have long-lasting effects on the state of Mississippi, as many of the Freedom School students remained active in protest movements long after Freedom Summer.

2000S

In the 21st century, technology became an instrumental component to Black-led resistance. The role of technology in resistance was twofold: Although it allowed word of protests and other acts of resistance to spread quickly, technology also put issues of police violence toward Black Americans front and center as cellphone videos posted to social media became headlines for national news. These videos captured by cellphone cameras allowed millions of Americans, and even more people worldwide, to bear witness to the state-sanctioned violence that Black Americans continued to suffer at the hands of police officers who have sworn to protect and serve the communities in which they work.

One example of a movement that was largely built with the tools of technology is #BlackLivesMatter. George Zimmerman, a vigilante neighborhood watchman, murdered Trayvon Martin after calling the police on him, claiming Martin looked suspicious while walking home from a gas station. Nearly a year and a half later, Zimmerman was acquitted of Martin's murder, despite admitting to shooting him and following him after a 911 operator advised him not to. Following Zimmerman's acquittal, activist Alicia Garza wrote about Black lives mattering on social media, and fellow activist Patrisse Cullors added the hashtag. This phrase has become a rallying cry following the extrajudicial police killings of Michael Brown, Tamir Rice, and far too many other Black Americans to name here. While it began as a social media hashtag, Black Lives Matter (n.d.) has morphed into a global network that continues to amplify anti-Black racism and state-sanctioned violence while working to dismantle systemic racism and affirming all Black lives.

CONCLUSION

It remains to be seen whether or not the Black Lives Matter protest movement of 2020 will have a lasting impact on race relations and policy in the

United States and beyond, but the fact that it is the largest protest movement in global history provides new possibilities. Like few other historical moments, the COVID-19 pandemic held a mirror to the nation, forcing Americans to take a long, hard look at the myriad ways racism persistently affects the lives of Black Americans, and forcing White Americans to grapple with their role(s) and complicity in racism.

We close out this chapter by calling on teachers to not let the lessons learned in this rare historical moment go to waste. One way teachers can keep the momentum of this movement going is by making the invisible visible to students. The COVID-19 pandemic revealed that Black communities suffer racial disparities that had previously been invisible to those outside them. Teachers can help students become aware of systemic racism by pointing out racial disparities and providing students with the opportunity to investigate how these disparities came to be and why they persist.

Another suggestion is to have students investigate the conditions that created the largest protest movement in world history. George Floyd, unfortunately, was not the first Black American to die at the hands of police on camera, but his death ignited a movement like none the world had ever seen. How is this similar to or different from the strategies that other activists have used in resistance? What conditions are typically in place for a racial reckoning in the United States? Can racial progress be achieved without such conditions? These suggestions are, of course, in addition to contextualizing the racism and subsequent Black-led resistance that has taken place for centuries. Student learning about such resistance could put social studies classrooms on a pathway from alienating Black students toward helping students develop effective tools and strategies for resistance.

REFERENCES

Alridge, D. P. (2006). The limits of master narratives in history textbooks: An analysis of representations of Martin Luther King, Jr. *Teachers College Record, 108*(4), 662–686. https://eric.ed.gov/?id=EJ733292

Anderson, C. B., & Metzger, S. A. (2011). Slavery, the Civil War era, and African American representation in U.S. History: An analysis of four states' academic standards. *Theory & Research in Social Education, 39*(3), 393–415. https://doi.org/10.1080/00933104.2011.10473460

Anderson, J. (1988). *The education of Blacks in the South, 1860–1935.* University of North Carolina Press.

Aptheker, H. (1937). Negro slave revolts. *Science & Society, 1*(4), 512–538.

Arias, E., Tejada-Vera, B., & Ahmad, F. (2021). *Provisional life expectancy estimates for January through June 2020.* Centers for Disease Control and Prevention, National Center for Health Statistics. https://www.cdc.gov/nchs/data/vsrr/VSRR10-508.pdf

Beezer, B. (1986). Black teachers' salaries and the federal courts before Brown v.

Board of Education: One beginning for equity. *Journal of Negro Education, 55*(2), 200–213. https://doi.org/10.2307/2294882

Berry, D., & Gross, K. (2020). *A Black women's history of the United States.* Beacon Press.

Black Lives Matter. (n.d.). *Herstory.* Author. https://blacklivesmatter.com/herstory/

Blassingame, J. W. (1972). *The slave community: Plantation life in the antebellum South.* Oxford University Press.

Brown, A., & Brown, K. (2010). Strange fruit indeed: Interrogating contemporary textbook representations of racial violence toward African Americans. *Teachers College Record, 112*(1), 31–67.

Buchanan, L., Bui, Q., & Patel, J. K. (2020, July 3). Black Lives Matter may be the largest movement in U.S. history. *The New York Times.* https://www.nytimes.com/interactive/2020/07/03/us/george-floyd-protests-crowd-size.html

Busey, C. L., & Walker, I. (2017). A dream and a bus: Black critical patriotism in elementary social studies standards. *Theory & Research in Social Education, 45*(4), 456–488. https://doi.org/10.1080/00933104.2017.1320251

Carter-Jackson, K. (2019). *Force and freedom: Black abolitionists and the politics of violence.* University of Pennsylvania Press.

Chilcoat, G., & Ligon, J. (1999). "Helping to make democracy a living reality": The curriculum conference of the Mississippi Freedom Schools. *Journal of Curriculum and Supervision, 15*(1), 43–68.

Cobb Jr., C. (2011, July). Freedom's struggle and Freedom Schools. *Monthly Review: An Independent Socialist Magazine, 63*(3). https://monthlyreview.org/2011/07/01/freedoms-struggle-and-freedom-schools/

Dillard, C. (2012). *Learning to (re)member the things we've learned to forget: Endarkened feminisms, spirituality, & and the sacred nature of research & teaching.* Peter Lang.

Du Bois, W. E. B. (1989). *The souls of Black folk.* Penguin Books. (Original work published in 1903)

Dunkley, D. A. (2013). *Agency of the enslaved: Jamaica and the culture of freedom in the Atlantic world.* Lexington Books.

Gates, Jr., H. L. (2013, May 20). *Which slave sailed himself to freedom?* The Root. https://www.theroot.com/which-slave-sailed-himself-to-freedom-1790896506/

Gould, E., & Wilson, V. (2020). *Black workers face two of the most lethal preexisting conditions for coronavirus—racism and economic inequality.* Economic Policy Institute. https://www.epi.org/publication/black-workers-covid/

James, J. (2005). *The new abolitionists: (Neo)slave narratives and contemporary prison writings.* State University of New York Press.

Kelley, R. D. G. (2002). *Freedom dreams: The Black radical imagination.* Beacon.

King, L. J. (2017). The status of Black history in U.S. schools and society. *Social Education 81*(1), 14–18.

Kirk, J. A. (2009). The NAACP campaign for teachers' salary equalization: African American women educators and the early civil rights struggle. *Journal of African American History, 94*(4), 529–552. https://www.jstor.org/stable/25653977

Mills, C. (1998). *Blackness visible: Essays on philosophy and race.* Cornell University Press.

Pellegrino, A., Mann, L., & Russell, W. (2013). To lift as we climb: A textbook analysis of the segregated school experience. *The High School Journal, 96*(3), 209–231.

Quarles, B. (1969). *Black abolitionists*. Oxford University Press.

Robbins, H. (2009). Fugitive mail: The deliverance of Henry "Box" Brown and antebellum postal politics. *American Studies, 50*(1/2), 5–25. https://doi.org/10.1353/ams.2011.0045

Robinson, J. (1987). *The Montgomery Bus Boycott and the women who started it: The memoir of Jo Ann Gibson Robinson*. University of Tennessee Press.

Sharpe, C. E. (2016). *In the wake: On Blackness and being*. Duke University Press.

Sinha, M. (2016). *The slave's cause: A history of abolition*. Yale University Press.

Smith, W. (2017). Why do we focus on firsts? Problems and possibilities for Black history teaching. *Social Education, 81*(1), 19–22.

Sojoyner, D. M. (2017). Another life is possible: Black fugitivity and enclosed places. *Cultural Anthropology, 32*(4), 514–36. https://doi.org/10.14506/ca32.4.04

Vasquez Heilig, J., Brown, K., & Brown, A. (2012). The illusion of inclusion: A critical race theory textual analysis of race and standards. *Harvard Educational Review, 82*(3), 403–424. https://doi.org/10.17763/haer.82.3.84p8228670j24650

Woodson, A. N. (2016). We're just ordinary people: Messianic master narratives and Black youths' civic agency. *Theory & Research in Social Education, 44*(2), 184–211. https://doi.org/10.1080/00933104.2016.1170645

Anti-Asian Violence Amid the COVID-19 Pandemic and Implications for Social Studies Education

Sohyun An and Noreen Naseem Rodríguez

After COVID-19 took root in the United States in January 2020, there was a surge in violence and discrimination against Asian Americans. Between February 9 and March 7, 2020, the number of news articles on anti-Asian harassment related to COVID-19 increased by 50% (Jeung et al., 2020). From its launch on March 19, 2020, through early August 2020, the self-reporting website Stop AAPI Hate (2020) received 2,583 reports of anti-Asian discrimination nationwide. These reported incidents included stories of Asian Americans who were verbally abused, yelled at, spat on, and beaten as they were baselessly accused of being coronavirus carriers or spreaders.

Disturbingly, this was not the first time in U.S. history that Asians and Asian Americans were targeted during a public health crisis (Mohr, 2005; Shah, 2001). Further, it was certainly not the first time a racially marginalized group was blamed for an epidemic (Kraut, 1994; Markel, 2004; Molina, 2006). In this chapter, we contextualize the surge of anti-Asian violence during the COVID-19 pandemic within the long history of racializing disease in the United States and draw implications for social studies education. We particularly underscore the urgency of teaching about race and racism in order to disrupt the ongoing manifestation of racism during public health crises.

RACIALIZING EPIDEMICS IN THE UNITED STATES

In the United States, placing blame on racially marginalized groups for the introduction and spread of disease is nothing new. In the 19th and early 20th centuries, for example, newly arrived immigrants from Europe were often blamed for epidemics. These incidents of discrimination include scapegoating of Irish immigrants for the 1832 cholera epidemic, Jewish immigrants for tuberculosis in the late 19th and early 20th centuries, and Italian immigrants for the 1926 polio epidemic. Although the Irish, Jewish, and Italian immigrants eventually became white,[1] they were not regarded as racially white when they first arrived in the United States (Lee, 2019). The dominant group—the native-born Anglo-Saxon Protestants—viewed the new European immigrants as racially inferior, dirty, and disease-ridden (Kraut, 1994; Lee, 2019). Thus, during epidemics, the dominant group was quick to blame the newcomers as a health threat to the country.

Of course, the new arrivals were not naturally sickly and diseased people. As poor newcomers, the Irish, Italian, and Jewish immigrants had few housing options and therefore lived in cramped city apartments or densely packed tenement buildings with limited access to clean water and uncontaminated food (Kraut, 1994; Rosenberg, 1987). These living conditions made them more vulnerable to diseases compared to those in better housing conditions. Yet the dominant group ignored these structural factors (e.g., poverty and deprived urban housing) and instead scapegoated the newcomers for the public health crises. The racist nativist accusations fueled further violence, such as the murder of Irish railroad workers by local nativist vigilantes (Rosenberg, 1987; Tucker, 2010), and discriminatory legislation, including restrictions on Jewish immigration in the 1920s and denying entry to Jewish refugees fleeing Europe in the 1930s and 1940s (Kraut, 1994).

Blaming racially marginalized groups for epidemics continued in the contemporary period, becoming an American tradition (Markel, 2004). Examples include the scapegoating of Haitian immigrants along with gay men during the 1980s AIDS epidemic, Mexican immigrants for H1N1 in 2009, and West Africans for the 2014 Ebola outbreak. During each of these crises, the dominant society responded similarly as it did in the earlier epidemics noted above. In other words, the dominant society acted upon long-held racism against the "Other" and blamed a racially marginalized group for a public health crisis. In contemporary cases, however, a new pattern has emerged due to the pivotal role of the media in escalating the troubling pattern of racializing disease.

Sensational news headlines such as "Alert over gay plague" and the heightened volume of media stories associating Haitians and gay men with AIDS demonized the Haitian and LGBTQ+ communities, fueling hate crimes against these groups (Clews, 2017; Kraut, 1994). In the case of the H1N1 outbreak, conservative media emphasized that the first case of H1N1 was found in Mexico and subsequently called the pandemic the "Mexican flu" (Media Matters, 2009). This media framing brought to the fore longstanding racism against Mexican Americans and exacerbated racial harassment against the group (Alexander, 2009). Similarly, when the first Ebola case in the United States was attributed to a Liberian who traveled from West Africa to Texas, a surge of media reports depicted Ebola as a stand-in for various combinations of African-ness, Blackness, foreignness, and "infestation" that were poised to ruin the perceived purity and health of white, western, U.S. bodies and borders. Feeding off the long history of deeply held anti-Black racism in the United States, racial discrimination against West African communities ensued (Abrams, 2014; Ohlheiser, 2014).

ANTI-ASIAN VIOLENCE DURING EPIDEMICS

Unsurprisingly, Asian Americans are no exception to this troublesome history of racialized disease. Since their earliest arrivals in the United States, Asian immigrants have been racialized as "perpetual foreigners" (Wu, 2002, p. 81) who are unassimilable to dominant white society and a "yellow peril" whose presence is a threat to U.S. culture, economics, politics, and health (Lee, 2019). In its 1876–1877 Municipal Reports, for example, the San Francisco Board of Supervisors described Chinese immigrants as "a social, moral, political curse to the [white] community" (as cited in Trauner, 1978, pp. 71–72). Similarly, in 1867, *The New York Times* described Chinese immigrants as "[a] population befouled with all the social vices, with no knowledge or appreciation of free institutions or constitutional liberty, with heathenish souls and heathenish propensities, whose character, and habits, and modes of thought are firmly fixed by the consolidating influence of ages upon ages" (as cited in Molina, 2006, p. 17). Such racialization of Asian immigrants as dangerous foreigners has been at the core of countless examples of discrimination against Asian Americans throughout U.S. history, many of which turned into outright violence during times of national crisis (Lee, 2019; Wu, 2020).

For example, amidst an economic downturn in 1885, a mob of white miners in Rock Springs, Wyoming, felt threatened by the Chinese laborers (who worked for lower wages), and massacred 28 Chinese workers. A century later, in 1982, two unemployed white auto workers in Detroit, Michigan, beat Chinese American Vincent Chin to death with a baseball bat. They assumed Chin was Japanese and consequently blamed him for their layoffs and the U.S. auto industry's meltdown at the time. The two white men who murdered Chin were never sent to jail.

During wartime, anti-Asian racism has also surged. After Japan's attack on Pearl Harbor and other U.S. colonies in the Pacific during World War II, long-held anti-Japanese racism resulted in the incarceration of 120,000 Japanese Americans by the U.S. government in the name of national security. Similarly, in the wake of the 9/11 terrorist attacks, there was a sharp rise in hate crimes and discrimination against South Asian, Muslim, Sikh, and

Hindu communities. As outlined previously, public health crises are also moments when deep-seated racism easily manifests into escalated violence and discrimination (Lee, 2019; Wu, 2020). Below, we describe a few examples of the racialization of disease in Asian American communities.

Chinese Immigrants During the 1876 Smallpox Epidemic

When the smallpox outbreak occurred in 1876 in San Francisco, California, 30,000 Chinese immigrants in the city were held medically responsible (Shah, 2001). Health officials were quick to condemn Chinatown as a laboratory of infection and to quarantine and fumigate homes throughout the neighborhood (Trauner, 1978). The measure, however, did little to stop the spread of smallpox, which infected more than 1,600 people and took nearly 45 lives. Unable to account for the severity of the epidemic, city health officer John Meares announced, "I unhesitatingly declare my belief that the cause is the presence in our midst of 30,000 of unscrupulous, lying and treacherous Chinamen, who have disregarded our sanitary laws, concealed and are concealing their cases of smallpox" (as cited in Trauner, 1978, p. 73).

Like Meares, health officials, politicians, and the public at large generally conceived of Chinatown as the preeminent site of urban sickness, vice, crime, poverty, and depravity, and they viewed Chinese immigrants as a filthy, diseased race who incubated incurable afflictions and infected white Americans. The public panic and fear of the disease exacerbated calls to bar all Chinese immigrants from entering the United States, which culminated in the Chinese Exclusion Act of 1882 (Shah, 2001).

Chinese Immigrants During the 1899–1900 Bubonic Plague

Similar scapegoating occurred during the bubonic plague outbreak (Markel, 2004; Mohr, 2005; Shah, 2001; Trauner, 1978). The plague was first detected in 1899 in Hawai'i, a U.S. colony at the time. After a shopkeeper in Honolulu's Chinatown was diagnosed with the bubonic plague and more cases were identified, Hawai'i's Board of Health declared a state of emergency (Mohr, 2005). C. B. Wood, a health board member, said: "Plague lives and breeds in filth and when it got to Chinatown, it found its natural habitat" (cited in U.S. National Library of Medicine, n.d.). Such anti-Chinese prejudice precipitated discriminatory measures in the fight against the plague, including the cordoning-off of the Chinese community in Honolulu by health authorities. Ten thousand people were imprisoned within the community, with its perimeter patrolled by armed guards. After cases began to spread, city officials decreed that any building where someone had contracted the plague be razed with fire. Forty-one buildings were identified, and fires were set. Tragically, winds fanned the flames, and the fires burned for 17 days, destroying 38 acres of Honolulu and almost all of Chinatown. Over 4,000 people were left homeless, most of whom were of Chinese descent (Mohr, 2005).

By 1900, the bubonic plague emerged in San Francisco (Markel, 2004; Shah, 2001; Trauner, 1978). When an autopsy suggested that a deceased Chinese immigrant in the city's Chinatown had died of bubonic plague, city authorities placed a rope cordon around Chinatown in an attempt to close off 14,000 Chinese residents from contact with the white residents of the city. Guards were placed at every point of exit from the city to examine any Chinese who attempted to leave, and a house-to-house inspection of Chinatown was ordered. Sewers and dwellings were disinfected with sulfur dioxide and bichloride of mercury, and the disinfection campaign also included forced vaccination. The Board of Health authorized physicians to forcibly inoculate Asians on the streets of Chinatown with an experimental serum that was still in the testing stage. When the plague killed white residents 7 years later, none of the disinfection measures used against the Chinese were repeated (McLaren, 2020).

The Chinese community of San Francisco resisted these racist government actions with boycotts, persuasive political speeches, and poems (McClain, 1996; Shah, 2001). When their protests went unacknowledged, they turned to the courts for help (McClain, 1996). In one example, a Chinese immigrant named Wong Wai challenged the orders in federal court in 1900, arguing that compulsory inoculation with an experimental drug constituted "a purely arbitrary, unreasonable, unwarranted, wrongful, and oppressive interference" with a citizen's personal liberty (Kraut, 1994, p. 91). In response, federal health officer Joseph Kinyoun and the San Francisco Board of Health argued that they had the right to compel behavior in the interest of public health, even if it meant regulating just the Chinese. The judge ruled in favor of Wai by stating that the compulsory inoculation was "boldly directed against the Asiatic or Mongolian race as a class, without regard to the previous condition, habits, exposure or disease, or residence of the individual on the unproven assumption that this race was more liable to the plague than any other" (Kraut, 1994, pp. 91–92). The court's decision not only saved the Chinese from future compulsory inoculations, but also set a legal precedent that limited the government's ability to override the rights of individuals in the name of public health (Kraut, 1994).

Another court case questioned the legality of the quarantines. In 1900, Jew Ho, a grocer in Chinatown, filed a complaint on behalf of other residents. He argued that placing Chinese residents under house arrest while white San Franciscans were allowed to enter and leave Chinatown as they pleased was discriminatory. He also noted that the Board of Health had made no provision to feed or care for isolated members of the Chinese community. The court agreed with Ho but nonetheless permitted the city to quarantine specific buildings that officials believed to be contaminated (McClain, 1996).

Chinese/Asian Americans During SARS in 2003

The condemnation of Asian Americans for disease outbreaks continues in the present century. The surge of anti-Asian racism in the wake of the 2003 SARS epidemic is one example. SARS was believed to have originated in China in the fall of 2002 and later spread to more than 30 countries (Person et al., 2004). SARS did not spread widely in the United States, as only 74 cases were classified as probable SARS with no deaths (Centers for Disease Control and Prevention, 2003). Anti-Asian rhetoric and racism ensued, nonetheless. *The Pittsburgh Tribune-Review* published an editorial cartoon featuring a Chinese food takeout container with "SARS" written on it and a caption that read "Bad Chinese Take-Out" (Hung, 2004). This anti-Asian rhetoric was accompanied by an avoidance of Chinese restaurants, some of which went out of business due to the lack of customers. Once again, East Asian Americans were socially humiliated and stigmatized as dirty disease carriers (Eichelberger, 2007; Fang, 2020; Hung, 2004).

Chinese/Asian Americans During the COVID-19 Pandemic

In 2020, East Asians and East Asian Americans were frequently held responsible for the COVID-19 pandemic, resulting in an uptick of anti-Asian violence. Then-President Trump, conservative politicians, and media personalities called the coronavirus a "Chinese virus," "foreign virus," "Wuhan virus," and "kung flu," as if the virus possessed a nationality. Their claims that such comments were "not racist at all" (Trump, 2020) have been disproven by history, which demonstrates that associating a disease with a group of people easily leads to hate, xenophobia, and violence.

Indeed, in the present moment, the United States has witnessed a surge of anti-Asian hate crimes and discrimination. In Texas, a Burmese American man and his two young children were stabbed by a 19-year-old man who believed they were "Chinese and infecting people with the coronavirus" (Kim, 2020, para. 1); the assailant was charged with attempted murder. In California, a 16-year-old student was sent to the hospital after his peers physically harmed him at school. His bullies accused the student of having the coronavirus simply because he was Asian American (Capatides, 2020). In New York, a 47-year-old Asian man was hit on the head in front of his 10-year-old son by a man screaming, "Where's your f-king mask?" (Bensimon, 2020, para. 4). In Minnesota, an Asian American family came home to find a hateful note taped to their front door, stating, "We're watching you f-king chinks. Take your Chinese virus back to China. We don't want you here infecting us with your diseases" (Yoo, 2020, para. 7). In North Carolina, a 9-year-old student was called "coronavirus" and taunted by his classmates (Hong, 2020). These are just a brief snapshot of the thousands of anti-Asian racist and violent acts documented since the beginning of the COVID-19 pandemic.

As this overview shows, the racialization of Asian Americans as dangerous foreigners is deep-rooted and still alive today in U.S. society. In spite of Asian Americans often being touted as a "model minority," "almost white," "near white," or a "successful minority," the longstanding racialization of Asians as a foreign threat has never been erased. During public health crises, such racist views are easily activated by public panic and anxiety into hypervisible forms such as physical and verbal violence and harassment.

IMPLICATIONS FOR SOCIAL STUDIES EDUCATION

The history of racializing disease and scapegoating racially marginalized groups during public health crises demonstrates that racism is normal, pervasive, and permanent in the United States. When epidemics arise, people immediately look for a target to blame, and groups already marginalized as "the Other" become easy targets. The recent surge of anti-Asian violence during the COVID-19 pandemic proves that we are far from an anti-racist society, as the equation of disease with "the Other" remains painfully prevalent.

How might social studies educators intervene in ways that disrupt and resist the racialization of disease? First, we note the critical need for teaching about race and racism in the field of social studies. As the home of citizenship education, social studies is an ideal site for students to develop racial literacy. Racial literacy is "the capacity to decipher the durable racial grammar that structures racialized hierarchies and frames the narrative of our republic" (Guinier, 2004, p. 100).

In education, racial literacy is a framework that recognizes the embedded nature of racism in the founding of the United States; exposes psychological, interpersonal, and structural racism; and considers relationships between race and power (King, 2016; Skerrett, 2011). The racialization of disease illustrated above cannot be adequately explained or understood if students do not have a clear understanding of white supremacy and racial hierarchies in U.S. history. The origin and spread of diseases are not and have never been race-based, but white supremacist discourse utilizes such arguments, whether scientifically accurate or not, to reinforce narratives of white superiority.

Second, educators must teach critical race media literacy. Yosso (2002) described critical race media literacy as a tool for students to develop critical racial consciousness that allows them to recognize and address racism in mainstream media. Given the pervasiveness of anti-Asian racist discourse on social media and news outlets during COVID-19, critical race media literacy easily weaves into social studies lessons about current events. Hawkman and Shear (2020) have urged social studies educators to help students recognize microaggressions and stereotypical representations in individual media as well as broader society. Once students have uncovered problematic representations, educators should encourage students to think critically about how different audiences might interpret media and consider how students can enact change beyond the classroom. In particular, social studies educators can ask students to consider the intentions behind racist discourse and the impact of such discourse on already marginalized communities.

Lastly, we insist on the need to teach Asian American history. Asian Americans rarely appear in social studies textbooks and curriculum standards and are often presented as a foreign threat or enemy to the nation (An, 2016; Hartlep & Scott, 2016; Suh et al., 2015). Such curricular practices suggest to students that Asian Americans are insignificant, foreign, and/or dangerous and can be punished for being a threat to "Americans" without due process or recourse. This message, along with media portrayals of Asians and Asian Americans as exotic Others, can then allow, ignore, or justify anti-Asian violence, as we saw during the COVID-19 pandemic (An, 2020).

We suggest two ways for educators to reimagine their pedagogy and teach Asian American history so that it counters stereotypes and racism found in textbooks and mainstream media. The first is for social studies educators to teach the two Asian American events most commonly included in U.S. history curriculum (Chinese immigration during the 1800s and Japanese American incarceration during World War II) in ways that center Asian American perspectives to complicate notions of citizenship and exploitation (Rodríguez, 2015, 2017, 2020). The second approach broadens the scope of Asian American history to go beyond these two events.

Students may learn, for example, about the creation of the Asiatic barred zone in 1917, but rarely learn about what happened after the age of Asian exclusion ended via the passage of the Immigration and Nationality Act of 1965. An examination of the breadth of Asian American history allows students to disrupt stereotypes as they learn about the diversity of Asian America. For example, teaching this history might include the influx of Filipino nurses into the United States post-1965 and could reveal the astonishing statistic that a third of the registered nurses who died due to COVID-19 in 2020 were Filipino (Powell, 2021). A critical race media literacy approach to teach this history would aid students to interrogate the conditions that led to such an appalling impact on an Asian American community as well as question why this statistic has been underreported.

CONCLUSION

Pandemics come and go. The way society responds to them, however, has rarely changed. It is time to stop the historical pattern of racializing disease and scapegoating marginalized groups during public health crises. Social studies education plays an important role in this intervention and should center race, racism, critical race media literacy, and ethnic studies, including Asian American history, in the teaching and learning of democratic citizenship and U.S. history.

NOTE

1. We deliberately leave *white* in lower case in an effort to disrupt the privileging of the term and its relationship to racial domination (Gotanda, 1991).

REFERENCES

Abrams, L. (2014, October 20). *Parents freak out over Ebola, keep Rwandan children from starting elementary school.* Salon. https://www.salon.com/control/2014/10/20/parents_freak_out_over_ebola_keep_rwandan_children_from_starting_elementary_school/

Alexander, B. (2009, May 1). *Amid swine flu outbreak, racism goes viral.* NBC News. http://www.nbcnews.com/id/30467300/ns/health-cold_and_flu/t/amid-swine-flu-outbreak-racism-goes-viral/#.XvZUs257mEd

An, S. (2016). Asian Americans in American history: An AsianCrit perspective on Asian American inclusion in state U.S. history curriculum. *Theory & Research in Social Education, 44*(2), 244–276. https://doi.org/10.1080/00933104.2016.1170646

An, S. (2020). Disrupting curriculum of violence on Asian Americans. *Review of Education, Pedagogy, and Cultural Studies, 42*(2), 141–156. https://doi.org/10.1080/10714413.2020.1753492

Bensimon, O. (2020, March 14). Asian man, son harassed in potential Queens hate crime. *New York Post.* https://nypost.com/2020/03/14/asian-man-son-harassed-in-potential-queens-hate-crime/

Capatides, C. (2020, February 14). *Bullies attack Asian American teen at school, accusing him of having coronavirus.* CBS News. https://www.cbsnews.com/news/coronavirus-bullies-attack-asian-teen-los-angeles-accusing-him-of-having-coronavirus/

Centers for Disease Control and Prevention. (2003). *Severe Acute Respiratory Syndrome: Worldwide and United States.* Author. https://www.cdc.gov/mmwr/preview/mmwrhtml/mm5228a4.htm

Clews, C. (2017). *Gay in the 80s: From fighting for our rights to fighting for our lives.* Troubador Publishing.

Eichelberger, L. (2007). SARS and New York's Chinatown: The politics of risk and blame during an epidemic of fear. *Social Science & Medicine, 65*(6), 1284–1295. https://doi.org/10.1016/j.socscimed.2007.04.022

Fang, J. (2020, February 4). The 2003 SARS outbreak fueled anti-Asian racism. Coronavirus doesn't have to. *The Washington Post.* https://www.washington-post.com/outlook/2020/02/04/2003-sars-outbreak-fueled-anti-asian-racism-this-pandemic-doesnt-have/

Gotanda, N. (1991). A critique of "Our Constitution Is Color-Blind." *Stanford Law Review, 44*(1), 1–68.

Guinier, L. (2004). From racial liberalism to racial literacy: Brown v. Board of Education and the interest-divergence dilemma. *The Journal of American History, 91*(1), 92–118.

Hartlep, N. D., & Scott, D. P. (2016). *Asian/American curricular epistemicide: From being excluded to becoming a model minority.* Sense Publishers.

Hawkman, A., & Shear, S. (2020). "Who made these rules? We're so confused.": An introduction to the special issue on critical race media literacy. *International Journal of Multicultural Education, 22*(2), 1–4. http://dx.doi.org/10.18251/ijme.v22i2.2645

Hong, A. (2020, March 12). *Amid the coronavirus outbreak, Asian-American students like my son face racist taunting. Let's change that.* Chalkbeat. https://www.chalkbeat.org/2020/3/12/21178748/amid-the-coronavirus-outbreak-asian-american-students-like-my-son-face-racist-taunting-let-s-change

Hung, H. (2004). The politics of SARS. *Asian Perspective, 28*(1), 19–44.

Jeung, R., Gowing, S., & Takasaki, K. (2020). *News accounts of COVID-19 discrimination.* Asian Pacific Policy & Planning Council & Chinese for Affirmative Action. https://drive.google.com/file/d/1mzNEU2ebTF_5OZUon-ovrt36x22nXcuE/view

Kim, J. (2020, April 8). *Sam's Club stabbing suspect thought the family was 'Chinese infecting people with coronavirus.'* KXAN. https://www.kxan.com/news/crime/report-sams-club-stabbing-suspect-thought-family-was-chinese-infecting-people-with-coronavirus/

King, L. J. (2016). Teaching Black history as a racial literacy project. *Race Ethnicity and Education, 19*(6), 1303–1318. https://doi.org/10.1080/13613324.2016.1150822

Kraut, A. (1994). *Silent travelers: Germs, disease, and the immigrant menace.* Basic Books.

Lee, E. (2019). *America for Americans: A history of xenophobia in the United States.* Basic Books.

Markel, H. (2004). *When germs travel: Six major epidemics that have invaded America since 1900 and the fears they have unleashed.* Pantheon Books.

McClain, C. (1996). *In search of equality: The Chinese struggle against discrimination in nineteenth century America.* University of California Press.

McLaren, J. (2020, February 12). *Coronavius: Vaccinate against racism.* Spring. https://springmag.ca/coronavirus-vaccinate-against-racism

Media Matters. (2009, April 27). *Paranoia pandemic: Conservative media baselessly blame swine flu outbreak on immigrants.* https://www.mediamatters.org/glenn-beck/paranoia-pandemic-conservative-media-baselessly-blame-swine-flu-outbreak-immigrants

Mohr, J. (2005). *Plague and fire: Battling Black Death and the 1900 burning of Honolulu's Chinatown.* Oxford University Press.

Molina, N. (2006). *Fit to be citizens? Public health and race in Los Angeles.* University of California Press.

Ohlheiser, A. (2014, October 15). Navarro College in Texas apologizes after rejecting Nigerian applicants over Ebola fears. *The Washington Post.* https://www.washingtonpost.com/news/to-your-health/wp/2014/10/15/navarro-college-in-texas-apologizes-after-rejecting-nigerian-applicants-over-ebola-fears/

Person, B., Sy, F., Holton, K., Govert, B., Liang, A., & National Center for Infectious Diseases/SARS Community Outreach Team. (2004). Fear and stigma: The epidemic within the SARS outbreak. *Emerging Infectious Diseases, 10*(2), 358–363. https://dx.doi.org/10.3201/eid1002.030750

Powell, L. (2021, January 17). 'It's starting again': Why Filipino nurses dread the second wave. *The New York Times.* https://www.nytimes.com/2021/01/15/nyregion/filipino-nurses-coronavirus.html

Rodríguez, N. N. (2015). Teaching about Angel Island through historical empathy and poetry. *Social Studies and the Young Learner, 27*(3), 22–25.

Rodríguez, N. N. (2017). "But they didn't do nothin' wrong!" Teaching about Japanese-American incarceration. *Social Studies and the Young Learner, 30*(2), 17–23.

Rodríguez, N. N. (2020). "Invisibility is not a natural state for anyone": (Re)Constructing narratives of Japanese American incarceration in elementary classrooms. *Curriculum Inquiry, 50*(4), 309–329. https://doi.org/10.1080/036267 84.2020.1831369

Rosenberg, C. E. (1987). *The cholera years: The United States in 1832, 1849, and 1866.* University of Chicago Press.

Shah, N. (2001). *Contagious divides: Epidemics and race in San Francisco's Chinatown.* University of California Press.

Skerrett, A. (2011). English teachers' racial literacy knowledge and practice. *Race Ethnicity and Education, 14*(3), 313–330. https://doi.org/10.1080/13613324.2 010.543391

Stop AAPI Hate Initiative. (2020, April 23). *Stop AAPI Hate national report 3.19.20 - 8.5.20.* Author. https://stopaapihate.org/national-report/

Suh, Y., An, S., & Forest, D. (2015). Immigration, imagined communities, and collective memories of Asian American experiences: A content analysis of Asian American experiences in Virginia U.S. history textbooks. *Journal of Social Studies Research, 39*(1), 39–51. https://doi.org/10.1016/j.jssr.2014.05.002

Trauner, J. (1978). The Chinese as medical scapegoats in San Francisco, 1870–1905. *California History, 57*(1), 70–87. https://doi.org/10.2307/25157817

Trump, D. (2020, March 18). *White House coronavirus task force's daily news briefing.* https://www.youtube.com/watch?v=7zatCqqRY_I

Tucker, A. (2010). Ireland's forgotten sons recovered two centuries later. *Smithsonian Magazine.* https://www.smithsonianmag.com/history/irelands-forgotten-sons-recovered-two-centuries-later-9194680/

U.S. National Library of Medicine. (n.d.). *1899: Bubonic plague diagnosed in Honolulu's Chinatown.* Author. https://www.nlm.nih.gov/nativevoices/timeline/708.html

Wu, F. (2002). *Yellow: Race in America beyond Black and white.* Basic Books.

Wu, F. (2020, March 25). *Coronavirus is not a "Chinese virus."* Diverse: Issues in Higher Education. https://diverseeducation.com/article/170580/

Yoo, S. (2020, March 26). *We can control the spread of hate during the coronavirus pandemic.* KARE 11 News. https://www.kare11.com/article/news/local/breaking-the-news/we-can-control-the-spread-of-hate-during-the-coronavirus-pandemic/89-b3d406e0-9e14-4794-9e5e-727b48d0d275?fb-clid=IwAR2Exv2FBrX_VZergaIXKJ_is480yNVl7MqxUk2EDgRmNI6JI19g_zlsD_E

Yosso, T. J. (2002). Critical race media literacy: Challenging deficit discourse about Chicanas/os. *Journal of Popular Film and Television, 30*(1), 52–62. https://doi.org/10.1080/01956050209605559

CHAPTER 12

Breathing Life Back Into Social Studies

Lessons From COVID-19

Jennifer Hauver

On March 12, 2020, at 2:45 p.m., sitting on a stool in front of my 6th-period seniors, I clicked off the projector. "Okay, that's it for today. I guess . . . I'll see you when I see you," I said with a smile. They gathered their things and began filing out the door, uncertain smiles on their faces. "Bye, Dr. H."

School districts to the east and west of us had already decided to close for a couple weeks as news of the COVID-19 virus spread. Our county had not yet made the call, but it seemed imminent. As students filed past me on their way out the door, none of us believed that we wouldn't see one another again. Later that evening, we learned that schools would be closed as of the following morning and would remain so through spring break (2 weeks away). Then, 11 days later, on March 23rd, the governor shut schools for the remainder of the academic year.

Spring sports, which had just completed tryouts: canceled. The spring play, *A Midsummer Night's Dream*, which had been days away from dress rehearsal: canceled. The spring band trip to Florida: canceled. The spring choral concert, for which students had already begun practicing: canceled. The spring picnic: canceled. Eventually we learned that prom, convocation, the all-night senior party, even graduation itself would be canceled. Then the stay-at-home order came from Richmond, the state capital.

In early April, a series of faculty meetings focused on helping teachers move their courses online, familiarizing us with tech tools we might use to deliver content and encouraging us to identify "essential standards" to be covered in this new abbreviated 4th quarter. Conversations were held at the state and county levels about grading, attendance policies, and graduation requirements. Little by little, this information trickled down to teachers and students. There would be no grades. No attendance requirements. No obligatory assignments going forward. No final exams. No state tests. No

Advance Placement or International Baccalaureate (IB) exams. Unequal access to the Internet made it impossible to hold students accountable for their presence or work during this time, not to mention the varying responsibilities students had picked up now that they were home full-time. Everyone wondered: Would students even bother to attend class?

In my house, my two daughters, a first-year and a senior in high school, struggled emotionally. My younger daughter had spent weeks practicing day and night in hopes of making the junior varsity softball team. Just 6 days before schools were closed, she had sat in a line outside the coach's classroom awaiting the verdict. She made the team. They distributed uniforms and had one practice. She was crushed. When would she see her friends again? My freshman's emotional downturn, however, paled in comparison to that of my senior. My older daughter hardly got out of bed. She stopped working out, lost all sense of routine, moped around the house, and cried at the drop of a hat. Everything she had been looking forward to had evaporated before her eyes. She had even just started seeing a boy. That boy's stepfather would soon be diagnosed with COVID-19 and admitted to the hospital. Her world was falling apart.

Emails started rolling in from anxious students who worried about their final grades. Student members of the Gay–Straight Alliance, a club I sponsored, reached out to me in fear and loneliness. Many of them were not out to their families and were desperately missing our shared safe space. Seniors wrote to me asking what was happening, expressing deep sadness at what they had lost. Some expressed worry that they wouldn't be able to attend distance learning because they had to take on full-time work to support their families or assume responsibilities for younger siblings since child-care centers were closed. Some shared that family members and friends were sick.

As a school, we bumbled our way into distance learning. The plan was set: I would meet my three sections of a freshman World History course and two sections of a senior-level IB Geography course online through Blackboard Collaborate. I would have one 45-minute synchronous session with each class per week. The rest would be asynchronous. I emailed and posted announcements on Google Classroom about our first meeting and sat down to plan the first week of classes. With none of the typical incentives (grades, assessments) in play, I decided to focus on topics my students would find relevant and meaningful in hopes of keeping them engaged.

My seniors, I believed, might be difficult to lure in. All, if not most, of them knew what they were doing next fall. No end-of-year exams meant they didn't really need to attend at all. More than my freshmen, they were working and caring for younger siblings now that school was not in session. We had one unit left when school closed. I wasn't so worried about completing this unit. Like my own daughter, my seniors were feeling sad and isolated and not a little bit angry; they had been robbed of rites of passage they had been looking forward to for a long time. Tanner had worked for 3 years to become captain of a soccer team that wouldn't get to play. Hermina was to be the first in her family to graduate high school in the United States, and she had never been to prom. Zadeer, who had been in danger of failing all year as he tried to balance supporting his family and attending school— what would happen to him now? I was concerned about my freshmen too, but email suggested that my seniors were struggling in ways others were not.

I told all of my students that we would have one assignment a week. Most importantly, though, I just wanted them to check in. Even if they didn't do the assignment, I wanted to see their faces, hear their voices, and know how they were doing. The first week, a handful of students read. A few submitted work. But nearly every one of them showed up for class. Even Zadeer called in on his phone from his car, checking in before beginning his shift at work. In our 45 minutes together that week, and each week that followed, we shared what we had been up to and talked about how we felt. Most often, students reported being tired, having little to no routine, feeling depressed, and watching a lot of YouTube. Many admitted to feeling hopeless and anxious. They returned each week just to say hello. We would talk about the reading some and then give the rest of our time to just being together. It was clear that what we all needed was to connect, to have someone ask how we were, to share our fear and disappointment.

My students' experience was reflected in stories about the pandemic's effect on students across the country and the world. Psychiatrists, pediatricians, and ethicists spoke out about the importance of attending to young people's well-being: "The COVID-19 pandemic may worsen existing mental health problems and lead to more cases among children and adolescents because of the unique combination of the public health crisis, social isolation, and economic recession" (Golberstein et al., 2020, para. 3). For many, in the spring of 2020, the loss of school meant a loss of routine, social isolation, increased loneliness, and greater access to social media (Thakur, 2020), as well as more incidents of domestic violence, furloughs and job cuts for families, and the all-pervading fear of contracting the virus. Articles were published by and for educators with suggestions for how to support students through this difficult time. Advice included checking in, listening, noticing their body language and mood, inviting students to express their feelings, remaining calm in the face of upset, maintaining routines and warm, welcoming spaces (American Psychological Association, 2020). As I tried to learn new technologies to deliver instruction, to reorganize and plan lessons, to tend to my own anxiety and struggling daughters, I sought to be a source of support and hope for my students from afar. We all did.

In this chapter, I describe how the focus on emotion due to COVID-19 also emphasized the need to recognize *affect* as an essential aspect of social studies education. I first briefly detail how the emotion associated with the pandemic created space for my students to better understand the limits of studying the dispassionate accounts of history found in their textbooks and state curriculum standards. Then I make a case for how, moving forward, teachers can better utilize emotion as a pathway to social studies education that is livelier and more relevant to students' lives.

A DOOR OPENS

It was in the midst of sharing our experiences and feelings with one another that an unexpected door opened for us to consider what roles lived experience and emotion played in social studies. We believed that understanding how we felt was essential to understanding life in 2020. By extension, we reasoned that if we wanted to understand why people in another time or another place acted as they did, we needed to understand how they felt, what motivated them, what information they had access to, and how their experience helped them to make sense of it. I asked students what they would want those in the future to know about the COVID-19 pandemic. Students believed that it would be impossible to truly understand this historic moment without knowing people's stories of what it was like to live it. Statistics about death tolls, analysis of state policy decisions about if and when to close schools or businesses, availability of EPP and testing—if the study stopped here, students said, people would miss the bigger picture.

We had been inquirers and historians all year, generating and investigating questions, piecing together answers to our questions, and trying to build understanding across time and space. "What kinds of artifacts would future historians need to truly understand what 2020 was like for us?" I asked. We decided to create our own individual scrapbooks and journals to capture our personal stories. Some wrote diary entries. Others copied popular memes into their digital journals. Some drew pictures. Some clipped news articles and glued them into their books. Others reported on friends' and neighbors' experiences, especially those on the front line who risked their lives every day as nurses, doctors, and emergency responders. This optional assignment was an effort to honor students' experience, to give them space to express themselves, and to serve as documentation for future generations who might want to learn about life during the COVID-19 pandemic.

As we turned, then, to our study of the Cold War (in World History), students were intrigued to learn what it must have been like to live through this period in history: to do duck-and-cover drills in school, to watch fall-out shelters being dug in their neighborhood, to see anticommunist propaganda, to have a family member investigated under suspicion of being a communist sympathizer. They were driven by the question, "What was it like?" Freed from the responsibility of "covering" content, I could go where their curiosity led us. We drew on resources from the Cold War Museum in Virginia that included personal reflections, documentaries, propaganda, instructions for preparing emergency provisions, and advertisements for bomb shelters. They talked to their parents and grandparents about their experience and compared the fear of living during the Cold War with the fear of living during a pandemic.

As we wrapped up our study, I shared with students the standards that we were meant to cover on the Cold War:

> The student will apply social science skills to understand the conflicts during the second half of the twentieth century by
> a) explaining the causes of the Cold War, including the competition between the American and Soviet economic and political systems and the causes of the collapse of communism in the Soviet Union and Eastern Europe;
> b) describing the major leaders and events of the Cold War, including the location of major conflicts;
> c) describing conflicts and revolutionary movements in Asia and their major leaders, including Mao Tse-tung (Zedong), Chiang Kai-shek, Deng Xiaoping, and Ho Chi Minh; and
> d) examining the political and economic shifts that led to the end of the Cold War, with emphasis on Margaret Thatcher, Mikhail Gorbachev, and Ronald Reagan. (Virginia SOLs, World History & Geography: 1500–Present; see https://www.doe.virginia.gov/testing/sol/standards_docs/history_socialscience/next_version/stds_worldhistory_geography_1500-present.pdf)

In sum, we had been meant to cover the causes of the Cold War and key political actors and events. When students read this standard, a few of my high-achieving students furiously took notes—no doubt things they would be looking up over the summer. Most, however, sat dumbfounded, staring into the screen. "That's about countries and leaders," Jack offered. "Yeah," Natalie agreed, "but what about the *people*? Like . . . what was it really *like*?" Students nodded in agreement.

"So, you're suggesting that something is lost when we focus exclusively on political and military history. You're not satisfied with the decisions the Department of Education has made on your behalf?" I asked students.

"It's like the life gets sucked out of history," Anna responded. "I mean, it would be like if we told the story of the pandemic and only talked about countries and leaders. The real story would be missing. It wouldn't be complete."

In IB Geography, students reached similar conclusions. As we learned about the 1918 Spanish influenza outbreak and the parade in Philadelphia following the end of World War I, students wrestled with the familiar dilemma of wanting to gather with others for important events and the need to be socially distant. They weren't so interested in the statistics I shared as they were in people's lived experience of navigating life at the time. Did schools close? Was there a lockdown? Did people wear masks and have to stay 6 feet apart? How did life change and when did it return to normal? Their own emotional and personal experience of living through a pandemic served as the source of purposeful and sincere questions about the feelings and experiences of those in the past. In the next section, I posit lessons that social studies teachers can take from this experience, even as COVID-19 fades into our collective memories.

LESSONS LEARNED

Emotion has an uneasy relationship with the teaching and learning of social studies (Helmsing, 2014; Sheppard et al., 2015). In their literature review on conceptualizations of emotion in the social studies, Sheppard et al. (2015) argued that emotion is both undertheorized and relegated to the shadows. When it is present in literature, either explicitly or implicitly, it is coupled with a "desire to control emotions to support more reasoned thought and action and to harness students' emotions to heighten engagement" (pp. 165–166).

We want students to be motivated, certainly, and so we design enticing hooks for lessons; we work to make content relevant and engaging. At the same time, we fear that emotion will get in the way of objective thinking or make things messy. Historians want us to bracket our feelings so that we can see the past more clearly on its own terms. Economists and political scientists want us to apply reason and rationality to solve problems and make predictions. As teachers, we feel that we ought to maintain neutrality on controversial issues and are forever worried that classroom discussions will get "heated." Emotion scares us. It makes us feel as if we are not in control. School is a place where control is highly valued: standards and pacing guides, common assessments, bell schedules, dress codes, and discipline practices. Emotion must tread lightly in such a place.

Yet whatever illusion of control we have under normal circumstances goes out the window in a pandemic. All norms and routines are shattered. The rules of engagement change. We are cut off from others. Even adults—who typically order and manage things—are uncertain about what tomorrow will bring. Life feels very out of control. Emotion is raw and visible and everywhere. Teachers and students alike feel vulnerable and anxious. Emotion cannot be checked at the virtual door or bracketed for the sake of objectivity.

As I reflect back on those few months of Spring 2020, and even now as we continue to navigate online schooling while awaiting the distribution of the vaccine, I am oddly grateful for many of the lessons COVID-19 and my students have taught me. Among them are reminders about the importance of emotion in the social studies classroom: Emotion ought to be honored; emotion can guide us toward genuine inquiry and powerful learning; and emotion should be part of the story.

Honoring Students' Emotions

Colleagues of mine who tried to carry on as if nothing was out of the ordinary lost students. My own daughter chose to continue attending only the two classes where the teachers took the time to ask how she was and to adjust the work to a new reality. The others, she said, kept scrolling through PowerPoint slides as if nothing had changed. "The world is ending," she said one morning as I tried to coax her to the computer. "What's the point?" She tuned in where she felt connected and cared for. She was experiencing tremendous loss and felt fearful. Teachers who validated her emotion and experience earned her trust and respect.

As with my daughter, my own students' need for social connection and opportunities to express their feelings kept them tuning in. The relationships we had developed prior to COVID-19 created a safe space that students wanted to return to when their world went off the rails. They trusted me. They trusted one another. At what was a scary and uncertain time, they sought out our community. For some, the emotions they were experiencing were so overwhelming that just showing up was all they could muster, and we were happy to have them. High levels of fear and sadness were not conducive to learning, but these emotions were worthy of our attention just the same. They were legitimate feelings, and we supported one another the best we could.

I have long taught about the importance of strong teacher–student relationships in my teacher education courses. I have come to understand high-quality teacher–student relationships as involving attunement (sensitivity to what students are feeling and thinking), relatedness (warmth, acceptance, belonging), supportiveness (affirmation and assistance), and openness (a commitment to honesty and reflection). Knowing our students in their own right—trying to understand their contexts, their perspectives, their feelings, their experiences—helps us to build meaningful curriculum, scaffold appropriately, and develop trust. When students trust us and their peers around them, they are more willing to take the risks necessary to learn (James et al., 2017).

I know these things intellectually, and I know them from years of teaching in various contexts. Last spring, however, COVID-19 reminded me just how important relationships are. For many young people, the synchronous sessions at school—as fraught as they were with technological issues—were their tether to the outside world and to whatever sense of normal still existed. They weren't so interested in doing school, but they were desperate for connection and a reminder that we were all still here—that we were in this together, and they weren't alone.

Students who had already suffered from anxiety or depression were exceptionally impacted by social isolation and disruption of school (where many received mental health services). Students who lived in abusive or violent situations felt trapped. Students who were not free to be themselves at home felt dreadfully alone. COVID-19 exacerbated the challenges students already faced and gave us all something new to worry about. Yet COVID-19 also served as a powerful reminder that students *always* need connection, belonging, acceptance, and safety. Caring and connection—honoring our students' emotions—must always come first.

Letting Emotion Guide Us in Inquiry

COVID-19 also reminded me that emotion can open the door to genuine inquiry and a desire to understand. For many students, the intensity of their experience prompted them to wonder about the experience of others. They wanted to understand the experience of those who had lived through the 1918 Spanish influenza outbreak. They recognized the importance of knowing *what it was like* to live through the Cold War. They were inspired to ask questions about the lived experiences of those in the past because they were determined that those in the future must understand their own lived experience of the history that was unfolding around us. Their emotion drove my planning, and fortunately, I had the freedom to let it.

It is not news that emotion matters for learning. The more powerfully we experience a moment, the more likely we are to remember it. As psychologists Linda Levine and David Pizarro (2004) noted, "Emotion appears to increase the salience of information much like a highlighter increases the salience of text. In short, emotion makes memory better" (p. 537). Physiologically speaking, when we are emotional, we release adrenaline that helps "forge the neural pathways that underlie memories" (Berry et al., 2008, p. 447). Furthermore, there is an association created between the feelings and the content that follows (Bower, 1970).

Emotions heighten our attention in the moment and contribute to motivation, which can lead to higher levels of understanding (Jung et al., 2014). Of course, differing types and degrees of emotion impact learning differently. We know that some stress can be motivating, for instance, while too much (as some of my students were experiencing) can be debilitating (Vogel & Schwabe, 2016). Emotion draws our attention to the thing we want to understand. Even in online learning environments, Cleveland-Innes and Campbell (2012) found that "Emotions create presence . . . they focus our perceptions on particular aspects of a situation and enable us to concentrate on specific situations, connect the affective to the cognitive, and arrive at thoughtful and appropriate decisions" (pp. 284–285). Emotion stimulates learning and keeps us engaged.

Emotions, then, absolutely *do* have a place in schools and in classrooms. When students express emotions, they are telling us what they care about. As social studies scholars Keith Barton and Linda Levstik (2004) wrote, "Care is the motivating force behind nearly all historical research. . . . Care-less history strikes us as a soulless enterprise. . . . We cannot interest students in the study of history . . . if we reject their cares and concerns or if we dismiss their feeling and emotions" (pp. 228–229). When students care about something, they are more likely to generate genuine questions and seek genuine answers. They *want* to learn. The students in my classes had real questions about people in the past, about policy, about economics that grew out of their experience, and emotions. Even in a space without grades and tests, many engaged with conversation, readings, and documentaries because they wanted to. Of course, having the freedom to follow students' curiosity and passion requires flexibility in planning and pacing, something I turn to next.

Making Emotion Part of the Story

History education scholar Sam Wineburg (2001) wrote, "Coming to know others, whether they live on the other side of the tracks or the other side of the millennium, requires the education of our sensibilities" (pp. 23–24). The social studies are uniquely suited to this charge. They are the collective studies of human experience. To strip them of emotion is to render them lifeless, devoid of humanity. It is the humanity that makes them interesting and relevant to us today. It is our curiosity about the human condition that, if engaged thoughtfully, allows us "to go beyond our own image, to go beyond our brief life, and to go beyond the fleeting moment in human history into which we have been born" (p. 24).

In two research studies conducted with upper elementary age children, Barton and Levstik (2004) found that students were routinely interested in topics that were relevant to their own lives: "They imagined themselves in the circumstances they read about, speculated about their own abilities to handle such dilemmas, and compared their imagined responses to those of people in history" (p. 231). Students wanted to learn about topics with personal connections to themselves or those they knew. They wanted to learn about daily life and how people "experienced dramatic events such as wars, violence, and criminal punishments" (p. 231). As Barton and Levstik surmised,

Students cared about topics that allowed them to explore the feelings and experiences of people in the past and relate them to their own. If we hope to motivate students to study history, then surely we must begin with the topics they care about, even when those topics focus on personal and emotional issues. (p. 232)

Yet, as with the Cold War standards in my own state, our social studies standards continue to emphasize political and military history. Such curricula are limited in their focus on the actions of countries and key individuals and exceedingly narrow in the histories they include. How are students to relate to the curriculum on the page? Where do they see themselves? Where do they see their cares and concerns reflected? Within our classrooms and at the level of policymaking, we must work to make our curricula flexible enough to respond to students' interests. The best examples of such curriculum that I have seen are the IB courses in which teachers organize inquiry around themes (such as civil rights or authoritarianism) or have choices of units that will make up their yearlong plan.

CONCLUSION

In time, COVID-19 will be a thing of the past. When it is, I hope we will remember the lessons it has taught us. COVID-19 reminds us that the students in our rooms are human—not widgets in need of processing. We must not be afraid to engage emotion when it is present, honoring the humans in our presence; empathizing when we can, respecting difference where it exists. Letting emotion into our classrooms is like letting the air back in, opening a window, letting everyone take a big, deep breath and exhale, knowing it is okay to allow our whole selves—not just our cognitive, intellectual, thinking selves—to come to school.

Doing so will allow us to know one another in new ways and to see what we care about. Together, we can explore our own and others' humanity, and develop "humility in the face of our limited ability to know, and awe in the face of the expanse of human history" (Wineburg, 2001, p. 24). It is because we feel and want and regret and hope that we can wonder about others in other times and other places. Our humanity ties us together. Emotion can be the conduit for inquiry and empathy, and greater humanity can be the product of our engagement. As scary as it might sound to let passion steer us, we should be inspired by the possibility of cocreating curriculum that is more meaningful and real for our students.

When we get there—to the heart of our shared inquiry—we should continue to let our interest guide the way. If daily life and experience—people's hurt, fear, pride, and hope—are what interest us, then let us linger there. Let us cultivate a love of asking questions and seeking answers and foster a desire to understand. COVID-19 has turned our world upside down, but not every piece should go back to the way it was. My hope is that our humanity remains at the forefront of our teaching.

NOTE

From December 2018 to June 2020, I was on leave from my college appointment and teaching high school social studies. I reflect here on my experience transitioning with students to distance learning and what it taught me about the central place emotion plays in the teaching and learning of social studies.

REFERENCES

American Psychological Association (2020). *8 ways teachers can continue supporting students during the COVID-19 era.* Author. https://www.apa.org/topics/covid-19/teachers-supporting-students

Barton, K. C., & Levstik, L. S. (2004). *Teaching history for the common good.* Lawrence Erlbaum Associates.

Berry, C., Schmied, L. A., & Schrock, J. C. (2008). The role of emotion in teaching and learning history: A scholarship of teaching exploration. *The History Teacher, 41*(4), 437–452.

Bower, G. H. (1970). Imagery as a relational organizer in associative learning. *Journal of Verbal Learning and Verbal Behavior, 9*(5), 529–533. https://doi.org/10.1016/S0022-5371(70)80096-2

Cleveland-Innes, M., & Campbell, P. (2012). Emotional presence, learning, and the online learning environment. *The International Review of Research in Open and Distance Learning, 13*(4), 269–292. https://doi.org/10.19173/irrodl.v13i4.1234.

Golberstein, E., Wen, H., & Miller, B. F. (2020). Coronavirus disease 2019 (COVID-19) and mental health for children and adolescents. *Journal of the American Medical Association, 174*(9), 819–820. https://doi.org/10.1001/jamapediatrics.2020.1456

Helmsing, M. (2014). Virtuous subjects: A critical analysis of the affective substance of social studies education. *Theory & Research in Social Education, 42*(1), 127–140. https://doi.org/10.1080/00933104.2013.842530

James, J. H., Kobe, J., & Zhao, X. (2017). Examining the role of trust in shaping children's approaches to peer dialogue. *Teachers College Record, 119*(10), 1–34.

Jung, N., Wranke, C., Hamburger, K., & Knauff, M. (2014). How emotions affect logical reasoning: Evidence from experiments with mood-manipulated participants, spider phobics, and people with exam anxiety. *Frontiers in Psychology, 5*(570), 1–12. https://doi.org/10.3389/fpsyg.2014.00570

Levine, L. J., & Pizarro, D. A. (2004). Emotion and memory research: A grumpy overview. *Social Cognition, 22*(5), 530–554. https://doi.org/10.1521/soco.22.5.530.50767

Sheppard, M., Katz, D., & Grosland, T. (2015). Conceptualizing emotions in social studies education. *Theory & Research in Social Education, 43*(2), 147–178. https://doi.org/ 10.1080/00933104.2015.1034391

Thakur, A. (2020). Mental health in high school students at the time of COVID-19: A student's perspective. *Journal of American Academy of Child and Adolescent Psychiatry, 59*(12), 1309–1310. https://doi.org/10.1016/j.jaac.2020.08.005

Vogel, S., & Schwabe, L. (2016). Learning and memory under stress: implications for the classroom. *Science of Learning, 1*, 1–10. https://doi.org/10.1038/np-jscilearn.2016.11

Wineburg, S. (2001). *Historical thinking and other unnatural acts.* Temple University Press.

CHAPTER 13

Taking Seriously the Social in Elementary Social Studies

Katherina A. Payne and Anna Falkner

Amidst the COVID-19 pandemic, schools and society faced massive change and loss. The everyday experience of negotiating how to live and learn with others in an embodied way shifted to virtual classrooms where teachers and students had to consider new interactional norms and questions. Systemic inequities in healthcare and other critical infrastructure (e.g., housing) compounded the detrimental effects of the pandemic for children and families in historically marginalized communities. Questions about the common good, how we care for and protect one another, and how institutions like schools support communities became acute in people's daily lives.

In this chapter, we consider what it would mean for elementary social studies to truly engage the question "How do we live together?" Elementary social studies can address this question in content and with the relational aspects of learning and living together in classrooms; teachers have the potential to engage in deep sociological thinking with young children. We recognize the important skills and content of other fields often listed as disciplines of social studies—history, geography, civics, and economics. Here, we urge teachers to see disciplines through a lens focused on people's relationships with one another, the places they inhabit, and the institutions created within those places.

A sociological lens allows elementary social studies to examine the historical roots that led to the events of 2020 and to envision different ways of living together post-pandemic. We raise the following questions: How do we care for one another at a moment like this? How do we protect the most vulnerable among us? How do we push forward voices that White-dominant society has traditionally discounted in public narrative and deliberation? How can we support younger generations as they enact a just society that recognizes everyone's humanity? To address these questions and make a case for a sociological approach to elementary social studies, we will examine three strands of inquiry around the following areas: social movements, social relations in everyday interactions, and anti-bias–anti-racist frameworks for curricula.

LEARNING ABOUT AND FROM SOCIAL MOVEMENTS

Education scholar Quentin Wheeler-Bell (2014) argued that we should encourage young people to develop a "spirit of activism" (p. 2) to guide their thinking about creating an ideal, just society. To do this, students should develop the skills and strategies to work collectively in social movements. Learning about and from social movements pushes back on typical "heroes and holidays" social studies approaches that overemphasize individual actions and present a decontextualized and whitewashed narrative. Study of social movements shows us how people work together to negotiate and enact their visions of an ideal and just society, and moves students away from the mythology of rugged individualism. During the COVID-19 pandemic, people acutely grappled with how their daily actions impacted the health and well-being of strangers; our work with children needs to help them develop the skills and dispositions to think beyond the individual and toward the collective good.

Elementary civic education has increasingly focused on how children take civic action, whether in the classroom and school communities (e.g., advocating for healthier lunches) or in the broader public (e.g., meeting with civic leaders). History education has examined learning about social movements as a way to develop children's democratic imagination and their capabilities for participation in social movements. Social studies scholars Christopher Martell and Kaylene Stevens (2021) argued that history education ought to develop students' perspective of "thinking like an activist." Connecting the study of historical social movements to current issues provides young children with spaces for both sociological inquiry and for enacting civic strategies within present movements.

To prepare children to "think like an activist" or to develop a "spirit of activism" requires engaging their democratic imagination to envision a just society drawing on diverse people's histories and assets (Martell & Stevens, 2021; Swalwell & Payne, 2019; Wheeler-Bell, 2014). Historical and sociological inquiry focused on social movements is one way to prepare children to learn about collective action strategies and equity issues and to do critical analysis of social structures that reinscribe inequities. Here, we offer ways for teachers to develop their knowledge of social movements for inquiry with young students. In particular, we highlight social movements inclusive of and led by children. As students return to schools and a more publicly engaged life post-pandemic, we offer a possible starting point to truly center the social in elementary classrooms.

BRINGING SOCIAL MOVEMENTS INTO ELEMENTARY SOCIAL STUDIES CURRICULUM

To include social movements, teachers must take an expansive approach to state standards. Social studies scholars Christopher Busey and Irenea Walker (2017) found that elementary social studies standards emphasized individual, rather than collective, civic acts. Teachers can focus on the social (i.e., the collective) rather than the individual by stretching the standards, building content knowledge, highlighting children's roles in social movements, and connecting inquiries to how students can take action now, even in socially distanced ways.

Stretching Standards and Building Content Knowledge

Stretching standards to include social movements in elementary social studies curricula requires building content knowledge of varied movements. We learned from one 5th-grade teacher who had her classes examine historical and current social movements, including the Black Lives Matter movement and women's rights (Falkner & Payne, 2021). The teacher, a White woman named Ms. Vine, and the students, primarily Black and Latinx youth, affirmed children's identities and attended to counternarratives by connecting historically marginalized people's current struggles and social movements. To do this work, Ms. Vine stretched the standards and bolstered her content knowledge. In the previous school year, Ms. Vine and her classes had examined the Black Civil Rights movement; we asked her about including the Chicano Rights movement, which Ms. Vine admitted she knew little about. So Ms. Vine sought out resources to develop her knowledge so that she could include that history as well.

Elementary teachers prepare as generalists, meaning they must acquire broad knowledge of multiple disciplines. Teachers face constraints on time and effort to develop deep knowledge in multiple areas of study. One way to develop content knowledge is through the young adult versions of historical texts. In our elementary teacher preparation courses, we often assign Ronald Takaki's (2012) *A Different Mirror for Young People* or Howard Zinn's (2011) *A Young People's History of the United States*. Both of these texts counter the individualized heroes and holidays approach, and they cover varied social movements. In recent years, a number of other history texts first written for an adult audience have been adapted to young adult versions, including *An Indigenous People's History of the United States for Young People* (Dunbar-Ortiz, 2019), *A Queer History of the United States for Young People* (Bronski, 2019), *Lies My Teacher Told Me: Young People's Edition* (Loewen, 2019), *Stamped: Racism, Antiracism, and You* (Reynolds & Kendi, 2020), and *Freedom Summer for Young People* (Watson, 2020).

As elementary teachers envision ways to center the social in social studies, they can build their content knowledge of varied social movements.

More concrete content knowledge supports the critical use of children's literature about social movements. Evaluating narratives presented in texts and other media is essential to refocus teachers' attention on the social, rather than the individual. For example, narratives about Rosa Parks tend to describe racism as a "a problem between individuals" rather than a "social problem" and force a happy ending to a complex justice movement (Kohl, 1994). Books have often focused on Parks as an individual instead of as a member of a social movement. Keeping a focus on the collective, we highlight children's literature book lists from sources such as Teaching for Social Change's Social Justice Books (https://www.teachingforchange. org/socialjusticebooks-org) and the Cooperative Children's Book Center (https://ccbc.education.wisc.edu/), as well as social media resources such as The Conscious Kid and Debbie Reese's *American Indian Children's Literature* blog (https://americanindiansinchildrensliterature.blogspot.com/) as critical recommendation sources. These spaces offer focused book lists that cover study of varied social movements, including the Chicano rights movement, the Black Lives Matter movement, the LGBTQ+ rights movement, women's rights movements, and disability rights movements.

Children's Role in Social Movements

Education scholar Herbert Kohl (1994) noted:

> As a tale of a social movement and a community effort to overthrow injustice, the Rosa Parks story opens the possibility of every child identifying herself or himself as an activist, as someone who can help make justice happen. (p. 6)

By recognizing children's capabilities, we can also highlight their role in social movements. Learning about how children are currently and historically involved in social movements creates references of actions toward a just society. Within social movements, children take the lead, participate alongside adults, or engage in parallel actions to adults. While there was not a large social movement directly related to the COVID-19 pandemic, there were collective actions with children in efforts to protect communities (e.g., working to make cloth masks to distribute). Acting alongside adults to encourage public health initiatives in many ways became a political movement during the waning days of the Trump administration.

To support students in seeing themselves in social movements, we offer three examples highlighting cultural and ancestral knowledges in youth movements. These examples disrupt over-romanticized representations of children in social movements and instead emphasize the ongoing nature of children and youth's anti-oppressive activism.

Youth Against Gun Violence. During the youth-led 2018 March for Our Lives rally against gun violence, 11-year-old Naomi Wadler (2018) spoke poignantly about gun violence and its impact on Black girls and women: "For far too long these names, these Black girls and women have been just numbers. I'm here to say 'NEVER AGAIN' for those girls, too. I am here to say that everyone should value those girls too" (para. 7). Recent school shootings have brought the movement into the foreground; yet youth activists including groups such as VOYCE, Peace Warriors, and Black Youth Project 100 have been working to counter the impact of gun violence on children—particularly among Black communities—for much longer. When exploring the role of children in the gun control movement, we suggest using youth activist–curated resources or primary sources from children, which highlight issues from their perspectives. Pairing primary sources with picture books or activism guides (e.g., Dias, 2018) allows students to explore how intersecting identities of age, racialized group, and gender influence the issues, strategies, and impact of child activists.

Indigenous Youth Activists for Ecological Justice. In an example of acting alongside adults, youth from the Standing Rock bands of the Sioux tribe played a central role in protesting the Dakota Access Pipeline. Aslan Tudor, a 10-year-old citizen of the Lipan Apache Tribe of Texas, participated in the protest and authored a children's book, *Young Water Protectors: A Story About Standing Rock*, describing those experiences:

> Youth from Standing Rock started a water protector's camp to protect their water. It was called Sacred Stone Camp. They asked people to come and join them to help them protect their water. A lot of people came to help and a new camp started. It was called Oceti Sakowin Camp. (Tudor & Tudor, 2018, p. 8)

Drawing on tribal traditions of activism and care for the land, Native youth have continued to fight for ecological justice, including advocacy for policy changes around oil drilling and climate change. Examining climate change in social studies often centers on civics—students learning about problem solving and activism toward policy change (Kissling et al., 2017; Seitz & Krutka, 2019). Teachers can expand their approach to include ideas of ecojustice and how learning to work in and with a community includes both human and nonhuman life. Centering inquiries around ancestral knowledge and community organizing to care for one another and the land is essential as we consider the question of living together in a more just society.

Birmingham Children's Crusade. As a movement within a movement, during the Birmingham Children's Crusade of 1963 children capably navigated the broader Civil Rights Movement (CRM). When parents were worried about losing their jobs if they took part in a "fill the jails" strategy, children and youth recognized their strengths and made plans to fill the jails themselves (Civil Rights Movement Archive, 2021). Children trained with adult movement leaders to learn nonviolent protest strategies (Houston, 2004). In considering how to explore the role of children and youth in the CRM, we amplify the recommendations of educational scholars Noreen Naseem Rodríguez and Amanda Vickery (2020), who argued for advancing racial realism by "allowing students to understand racial progress as an ongoing project involving constant steps forward and backward at multiple levels and with a wide range of actors" (pp. 112–113). Using primary sources along with narratives that include personal accounts, such as the one in Hoose's (2001) book *We Were There Too! Young People in US History*, the *Mighty Times* documentary (Houston, 2004), or the website *Kids in Birmingham, 1963* (KidsinBirmingham1963.org), can help highlight children's roles in the movement while avoiding a reductionist, romanticized view of children's participation.

We suggest pairing the story of the Children's Crusade with primary sources showing youth participating in the summer of 2020 protests after the murder of George Floyd. Teachers may ask critical historical thinking (Salinas et al., 2012) questions such as, "Has our society changed enough?" and invite civic inquiry by asking, "What can we learn from these children?" and "What do you want to try now?" A sociological lens pushes us to ask, "Why do we need movements for racial justice in our society?" and "What would a just society that listens to the voices of these movements look like?"

SOCIAL RELATIONS IN EVERYDAY ACTIONS

Educational theorists have long considered the classroom a microcosm for society; we ask: How can our classrooms forward a just society rather than replicate current inequities? Classrooms are ripe with interactions (with people, materials, and spaces) that shape and are shaped by ideas of community. The COVID-19 pandemic upended our long-held ideas about shared community materials, multiple spaces for work in a classroom, and collectively shaping the classroom space—from the placement of furniture to what hangs on the walls. With public health concerns at the forefront, teachers and school leaders have had to rethink how children interact with one another, their teachers, and classroom materials. As we ease into a post-pandemic world, how can we envision classroom spaces that move toward a just society? How can we think about our roles in protecting our communities? What can we explore with young children as we negotiate living and learning in the same physical space?

We advocate engaging children in establishing what their classrooms look like and how they function on a daily basis (see Falkner & Payne,

2020). Establishing rules of living and learning together is not a one-day, 45-minute activity, but an involved (and continual) process that asks children to envision what they need to live and learn with joy. As students gather amidst and after the pandemic, these questions take on new meaning. Many students have had to avoid seeing family members outside of their home, and they are returning to classrooms that might include health procedures like wearing masks, keeping work areas separate, and limiting physical interaction. Teachers must be ready to help children navigate, negotiate, and make sense of these new learning and social configurations.

We urge educators to be more attentive to the social curriculum represented in children's everyday interactions with one another. Recent years have seen a surge in social–emotional learning programs; however, most often these approaches focus on the prosocial development of the individual child's skills rather than seeing the child as part of the collective classroom community (Payne et al., 2020). We advocate that teachers focus on the student in relation to the classroom community and larger structural issues that impact schools, rather than pursue an individualistic approach that seeks to fix the child. Foregrounding a collective ideal in the social curriculum can also emphasize non-Western ways of being and knowing, such as Afrocentric, Indigenous, and global south pedagogies (e.g., Johnson et al., 2019; Nxumalo, 2019; Pérez & Saavedra, 2017). Wrestling with the questions of living and learning together is essential as students return to collective spaces post-pandemic.

The social curriculum of classrooms includes everything that affects how children interact with one another. For example, when developing rules with children at the start of the year, the process should authentically represent what they (and the teacher) need to operate as a community. Classrooms often begin the year talking about children's hopes and, consequently, what the community needs to do to support those goals (see Charney, 2002). A child might hope to "read more books," which offers space to consider classroom norms during reading times, from noise levels (e.g., silent, music, low chatter), to types of spaces (e.g., open rug spaces, tables, small couches), to how children access books. We note here that the rules ought to be open to some process for negotiation, as community needs evolve. Engaging in rule negotiation can also result in children's creative solutions for pandemic-era rules, like one class we saw using paper airplanes to share ideas across a socially distanced classroom.

Another area ripe for the social studies curriculum is developing problem-solving strategies that support students' relationships and attend to restorative justice as a framework to prioritize students' relationships with community (e.g., Hopkins, 2002; Winn, 2020). Class meetings are one way that teachers engage in ongoing problem solving that helps children learn how "to build consensus [and] collective agreements that contribute to a more peaceful classroom" (Angell, 2004, p. 99). This type of experience gives children the opportunity to understand their lived experiences and imagine a more just way of being in community.

SOCIAL INQUIRY THROUGH AN ANTI-BIAS AND ANTI-RACIST (ABAR) FRAMEWORK

Young children actively make sense of their multiple identities and the identities of others through inquiry and embodied learning practices (Hirsh-Pasek et al., 2009; Kamii, 1984). As we return to in-person schooling, we want to imagine better possibilities for how to support the social inquiry always present in children's lives. In the United States, we have experienced the twin "pandemics" of COVID-19 and ongoing racial injustices laid bare. We wonder: How can schools center anti-bias–anti-racist (ABAR) early education, which "honors the centrality of race in shaping children's . . . worlds" (Escayg, 2020, p. 5) and engages issues of equity, diversity, and justice, centering children's multiple intersectional identities (Escayg, 2020; Iruka et al., 2020)? Drawing on an ABAR framework recognizes children's capabilities to interrogate oppression through both curriculum and pedagogy.

An ABAR approach to social inquiry includes the active, embodied, and ongoing investigation of social processes, including how people live and work together, how power influences decisions and systems, and how people collectively fight oppression. Social inquiry is embedded in and an extension of work children do in their classroom communities. Using an ABAR framework allows teachers to collaborate with children on social inquiry, to honor children's questions while extending inquiries with historical content, geographical and civic context, and economic implications. We suggest three cyclical steps for teachers: reflection and revision, observation and investigation, and extension and application.

Reflection and Revision

An ABAR approach to social inquiry requires personal reflective work. In the reflection and revision stage, educators first consider their positionalities, privileges, and experiences (Matias, 2013). Teachers may also reflect on their pedagogy and content, acknowledging how they might have done harm in the past, considering how they have or have not employed anti-oppressive frameworks in their teaching, and intentionally planning how they intend to grow. Resources like the Abolitionist Teaching Network (n.d.) podcast, "Teaching to Thrive," help teachers engage in reflexive praxis about how race and power show up in teaching, what opportunities for agency students have in their learning (Adair, 2014; Adair & Colegrove, in press), and how race operates in curricular content.

Revision, then, applies abolitionist thinking to our teaching practice; teachers work in solidarity "to achieve incremental changes in their class-rooms and schools for students in the present day, while simultaneously freedom dreaming and vigorously creating a vision for what schools will be" (Love, 2019, p. 89). Teachers actively seek out and use pedagogy that can support student inquiry and curiosity (Leu et al., 2016; Souto-Manning, 2013), build racial literacy and critical content knowledge (King & Chandler, 2016), and critically examine how their classroom might contribute to children's anti-oppressive social inquiries.

Observation and Investigation

During the observation and evaluation stage, teachers engage in close learning about how children are already doing social inquiry. Teachers should consider what social ideas/theories children try out, what resources they choose, and what strategies they already use to learn about social issues. Teachers consider what books children are reading, talk with families about what conversations they have been having, and make time and space for open-ended conversations among children. In doing so, teachers might observe children sharing experiences about personal and social issues, such as how the pandemic impacted their families and communities. Close attention to children's joys, interests, and lives is an essential part of an ABAR approach to inquiry, as it offers educators time to acknowledge and learn from children's cultural repertoires of learning (Gutiérrez & Rogoff, 2003) and funds of knowledge (Gonzalez et al., 2006). Additionally, when educators pay close, curious attention to children, they communicate that children are loved and that their ideas, wonderings, experiences, and lives matter (Love, 2019).

After observing what social ideas children are working on, teachers can engage in investigation. They may gather information through questioning and informal interviewing (see Paley, 1986), offer writing prompts on a topic, ask children to illustrate an idea or question, or engage in discussion with children. Questions such as "What else do you want to know about this?" and "How do you think we could learn more about this?" prompt students' investigations and provide teachers with insight into appropriate next steps. Early childhood scholars have noted that young children—particularly those who identify as Black, Indigenous, and Children of Color—often have limited control over what and how they learn at school (Adair et al., 2018; Dumas & Nelson, 2016; Yoon & Templeton, 2019) During the pandemic, as schools tried to adapt in-class lessons to remote learning, children may have experienced further restrictions on agency. To engage in ABAR, social inquiry requires disruption so that teachers may become collaborators with their students.

Extension and Application

The extension and application stage involves offering time, skills, and resources so children can build on their inquiries. Teachers can incorporate lessons that offer new information directly related to the questions and theories that children are exploring. Teachers can also offer lessons that provide students with opportunities to build inquiry skills or time to explore new ideas. These lessons provide students with sociohistorical context or ideas from other disciplinary perspectives. For instance, educators may notice children discussing the pandemic and offer inquiry resources about how the pandemic revealed racialized healthcare disparities. Teachers may also offer opportunities for students to take action. As with any inquiry process, sociological inquiry through an ABAR lens is cyclical. Each new experience with children can offer opportunities for reflection and observation, prompting teachers to make revisions or to invite children to engage in their inquiry in new ways.

CONCLUSION

At its core, our calls draw on education scholar Farima Pour-Khorshid's (2020) philosophy,

> To create humanizing learning experiences that allow students to think critically about what freedom is and what it is not; what love is and what it is not; what solidarity is and what it is not; because understanding these distinctions helps us move closer to our collective liberation one moment, one lesson, one classroom at a time. (p. 17)

Engaging children seriously around the broad social inquiry "How do we live together?" opens multiple spaces for developing a "spirit of activism," particularly as it relates to imagining a more just society. At a moment when there is an opportunity to reset after a mass societal shutdown during the pandemic, we owe children opportunities to draw lessons from the past as they imagine a more just future. Learning from social movements, everyday interactions, and an ABAR framework provides spaces for resistance to injustices and the practice of hope.

REFERENCES

Abolitionist Teaching Network. (2020). *Teaching to thrive.* Author. https://abolitionistteachingnetwork.org/podcast
Adair, J. K. (2014). Agency and expanding capabilities in early grade classrooms:

What it could mean for young children. *Harvard Educational Review*, *84*(2), 217–241. http://dx.doi.org/10.17763/haer.84.2.y46vh546h41l2144

Adair, J. K., & Colegrove, K. S.-S. (in press). *Segregation by experience: Agency, racism, and learning in the early grades*. University of Chicago Press.

Adair, J. K., Colegrove, K. S.-S., & McManus, M. E. (2018). How the word gap argument negatively impacts young children of Latinx immigrants' conceptualizations of learning. *Harvard Educational Review*, *87*(3), 309–334. http://dx.doi.org/10.17763/1943-5045-87.3.309

Angell, A. V. (2004). Making peace in elementary classrooms: A case for class meetings. *Theory & Research in Social Education*, *32*(1), 98–104. https://doi.org/10.1080/00933104.2004.10473245

Bronski, M. (2019). *A queer history of the United States for young people* (R. Chevat, adapted). Beacon Press.

Busey, C. L., & Walker, I. (2017). A dream and a bus: Black critical patriotism in elementary social studies standards. *Theory & Research in Social Education*, *45*(4), 456–488. https://doi.org/10.1080/00933104.2017.1320251

Charney, R. (2002). *Teaching children to care: Classroom management for ethical and academic growth, K–8*. Center for Responsive Schools, Inc.

Civil Rights Movement Archive. (2021). *The movement*. Author. https://www.crmvet.org/

Dias, M. (2018). *Marley Dias gets it done: And so can you!* Scholastic.

Dumas, M. J., & Nelson, J. D. (2016). (Re)Imagining Black boyhood: Toward a critical framework for educational research. *Harvard Educational Review*, *86*(1), 27–47. http://dx.doi.org/10.17763/0017-8055.86.1.27

Dunbar-Ortiz, R. (2019). *An Indigenous peoples' history of the United States for young people*. (D. Reese & J. Mendoza, adapted). Beacon.

Escayg, K.-A. (2020). Anti-racism in US early childhood education: Foundational principles. *Sociology Compass*, *14*(4), 1–15. https://doi.org/10.1111/soc4.12764

Falkner, A., & Payne, K. A. (2020). "But all your walls are blank!" Using the classroom environment to promote civics in the primary grades. *YC Young Children*, *75*(4), 32–37.

Falkner, A., & Payne, K. A. (2021). "Courage to take on the bull": Cultural citizenship in fifth-grade social studies. *Theory & Research in Social Education*, *49*(1), 78–106. https://doi.org/10.1080/00933104.2020.1831675

Gonzalez, N., Moll, L. C., & Amanti, C. (2006). *Funds of knowledge: Theorizing practices in households, communities, and classrooms*. Routledge.

Gutiérrez, K. D., & Rogoff, B. (2003). Cultural ways of learning: Individual traits or repertoires of practice. *Educational Researcher*, *32*(5), 19–25. https://dx.doi.org/10.3102/0013189X032005019

Hirsh-Pasek, K., Berk, L. E., & Singer, D. (2009). *A mandate for playful learning in preschool: Applying the scientific evidence*. Oxford University Press.

Hoose, P. (2001). *We were there, too! Young people in U.S. history*. Macmillan.

Hopkins, B. (2002). Restorative justice in schools. *Support for Learning*, *17*(3), 144–149.

Houston, R. (2004). *Mighty times: The children's march*. HBO.

Iruka, I. U., Curenton, S. M., Durden, T., R., & Escayg, K.-A. (2020). *Don't look away: Embracing anti-bias classrooms*. Gryphon House.

Johnson, L. L., Bryan, N., & Boutte, G. (2019). Show us the love: Revolutionary teaching in (un)critical times. *The Urban Review, 51*(1), 46–64. https://doi. org/10.1007/s11256-018-0488-3

Kamii, C. (1984). Autonomy: The aim of education envisioned by Piaget. *Phi Delta Kappan, 65*(6), 410–415.

King, L. J., & Chandler, P. T. (2016). From non-racism to anti-racism in social studies teacher education: Social studies and racial pedagogical content knowledge. In A. R. Crowe & A. Cuenca (Eds.), *Rethinking social studies teacher education in the twenty-first century* (pp. 3–21). Springer.

Kissling, M. T., Bell, J. T., Beltrán, A. C. D., & Myler, J. L. (2017). Ending the silence about the Earth in social studies teacher education. In C. C. Martell (Ed.), *Social studies teacher education: Critical issues and current perspectives* (pp. 193–220). Information Age.

Kohl, H. (1994). *Rethinking our classrooms*. Rethinking Schools.

Leu, K.-H., Templeton, T., & Yoon, H. (2016). Co-inquiry, co-construction, collaboration: The emergence of curriculum. *Language Arts, 94*(1), 54–57.

Loewen, J. (2019). *Lies my teacher told me: Young readers' edition: Everything American history textbooks get wrong* (R. Stefoff, adapted). The New Press.

Love, B. L. (2019). *We want to do more than survive: Abolitionist teaching and the pursuit of educational freedom*. Beacon.

Martell, C. C., & Stevens, K. M. (2021). *Teaching history for justice: Centering activism in students' study of the past*. Teachers College Press.

Matias, C. E. (2013). Check yo'self before you wreck yo'self and our kids: Counterstories from culturally responsive white teachers? . . . To culturally responsive white teachers! *Interdisciplinary Journal of Teaching and Learning, 3*(2), 68–81.

Nxumalo, F. (2019). *Decolonizing place in early childhood education*. Routledge.

Paley, V. G. (1986). On listening to what the children say. *Harvard Educational Review, 56*(2), 122–132. http://dx.doi.org/10.17763/haer.56.2.p775487x30t-k69m8

Payne, K. A., Adair, J. K., & Sachdeva, S. (2020). Creating classroom community to welcome children experiencing trauma. *Occasional Paper Series, 2020*(43), 113–121.

Pérez, M. S., & Saavedra, C. M. (2017). A call for onto-epistemological diversity in early childhood education and care: Centering global south conceptualizations of childhood/s. *Review of Research in Education, 41*(1), 1–29. http://dx.doi.org/10.3102/0091732X16688621

Pour-Khorshid, F. (2020). Teaching to heal, healing to teach: Ethnic studies as a healing endeavor in and out of the classroom. In R. Agarwal-Rangnath (Ed.), *Planting the seeds of equity: Ethnic studies and social justice in the K–2 classroom* (pp. 17–26). Teachers College Press.

Reynolds, J., & Kendi, I.X. (2020). *Stamped: Racism, antiracism, and you. A remix of the National Award-winning Stamped from the Beginning*. Little, Brown and Company.

Rodríguez, N. N., & Vickery, A. E. (2020). Much bigger than a hamburger: Disrupting problematic picturebook depictions of the Civil Rights Movement. *International Journal of Multicultural Education, 21*(2), 109–128. http://dx.doi.org/10.18251/ijme.v22i2.2243

Salinas, C., Blevins, B., & Sullivan, C. C. (2012). Critical historical thinking: When official narratives collide with other narratives. *Multicultural Perspectives*, 14(1), 18–27. https://doi.org/10.1080/15210960.2012.646640

Seitz, R. Z., & Krutka, D. G. (2020). Can the Green New Deal save us? An interdisciplinary inquiry. *The Social Studies*, 111(2), 74–85. http://dx.doi.org/10.1080/00377996.2019.1677547

Souto-Manning, M. (2013). *Multicultural teaching in the early childhood classroom: Approaches, strategies, and tools, preschool-2nd grade.* Teachers College Press.

Swalwell, K., & Payne, K. A. (2019). Critical civic education for young children. *Multicultural Perspectives*, 21(2), 127–132. https://doi.org/10.1080/15210960.2019.1606641

Takaki, R. (2012). *A different mirror for young people: A history of multicultural America.* Seven Stories Press.

Tudor, A., & Tudor, K. (2018). *Young water protectors: A story about standing rock.* CreateSpace.

Wadler, N. (2018, March 25). *Read 11-year-old Naomi Wadler's full speech from March for Our Lives DC.* Amy Poehler's Smart Girls. https://amysmartgirls.com/read-naomi-wadlers-11-yrs-full-speech-from-march-for-our-lives-dc-e729940f30be

Watson, B. (2020). *Freedom summer for young people: The violent season that made Mississippi burn and made America a democracy* (R. Stefoff, adapted). Triangle Square.

Wheeler-Bell, Q. (2014). Educating the spirit of activism: A "critical" civic education. *Educational Policy*, 28(3), 463–486. https://doi.org/10.1177%2F0895904812465113

Winn, M. T. (2020). *Justice on both sides: Transforming education through restorative justice.* Harvard Education Press.

Yoon, H. S., & Templeton, T. N. (2019). The practice of listening to children: The challenges of hearing children out in an adult-regulated world. *Harvard Educational Review*, 89(1), 55–84. http://dx.doi.org/10.17763/1943-5045-89.1.55

Zinn, H. (2009). *A young people's history of the United States* (R. Stefoff, adapted). Triangle Square.

CHAPTER 14

Rethinking the American Value of Freedom in the Post–COVID-19 Social Studies Curriculum

An Altruism Perspective

Yun-Wen Chan and Ya-Fang Cheng

Freedom and liberty are essential values grounded in the U.S. Constitution, and for many Americans, these values are prioritized in various aspects of their lives. Yet devotion to the concepts of freedom and liberty may be a danger when a nation requires its citizens to unite to fight against global crises. The COVID-19 pandemic is an obvious example that showcases the tensions between public safety and personal freedom, which led to the failure of pandemic control in the United States (Leng & Lemahieu, 2021a).

Since the COVID-19 outbreak in March 2020, federal, state, and county-level governments have implemented policies to prevent the spread of COVID-19 in the United States. These policies included stay-at-home orders, washing hands frequently, distancing six feet in social interactions, and wearing face masks in public areas. These regulatory policies, however, have led to tensions between claims regarding public health and private liberty (McKeever, 2020).

As an example, in Florida, a state with a high rate of COVID-19 transmission, a group of citizens at the Palm Beach County Commission meeting opposed the county's proposed policy in June 2020. These opponents argued that wearing masks offends God's divine creation of a human being's breathing systems and, thus, restricts individuals' natural rights. Another citizen invoked freedom and liberty in opposition to the policy, claiming that the six-foot social distance regulation was a military protocol associated with communist nations (NowThis News, 2020).

Protecting the public's welfare has been a pretext for governments to curtail or erode fundamental rights, and this tension has long been debated within the context of U.S. public health. As noted by sociomedical scientist Ronald Bayer (2007), these conflicts have been "animated by a deep-rooted mistrust of overreaching authorities, concerns about arbitrary exercises of power, and by the anti-authoritarian ethos that is a historically prominent feature of U.S. politics and civic culture" (p. 1099). This deep-rooted mistrust of the government, while appropriate at times, has been shown to be problematic during the pandemic through anti-regulation protests, vaccine conspiracy narratives, and direct threats to elected officials. The pandemic crisis, then, provides an opportunity to reexamine these central features of American values: What are the meanings of *freedom* and *liberty*? How do we balance the tensions between public safety and personal liberty in the face of a global pandemic crisis? Recognizing that individual freedom and liberty come at a cost, we suggest that an altruistic perspective is needed to balance these imperative values.

Our argument is developed by first illuminating the concept of *altruism* and how altruism lays a strong foundation for human beings to lead a good society. The practice of altruism helps to build trust, cooperation, and solidarity in our societies. A trusting, cooperative, and united environment, then, would allow more personal freedom. To strengthen our argument, we discuss two successful cases of national pandemic prevention: New Zealand and Taiwan. In contrast to the individual freedom–based American society, both New Zealand and Taiwan are more altruistic-oriented societies, which is an essential feature that has led to their success in COVID-19 control. While these two nations have significant cultural differences, we apply our argument to reflect on how these two cases balanced public safety and personal freedom to prevent COVID-19 from spreading. We believe that the United States could learn from these two nations, and we argue that U.S. civic education should take an altruistic approach when discussing the notion of individual freedom.

ALTRUISM

Altruism is a phenomenon that involves taking the interests of the other as one's own. This term is usually identified with the Golden Rule, as it exists in several ethical and religious traditions: Do unto others as you would have them do unto you. The Golden Rule seems to identify altruism with morality, though whether acting upon the Golden Rule is always moral is far from clear (Scott & Seglow, 2007).

Altruism has been discussed from different disciplinary perspectives, including evolutionary theory, social psychology, and economics. Scholars have debated what behaviors count as altruistic behaviors, whether emotions or reasons motivate altruistic behaviors, and what motivations or intentions are altruistic. From an evolutionary lens, Trivers (1971) identified an altruistic behavior as "behavior that benefits another organism, not closely related, while being apparently detrimental to the organism performing the behavior, benefit, and detriment being defined in terms of contribution to inclusive fitness" (p. 35).

A common example is helping a beggar by giving him money or food. This altruistic behavior can be made by a rational decision that one should promote others' interests, not one's own self-interest, to achieve a better society. It can also be motivated by one's passionate feeling toward helping the beggar who stands in front of them. This passionate feeling could be that one feels a duty to help people because of one's religious beliefs or that one feels good helping the beggar because one has lived a more fortunate life. The behavior can also be caused by empathy, along with a sense of guilt that one has a comfortable life, while the beggar suffers from hunger. Whether driven by reasons or emotions, a person who acts to help others could be identified as behaving altruistically.

Altruism as a Solid Foundation for Sustaining the Common Good

We believe that altruism lays a solid foundation for sustaining the common good in society. The pandemic provides a useful case to test that theory. Altruism serves to achieve the common good, which in the case of the pandemic we define as people living in a safe environment without their lives being threatened by COVID-19.

Many altruists believe that altruism can be enforced by social expectations (Piliavin & Charng, 1990). When more people share and act on perceived social expectations, these expectations become social norms. With regard to the pandemic, following public health guidelines is essential to promote public safety; conformity may be driven either by taking others' interests into account or through self-interest. To compare with an everyday example, if one has to follow traffic signs to drive a car, it makes sense to wear a face mask to go out among a population where disease is spreading. Following traffic signs and wearing face masks are both altruistic behaviors. In both cases, the acts protect oneself, as well as others.

Though it may be too optimistic for the welfare edifice to build solely on the basis of altruistic fellow-feeling, altruistic behaviors to maintain public safety are essential in order to achieve the common good. Cooperative behaviors, thus, have evolved and are reinforced by cultural and social norms in different communities. One example is the service industry responding to the reopening policy enacted by states. To revive the U.S. economy, since May 2020, most states developed guidelines for reopening. Most business owners (apparently not all, based on the increase of COVID-19 cases after reopening) followed the guidelines in order to revive their business and appeal to consumers. Following these rules steadily became social norms in business during the pandemic. This changing situation was aimed at economic recovery so that everyone could return to a sense of normalcy.

Another example is a student-led grocery store to support families in need. Linda Tutt High School in Sange, Texas, opened a grocery store for struggling families where good deeds were accepted as payment (Elassar, 2020). Partnered with First Refuge Ministries and Texas Health Resources, this school's students managed the inventory to support students and their families suffering from the pandemic. Students were given award points depending on their family size. They could use these points to purchase necessities, including toilet paper, meat, and basic food items. Students could also earn additional points from their outstanding performance in school and doing good deeds, such as volunteering in the library or mentoring elementary school students. Both of these examples showcase how altruism serves to promote public health and social stability.

Personal Freedom Should be Grounded in Altruism

We propose that altruism plays an essential role in navigating the tension between public safety and personal freedom, and we believe that personal freedom should be grounded in altruism. The practice of altruism helps to build trust, cooperation, and solidarity in society, and a trusting, cooperative, and united environment would ultimately allow for more personal freedom.

Here we draw on the Christian philosopher Auguste Comte, who was an innate altruist (Lévy-Bruhl & Harrison, 2018). In the tradition of Christian ethics, altruism is perceived as a moral concept. For Comte, altruism was central in advocating other people's interests, and morality was the triumph of altruism over egoism (Scott & Seglow, 2007). Comte believed that through education a person's self-egoism could evolve and develop to altruism in social relationships. In addition, the development of altruism and sympathy started with the family. Comte's notions of altruism and sympathy have provided a rationale to reexamine the opposition to wearing face masks.

Consider a heartbreaking story that has happened too many times in the United States since the start of the pandemic. An old grandmother with diabetes under long-term care in a hospital or nursing home got infected with coronavirus and died alone without familial companions. This tragedy could have been avoided if we were sympathetic to our elders' health and safety by engaging in simple acts, such as wearing a face mask. Deciding to wear a face mask is a truly altruistic behavior to benefit our families, friends, and even strangers, but it requires considering others' safety as a priority. Temporarily limited liberty is often necessary for public health. Wearing face masks is not an attack on one's freedom; instead, an altruistic perspective would argue that wearing face masks protects us in the short term to keep us, and those around us, alive, which allows for greater freedoms in the long term.

In sum, we believe that altruism is the foundation for sustaining the common good in our societies. During the pandemic crisis, arguments based on altruism could have served as a mediator to balance the tensions between public health and private freedom in the United States. If people could reconsider their personal freedom based on altruism, there is a possibility we could ease the tension between personal freedom and public safety and build a positive relationship between them. In the next section, we discuss two successful cases of national pandemic prevention, New Zealand and Taiwan, to illuminate our argument.

TWO CASES: NEW ZEALAND AND TAIWAN

New Zealand and Taiwan have been recognized as among the most successful countries at containing COVID-19 (Leng & Lemahieu, 2021a; Summers et al., 2020). Although their geographical advantage as island states contributes to mitigating the spread of the virus (Leng & Lemahieu, 2021b), an international comparison study reports that effective leadership, cohesive societies, and trusting relationships between the government and citizens are key factors that allowed countries to outperform others in this global crisis (Leng & Lemahieu, 2021a, 2021b). These factors are characteristics of an altruistic society. Through the lens of altruism, we examine how New Zealand and Taiwan balanced public safety and personal freedom to succeed in pandemic prevention.

New Zealand

New Zealand has shown remarkable achievement in defeating COVID-19. The government successfully eliminated virus transmission twice during 2020. Many factors contributed to their success, including the country's early interventions, targeted testing, surveillance systems (Robert, 2020), and outstanding governmental leadership and communication (Cameron, 2020). Our analysis showcases that New Zealanders' altruism was also an essential factor to success.

Throughout the COVID-19 outbreak, the New Zealand government emphasized that the most effective strategy to defeat the virus relied on societal cooperation. This spirit of cooperation was even more important given that New Zealand has relatively limited medical resources. According to the 2019 Global Health Security Index report, New Zealand is ranked lower and has less than one-seventh the intensive care beds per capita than the United States. The government used several slogans, such as "Unite against COVID-19" (New Zealand Government, n.d.) and "A team of 5 million," to encourage people to be kind, respectful, and caring for one another (Cameron, 2020).

Calling for public altruistic behaviors appeared to work. Cameron (2020) reported that only a small number of people came into contact with COVID-19-infected patients during the first lockdown. This evidence shows that the general public was looking after one another and firmly followed the stay-at-home restriction to lower the possibility of disease transmission in the community. Because people complied with the lockdown regulation, tracking people who were exposed to or infected by COVID-19 became manageable. The government could monitor people who were under quarantine or isolation utilizing traditional methodologies, such as phone calls, during the early outbreak of the pandemic (Cameron, 2020; New Zealand Ministry of Health, n.d.). Hence, the society was able to exit the lockdown within 4 weeks and minimize social costs and harm to the economy.

New Zealanders also strived to help one another during the pandemic. Many citizens volunteered to ship grocery parcels to those vulnerable populations who have limited access to resources (Graham-McLay, 2020). In addition, New Zealand medical experts demonstrated their altruistic behaviors even before the outbreak. They volunteered to build prediction models and serve on governmental advisory boards (Cameron, 2020). During the second outbreak in August 2020, they also helped develop a genomic sequencing–based model to trace outbreak resources, which helped the government defeat the virus a second time without implementing another large-scale lockdown (Geoghegan et al., 2020).

Taiwan

Despite its geographical proximity to China and high number of travelers from that country, Taiwan has been able to contain the spread of COVID-19 within the country. Taiwan is also one of the rare countries that never issued a stay-at-home lockdown order (Cameron, 2020). This substantial achievement has drawn the attention of both global society and the academy.

Many factors contributed to Taiwan's success in combating COVID-19, including timely border control, utilizing big data, information transparency, and the Taiwanese people's shared altruistic values (Taiwan Ministry of Health and Welfare, 2020a; Wang et al., 2020). Even before the pandemic, the Taiwanese people were willing to compromise their privacy and freedom to work with the government for the greater good of society. Since 2007, a law grants the government, in the face of a pandemic, the power to use individual information to contain the virus spread without the consent/authorization of individuals (Chen et al., 2020). This law was a reaction to the 2002–2003 SARS pandemic, during which Taiwan was the country/region with the third-most cases in the world. This tragic experience taught the Taiwanese people the importance of wearing masks and actively cooperating with government policies to promote public health (Taiwan Ministry of Health and Welfare, 2020b, 2020c).

Since March 2020, any citizens returning to Taiwan are subject to mandatory 14-day home quarantine. During the quarantine, people are required to respond to daily check-in text messages and phone calls and have their location tracked by the Digital Fencing Tracking System, a system that allows the government to cooperate with telecom operators to monitor individuals' smartphone signals to determine if individuals leave the quarantine location (O'Flaherty, 2020; Taiwan Ministry of Health and Welfare, 2020d). Moreover, Taiwanese people allow the government to retrieve their travel history from the NHI-MediCloud System (Taiwan Ministry of Health and Welfare, 2020d). The travel information makes it possible for doctors to conduct proactive medical treatments and report suspicious cases to the Central Epidemic Command Center. In addition, to prevent potential community transmission, Taiwanese people must present identification cards, and their location will be recorded in the surveillance system when participating in large gatherings such as baseball games, concerts, and movies in theaters. Although the above policies have considerably limited personal freedom and compromised personal privacy, large-scale protests for the sake of freedom like the ones that occurred in the United States are unheard of in Taiwan. There appears to be a social consensus among Taiwanese society that reaching the common good supersedes personal freedom.

In addition to their compliance with the government's policies, the Taiwanese people's altruistic behaviors were commonly seen during the pandemic. For example, a group of software engineers invested their own time to develop apps to help people track updated locations for government-distributed masks so people could purchase face masks in nearby pharmacy stores (O'Flaherty, 2020). Hotels and small businesses actively collaborated with local and national governments to identify quarantine hotels for travelers who had returned to Taiwan and families who may have contacted patients. Taiwanese people also initiated the "I'm okay, you go first" activity to give up their opportunity of receiving the distributed face masks to people who needed them the most (Taiwan Ministry of Health and Welfare, 2020c).

In sum, New Zealand and Taiwan's successful experiences in containing COVID-19 have taught us how altruism can contribute to public health and a cohesive society. Both the New Zealand and Taiwan governments strived to create a mutually trusting relationship with their citizens during the fight to combat the virus. They held daily press conferences or briefings to communicate the outbreak situation and respond to people's questions (Cameron, 2020; Taiwan Ministry of Health and Welfare, 2020e). The governments showed their commitment to supporting individuals and businesses who may have suffered from the pandemic by providing unemployment compensation, stimulus vouchers, and educational resources.

Because of the transparent communications, people understood the government's efforts and their responsibilities as citizens. As a result, defeating the virus and promoting public health became a common goal and social norm in which society had a shared expectation with the government. Individuals were willing to temporarily give up their freedom and personal privacy by wearing masks, staying at home, and sharing their personal information to promote the common good. New Zealand and Taiwan's cases have shown the potential to find a balance between public health and personal freedom to build a safe and trusting society.

CONCLUSION

Public trust in the U.S. federal government has remained at near-record lows for years. Today, as the United States struggles with a pandemic and economic recession, only 20% of adults trust the federal government to "do the right thing" just about always or most of the time (Pew Research Center, 2020). This phenomenon increases the tensions between public health and private liberty, making it challenging both to eliminate COVID-19 and to prevent the next pandemic or national crisis.

We believe now is the time to seriously rethink the imperative values of American freedom and liberty, especially within social studies curriculum. New Zealand and Taiwan's successful experiences have demonstrated how altruism can contribute to reaching a balance between public health and personal freedom. We believe that altruism lays a strong foundation for human beings to sustain the common good. As such, we also believe it is important to guide students to rethink the meaning of freedom in our social studies curriculum, especially in the wake of the COVID-19 crisis.

While the values of freedom and liberty are fundamental to U.S. democracy, those freedoms should not be framed as absolute within the social studies curriculum. By reexamining civic education through an altruistic lens, students can engage in complex discussions over the relationship between public safety and private freedoms, using the COVID-19 pandemic as a salient case study. Some questions for deliberation could be: What was most important to Americans during the global pandemic? What are the meanings of *freedom* and *liberty*? Did the country successfully balance the tensions between public safety and personal liberty during the pandemic? If not, how can and should the United States move forward based on what we have learned?

Using students' experiences during the pandemic, as well as contrasting those experiences with cases from more altruistic nations such as New Zealand and Taiwan, can help students think more deeply about what is truly valued in society. If the COVID-19 pandemic has taught us anything, it is that a successful society requires all members to be able and willing to think beyond personal interests to consider the common good of all human beings.

REFERENCES

Bayer, R. (2007). The continuing tensions between individual rights and public health: Talking point on public health versus civil liberties. *EMBO Reports, 8*(12), 1099–1103.

Cameron, B. (2020). *Captaining a team of 5 million: New Zealand beats back COVID-19, March–June 2020.* Innovations for Successful Societies, Princeton School of Public & International Affairs. https://successfulsocieties.princeton.edu/publications/captaining-team-5-million-new-zealand-beats-back-covid-19-march-%E2%80%93-june-2020

Chen, C.-M., Jyan, H.-W., Chien, S.-C., Jen, H.-H., Hsu, C.-Y., Lee, P.-C., Lee, C.-F., Yang, Y.-J., Chen, M.-Y., Chen, L.-S., Chen, H.-H., & Chan, C.-C. (2020). Containing COVID-19 among 627,386 persons in contact with the Diamond Princess cruise ship passengers who disembarked in Taiwan: Big data analytics. *Journal of Medical Internet Research, 22*(5), 1–9. https://doi.org/10.2196/19540

Elassar, A. (2020. December 6). *A high school in Texas opened a grocery store for struggling families where good deeds are accepted as payment.* CNN. https://edition.cnn.com/2020/12/06/us/texas-high-school-grocery-store-good-deeds-trnd/index.html?fbclid=IwAR2T6vgB3CusuvAnx57HRwDXq5pX95bdbF_wPEAI2t664eZ82RhXIW9M1WM

Geoghegan, J. L., Ren, X., Storey, M., Hadfield, J., Jelley, L., Jefferies, S., Sherwood, J., Paine, S., Huang, S., Douglas, J., Mendes, F. K., Sporle, A., Baker, M. G., Murdoch, D. R., French, N., Simpson, C. R., Welch, D., Drummond, A. J., Holmes, E. C. . . . de Ligt, J. (2020). Genomic epidemiology reveals transmission patterns and dynamics of SARS-CoV-2 in Aotearoa New Zealand. *Nature Communications, 11*(6351), 1–7. https://doi.org/10.1038/s41467-020-20235-8

Global Health Security Index. (2019). *2019 global health security index.* Author. https://www.ghsindex.org/

Graham-McLay, C (2020, April 21). New Zealand lockdown releases charity spirit as Ardern 'be kind' mantra kicks in. *The Guardian.* https://www.theguardian.com/world/2020/apr/22/new-zealand-lockdown-releases-charity-spirit-as-ardern-be-kind-mantra-kicks-in

Leng, A., & Lemahieu, H. (2021a, January 9). *Covid performance index: Deconstructing pandemic responses.* The Lowy Institute. https://interactives.lowyinstitute.org/features/covid-performance/#region

Leng, A., & Lemahieu, H. (2021b, February 1). *Looking for the keys to Covid "success."* The Interpreter. https://www.lowyinstitute.org/the-interpreter/looking-for-keys-covid-success

Lévy-Bruhl, L., & Harrison, F. (2018). *The philosophy of Auguste Comte.* Sonnenschein.

McKeever, S. (2020, May 22). *Ethicist weighs in on tension between public health and private liberty.* Davidson College. https://www.davidson.edu/news/2020/05/22/ethicist-weighs-tension-between-public-health-and-private-liberty

New Zealand Government. (n.d.). *Unite against Covid 19.* Author. https://covid19.govt.nz

New Zealand Ministry of Health. (n.d.). *Contact tracing for COVID-19.* Author. https://www.health.govt.nz/our-work/diseases-and-conditions/covid-19-novel-coronavirus/covid-19-health-advice-public/contact-tracing-covid-19

NowThis News. (2020, June 26). *Florida's anti-maskers are taking a stand*. Author. https://www.youtube.com/watch?v=433b5RJ9BME

O'Flaherty, K. (2020, November 14). How Taiwan beat Covid-19. *Wired*. https://www.wired.co.uk/article/taiwan-coronavirus-covid-response

Piliavin, J. A., & Charng, H. W. (1990). Altruism: A review of recent theory and research. *Annual Review of Sociology, 16*(1), 27–65. https://doi.org/10.1146/annurev.so.16.080190.000331

Pew Research Center. (2020). *Americans' views of government: Low trust, but some positive performance ratings*. Author. https://www.pewresearch.org/politics/2020/09/14/americans-views-of-government-low-trust-but-some-positive-performance-ratings/

Robert, A. (2020). Lessons from New Zealand's COVID-19 outbreak response. *The Lancet Public Health, 5*(11), e569–e570. https://doi.org/10.1016/S2468-2667(20)30237-1

Scott, N., & Seglow, J. (2007). *Altruism*. McGraw-Hill Education.

Summers, J., Cheng, H. Y., Lin, H. H., Barnard, L. T., Kvalsvig, A., Wilson, N., & Baker, M. G. (2020). Potential lessons from the Taiwan and New Zealand health responses to the COVID-19 pandemic. *The Lancet Regional Health-Western Pacific, 4*, 1–6. https://doi.org/10.1016/j.lanwpc.2020.100044

Taiwan Ministry of Health and Welfare. (2020a.) *Key success factors*. Author. https://covid19.mohw.gov.tw/en/np-4769-206.html

Taiwan Ministry of Health and Welfare. (2020b). *SARS experience*. Author. https://covid19.mohw.gov.tw/en/cp-4770-53679-206.html

Taiwan Ministry of Health and Welfare. (2020c) *Good etiquette of citizens*. Author. https://covid19.mohw.gov.tw/en/cp-4867-53763-206.html

Taiwan Ministry of Health and Welfare. (2020d). *Smart community transmission prevention*. Author. https://covid19.mohw.gov.tw/en/cp-4775-53739-206.html

Taiwan Ministry of Health and Welfare. (2020e). *Open and transparent information*. Author. https://covid19.mohw.gov.tw/en/cp-4772-53699-206.html

Trivers, R. L. (1971). The evolution of reciprocal altruism. *The Quarterly Review of Biology, 46*(1), 35–57. https://doi.org/10.1086/406755

Wang, C. J., Ng, C. Y., & Brook, R. H. (2020). Response to COVID-19 in Taiwan: Big data analytics, new technology, and proactive testing. *Journal of the American Medical Association, 323*(14), 1341–1342. https://doi.org/10.1001/jama.2020.3151

CHAPTER 15

Global Learning for Global Citizenship Education

The Case of COVID-19

Sarah A. Mathews

I first heard about the coronavirus in fall 2019, as media outlets began to report on a new disease impacting the Wuhan region of China. At the time, like many in the United States, I did not see COVID-19 as a threat. We were geographically separated from those impacted by the disease. Fast-forward to February 2020, when I was escorting five undergraduate students completing a student teaching internship in Ecuador as part of a global learning initiative at my university (Florida International University in Miami). I noticed a few isolated passengers with masks, marking my first encounter with the virus's possible risk and spread to the Western Hemisphere.

While in Ecuador, we learned that COVID-19 had reached Italy and was rapidly spreading throughout that nation. I found myself staring at the international news, watching the death count rise. At this point, the virus still seemed like an issue impacting people on the other side of the world. Three weeks later, in early March, my university announced it was transitioning to remote work. At the same time, I was arranging to bring the five students back from South America before the Ecuadorian president restricted air travel. Weeks later, under stay-in-place orders, South Florida surpassed the number of cases and the death toll in New York, becoming the newest coronavirus hotspot in the United States. As a global educator, I should have seen the worldwide spread of this virus coming; yet, like most, I was unprepared for this global pandemic.

In this chapter, I argue that the COVID-19 pandemic has made apparent the importance of placing *global learning for global citizenship* at the heart of social studies education. Global learning emerged from the overarching umbrella of global education, a field deeply rooted in social studies education, with scholars theorizing and advocating for this process as a form of global citizenship education. This approach is an interdisciplinary, problem-solving process drawing from history, science, the humanities, and the social sciences. Unfortunately, there is little evidence of global learning in K–12 settings (Gaudelli & Wylie, 2012; Mitchem et al., 2020).

If we use COVID-19 as an impetus to reimagine social studies education, it is imperative to place global learning for global citizenship at the center of the curriculum. In this chapter, I will outline *global learning* as the process and product of global citizenship education and as a mechanism to respond to and critique globalization. Finally, this chapter makes the argument that the COVID-19 pandemic is the quintessential case study to demonstrate the central role global learning for global citizenship should play in social studies education.

GLOBALIZATION, GLOBAL CITIZENSHIP EDUCATION, AND GLOBAL LEARNING FOR GLOBAL CITIZENSHIP

Global education in social studies emerged during the Cold War period of U.S. history and was used to promote a sense of world-mindedness that encourages empathy and sympathy for people of other nations and cultures (Becker, 1979). Social studies educators began advocating for different citizenship models, suggesting that competence in world citizenship is not distinct from competence in national and local citizenship (Anderson, 1968). Most global educators refer to Robert Hanvey's (1976/2004) scholarship, particularly his notion of a global perspective, as foundational to the conceptualization of global citizenship education (Harshman, 2016, 2017; Landorf et al., 2018; Merryfield & Wilson, 2005; Myers, 2006; Nganga et al., 2020). Hanvey (1976/2004) outlines the following five dimensions of global education: Perspective consciousness, or awareness, and appreciation for other perspectives of the world; cross-cultural awareness or an understanding of global cultural characteristics with a focus on similarities and differences among people; "State of the Planet" awareness; systemic awareness, or the ability to view the world's complex and interdependent systems; and options for participation at the local, national, and international level. Unlike national citizenship, which is related to legal status, global citizenship is a disposition and willingness to assume rights and responsibilities for the good of the world (Steenburgen, 1994).

This scholarship navigated global education away from merely teaching about the world and toward teaching students how to participate as active global citizens. A global citizenship education curriculum would examine issues resulting from globalization and propose that education can help individuals deal with global problems. Global issues include economic gaps between the poor and the rich, racism and discrimination, depletion of resources and environmental degradation resulting from human decisions, violations of human rights, the transmission of infectious diseases, nuclear proliferation, and terrorism (Diaz et al., 1999; Myers, 2006; Parker, 2004;

Suárez-Orozco & Michkiyan, 2016; White & Meyers, 2016). We need the social studies disciplines to address these issues.

The forces of globalization that emerged in the late 20th century have also shaped different approaches to global education. For example, journalist Thomas Friedman (2007) argued that nation-states that do not adapt to globalization, the uncontrollable "electronic herd" (p. 113), are going to be left behind, constricted by the "golden straitjacket" of capitalism (p. 105). According to this approach, graduates would need 21st-century skills for success in a global marketplace (e.g., critical reasoning; information literacy; intercultural competency; the capacity to work collaboratively with others; and ethical, social, and professional responsibility [Association of American Colleges and Universities, 2007; Engel & Siczek, 2018]).

Other scholars critique this notion of globalization's influence on education for promoting Eurocentric, Western, and colonial perceptions of the world. These critiques argue that economic and political theories of globalization often create a binary between the "haves" and the "have nots," placing blame on those nations that have not adapted to global forces (Merryfield & Subedi, 2006). These scholars argue that global education must go beyond teaching about the global Other or training individuals to compete in a global marketplace and move toward efforts to deconstruct globalization's dominant and oppressive discourse surrounding economic and political theories (e.g., Pais & Costa, 2020; Subedi, 2010).

These diverse perspectives suggest that global citizenship education can function as both a response to and a critique of globalization. However, regardless of the motive, scholarship in the field of global citizenship education acknowledges multiplicity in identity (Jaffee, 2016; McCarthy et al., 2003; Rodríguez, 2018) resulting from increased international migration and the influence of multinational corporations (Banks, 2016; Castles, 2004), and redefines traditional notions of what it means to be a "good citizen" (Cary, 2001; Dilworth, 2004; Ladson-Billings, 2004; Torres, 2017).

GLOBAL LEARNING FOR GLOBAL CITIZENSHIP: THE CASE OF COVID-19

Global education for global citizenship is an interdisciplinary concept serving as an "umbrella term that brings together the agendas of different fields of education [including] development education, human rights education, education for peace and conflict resolution, and education for sustainability" (Lourenço, 2018, p. 62). It includes both cognitive tools (e.g., knowledge and skills) and affective factors (e.g., intercultural competence, respect for others, and a disposition for engagement). It can be used to adjust to a perceived "uncontrollable herd" of political and economic forces (Friedman, 2007) by developing 21st-century skills (Engel & Siczek, 2018) or to provide resistance through counternarratives and antiglobalization policies (Pais & Costa, 2020; Subedi, 2010). Therefore, global education for global citizenship is a product of and reaction to globalization's impact through the media, markets, and migration.

Because global citizenship education transcends disciplines, theories, and geographic borders, *global learning* requires an interdisciplinary approach. According to global education scholars Hilary Landorf and Stephanie Doscher (2015), global learning is both a process and a product. They define global learning as "the process of diverse people collaboratively analyzing and addressing problems that transcend borders" (p. 24). Social studies educators recognize that global citizens must draw on the social studies disciplines to address most complex problems transcending borders (e.g., immigration, global warming, foreign relations, health and sanitation, human rights, and the distribution of resources).

In education-speak, we are often tasked with identifying student learning outcomes (i.e., the product of global learning). While one may argue that global learning is never-ending, this process can lead to three global learning outcomes. The first global learning outcome is *global awareness*. At Florida International University (2014), we define global awareness as "knowledge of the interrelatedness of local, global, international, and intercultural issues, trends, and systems" (p. 3). The idea is that it is not enough to point to a location on a map or recite a geographical region's cultural aspects. Global citizens must understand the interconnectedness of complicated systems that add complexity to current issues.

The second global learning outcome is *global perspective*. Global perspective rests on the assumption that one's view of the world is not universally shared and is often shaped by unconscious factors (Hanvey, 1976/2004, p. 5). Developing a global perspective requires the willingness to expand, interrogate, revise, or reaffirm one's perspective based on information from a variety of different sources. Therefore, global citizenship requires the ability to analyze issues from multiple perspectives.

The final global learning outcome is *global engagement*. This outcome includes one's willingness to participate in problem solving at local, national, and global levels (American Council on Education, 2012; Landorf & Doscher, 2015). Engagement forces individuals into spaces that provide them access to diverse perspectives and may facilitate the paradigm shifts necessary for developing a global perspective. Global citizenship requires the ability, the disposition, and the social responsibility to act.

When I teach my "Global Perspectives in Education" course, I shape the syllabus around one essential question: "What role should the United States play in world affairs?" I organize the course using the Jig-Saw method (Obenchain & Morris, 2014) and model it after Brown University's (2018) Choices Curriculum. I assign participants to "home groups" around specific foreign policy responses. Each group member must also become an "expert" on a specific current global issue (e.g., immigration, trade, terrorism, or climate change), and each home group must work together to design a policy statement addressing how the United States should respond to different current issues based on their assigned foreign policy platform.

Once groups have defended their position statements, often in front of a panel simulating a congressional committee, students drop their assigned position. The class then engages in deliberation to pose real-world solutions to real-world problems. This process can be used to theorize global learning as a core component of social studies education while also setting up the argument that the COVID-19 pandemic is the quintessential global learning case study.

What Roles Should the United States Play in the COVID-19 Response?

In my course, I divide students into groups that represent four different foreign policy responses. The first approach represents *isolationism,* or strict noninvolvement with the affairs of other nations. The second group takes on the position of *collective security*, emphasizing mutual collaboration with other countries. The third option, *internationalism,* rests on the notion that one or a few nations act as the world's police officers to promote their national interest or safeguard national security. The final group represents *imperialism,* an approach that exploits weaker entities to benefit one nation's interests. In current times, this exploitation can include political, economic, and cultural aspects. Although I recognize that foreign policy options are not reduced to these approaches and that policy decisions are never cut-and-dried, these four options help students try out various responses to imagine different outcomes.

COVID-19 is the perfect example of a current, interdisciplinary, and complex problem that transcends borders and requires diverse people's perspectives to solicit solutions. We can use this scenario to theorize what it would be like to explore the question, "What role should the United States play in a global pandemic?" As an overarching question, there are many different dimensions to consider when developing a "response to the pandemic" (e.g., migration, economic stability, human rights issues, access to universal health care, and the moral responsibility for others). Citizens can explore these aspects from different positions. In this next section, I focus on two global issues that have been impacted by COVID-19—global migration and human rights—and explore how each foreign policy approach produces different responses to this pandemic.

Movement, Migration, and Immigration

A great example of a nuanced component of COVID-19 involves the impact of migration during the pandemic. One of the most critical decisions involves whether a country will restrict or regulate travel both within and across borders. Should individual countries entirely restrict migration during COVID-19 due to a potential global spread of the virus or selectively choose to allow those who are safe and deemed "necessary" to enter a nation?

From a health safety perspective, closing borders and isolating migration and movement at the micro level appears to be the most obvious choice to contain the virus. Based on this rationale, an isolationist's position would restrict all migration, prohibiting tourists, refugees, and immigrants from entering the country. To some extent, this mirrors U.S. policies in 2020 in which visa processing overseas, as well as the dispensation of most immigration benefits, had virtually stopped (Loweree et al., 2020). Australia and New Zealand also barred entry to anyone who is not a citizen or resident (Letzing, 2020).

Economic analyst Erol Yayboke (2020) pointed out that limitations to migration during a pandemic can restrict the workforce, preventing those who need to work outside of the country from exiting or entering. Governments could use internationalism as an approach to make decisions about migration, allowing the immigration of essential workers such as scientists, doctors, journalists, and government officials. Countries would base these decisions on what is best for an individual nation, with nations holding economic power most likely having access to the most talented group. Canada, for example, has used this strategy to make exemptions for caregivers and seafood processors (Letzing, 2020).

However, an approach that restricts immigration to the most essential or talented population may not consider additional economic fallout. In 2016, the McKinsey Global Institute reported that global migration accounted for over 10% of the world's gross domestic product (Woetzel et al., 2016). Yayboke (2020) also highlighted the negative impact on global food supply chains when agricultural workers cannot migrate. Finally, nations or regions relying on tourism are economically challenged when migration is restricted. As of fall 2020, countries like Thailand have opened their borders and require 14-day quarantines, while others demand proof of a negative COVID-19 test, as is the case in Barbados, Cambodia, Costa Rica, Greece, and the Maldives (World Nomads, 2020). Many of these countries also require travelers to purchase special travel insurance in case they need access to health care services once they arrive.

Even before the world recognized the first case of COVID-19, the global refugee situation had reached humanitarian crisis status. In 2019, the United Nations High Commissioner for Refugees (UNHCR) classified 1% of the world's population as displaced, reporting that over 26 million people held refugee status (Lee & Wehrli, 2020; UNHCR, 2020). Refugee and displacement conditions have worsened, increasing the risk of catching COVID-19, as social distancing recommendations are often impossible to follow, limited water sources make personal hygiene impossible, and aid workers lack resources to contain any outbreak within camps. Aid workers have reported outbreaks at refugee camps in Greece, Bangladesh, the Gaza Strip, and Turkey (Lee & Wehrli, 2020; Letzing, 2020).

In many of these situations, transnational organizations, such as the United Nations (UN) and the World Health Organization (WHO), offer decision-making mechanisms through mutual collaboration. For example, the WHO has issued protocols to test for COVID-19 at borders and publishes weekly epidemiological updates about infection rates. The WHO also facilitates the Country Cooperation Strategy, providing countries with individualized frameworks that consider national and global needs. The United Nations Sustainable Development Cooperation Framework offers a similar structure and guidance, and the UN has proposed policies that provide both social and economic protection during the pandemic. Unfortunately, both cooperative organizations offer frameworks that are not enforceable policies, especially for countries that do not recognize these organizations. The UN and WHO are limited in terms of how they can enforce governance at the global level.

The Interconnectedness of Systems and Impacts on Human Rights

Each of these four foreign policy responses has overall health safety implications, economic impacts, and the potential to violate human rights. For example, a position like isolationism that puts overall health safety at the heart of the decision-making process may restrict all migration as a mechanism to save lives. However, policies enforcing stay-in-place efforts and restricting transregional and transnational movements have led to negative economic trends. When individuals in countries without universal healthcare lose their jobs, they also risk losing their health coverage, straining their economic situation if they catch COVID-19 or have any other health conditions.

The most current Human Rights Watch World Report (2020), based on data from 2019, indicates that no country honored or protected its citizens' universal human rights before the COVID-19 pandemic. As history demonstrates, human rights are often infringed upon during global catastrophes under the guise of national security or to promote "the common good." Different national and international responses to COVID-19 have had this same impact, raising awareness of various preexisting human rights violations.

As authors throughout this book demonstrate, the high infection and death rates of Black, Indigenous, and People of Color (BIPOC), as well as those of lower socioeconomic status, highlight the disproportional access to health care in the United States (see also Kolata, 2020; Ogedegbe et al., 2020). BIPOCs also comprise a large proportion of the "essential workers" delivering much-needed services to sustain both the U.S. and the global economy. These disparities are observed throughout the world, demonstrating human rights issues emerging from global COVID-19 responses.

As already noted, the displaced 1% of the population is also at increased risk of catching COVID-19 through their placement in refugee camps or their inability to find stable living situations. U.S. researchers have also suggested that mass incarceration, a situation in which individuals are confined to buildings and small, densely populated spaces, has contributed to over a million COVID-19 cases in the United States (Weill-Greenberg & Corey, 2020).

In December 2020, pharmaceutical companies announced the approval of COVID-19 vaccines. Governments' decisions about the distribution of these potentially life-saving vaccines are also human rights issues. This announcement raises questions such as: In the wake of COVID-19, should there be universal healthcare for all, including noncitizens and displaced individuals? What criteria should governments use to determine whether immigrants, inmates, or detainees receive vaccines? Who subsidizes the distribution of vaccines?

CONCLUSION

I began this chapter admitting to my own inability to predict the global impact of the COVID-19 pandemic. Although global learning may not prepare individuals to foresee all global issues, it does serve as a decision-making tool to conceptualize and theorize problems often encountered due to globalization. These complex problems require the willingness to seek out information and perspective-take with views that are different from one's own. This process involves media literacy skills such as verifying sources and synthesizing information. A more critical approach requires counternarratives to challenge representations often projected from the Western world or Global North (Harshman, 2017). Finally, this pandemic reminds us that global learning requires a form of action. This action can include choosing politicians based on their response to COVID-19, raising money for or supporting an organization working to address a pandemic-related issue, or even taking the responsibility to wear a mask and social-distance.

Because global learning involves a process of collaboratively analyzing and addressing complex problems, global citizenship education must include cooperative and active learning strategies. Active learning strategies can include Socratic circles, visual thinking strategies, team-based learning, place-based projects, role-playing and simulations, and service learning. As noted earlier in the chapter, I incorporate deliberation into the classroom. According to social studies educators Paula McAvoy and Diana Hess (2013), democratic deliberation "means that when the public discusses policies, knowledge is expanded, self-interest is diminished, and the result is a policy that a community can legitimately expect members to follow" (p. 18). Students are first assigned to a platform and gather information to defend that position. Each group presents their justification of the role it believes the United States should play in foreign affairs. Then we drop our prescribed platform and deliberate on possible real-world solutions that sometimes strengthen, blend, or reject different positions. I used COVID-19 to demonstrate theorizing through different foreign policy approaches related to the role the United States may play in a global pandemic, though many of the other issues presented in this book can also facilitate the global learning process.

The *C3 Framework*, published by the National Council for the Social Studies (2013), supports global learning through the inquiry arc, the use of disciplinary tools to gather and evaluate sources, and a commitment to taking informed action (Harshman, 2016). Unfortunately, global learning is either missing or introduced superficially at the K–12 level (Mitchem et al., 2020) and has a minimal presence in state curricula (Rappaport, 2009). However, the events of 2020, especially the COVID-19 pandemic, have demonstrated that we need to reconceptualize education. Living during this pandemic reveals that we need global citizenship education to prepare students to take action, even if this action is at the local level and involves staying informed and adhering to the Center for Disease Control's recommendations. Finally, COVID-19 has demonstrated that we need, as Landorf and Doscher (2015) suggested, "diverse people working collaboratively to address these problems that transcend borders" (p. 24). Global learning provides individuals the ability to respond to, and hopefully critique, the impacts of globalization. Therefore, reimagining social studies education should place global learning for global citizenship at the center of the curriculum.

REFERENCES

American Council on Education. (2012). *Mapping internationalization on U.S. campuses, 2012 edition*. Author.
Anderson, L. (1968). Education and social science in the context of an emerging global society. In J. M. Becker & H. D. Mehlinger (Eds.), *International dimensions in the social studies* (pp. 78–97). National Council for the Social Studies.
Association of American Colleges and Universities. (2007). *College learning for the new global century*. Author.
Banks, J. A. (2016). Civic education in the age of global migration. In J. A. Banks, M. M. Suárez-Orozco, & M. Ben-Peretz (Eds.), *Global migration, diversity, and civic education: Improving policy and practice* (pp. 29–52). Teachers College Press.
Becker, J. M. (Ed.). (1979). *Schooling for a global age*. McGraw-Hill.
Brown University. (2018). *The U.S. role in a changing world*. The Choices Program.
Cary, L. J. (2001). The refusals of citizenship: Normalizing practices in social educational discourse. *Theory & Research in Social Education, 29*(3), 405–430. https://doi.org/10.1080/00933104.2001.10505949
Castles, S. (2004). Migration, citizenship, and education. In J. A. Banks (Ed.),

Diversity and citizenship education (pp. 17–48). Jossey-Bass.

Diaz, C. F., Massialas, B. G., & Xanthopoulos, J. A. (1999). *Global perspectives for educators*. Allan and Bacon.

Dilworth, P. P. (2004). Multicultural citizenship education: Case studies from social studies classrooms. *Theory and Research in Social Education, 32*(2), 153–186. https://doi.org/10.1080/00933104.2004.10473251

Engel, L. C., & Siczek, M. (2018). A cross-national comparison of international strategies: Global citizenship and the advancement of national competitiveness. *Compare: A Journal of Comparative and International Education, 48*(5), 749–767. https://doi.org/10.1080/03057925.2017.1353408

Florida International University. (2014). *Global learning for global citizenship: Annual impact report of Florida International University's quality enhancement plan*. Author. https://goglobal.fiu.edu/_assets/docs/qep-impact-report-2013-14-final.pdf

Friedman, T. (2007). *The world is flat: A brief history of the twentieth century*. Farrar, Straus, and Giroux.

Gaudelli, W., & Wylie, S. (2012). Global education and issues-centered education. In S. Totten & J. E. Pedersen (Eds.), *Educating about social issues in the 20th and 21st centuries* (pp. 293–320). Information Age.

Hanvey, R. G. (2004). *An attainable global perspective*. The American Forum for Global Education. (Original work published 1976)

Harshman, J. (2016). Critical global competence and C3 in social studies education. *The Social Studies, 107*(5), 160–164. doi:10.1080/00377996.2016.1190915

Harshman, J. (2017). Developing a globally minded, critical media literacy. *Journal of Social Studies Education Research, 8*(1), 69–92.

Human Rights Watch. (2020). *The Human Rights Watch 2020: Events of 2019*. Author. https://www.hrw.org/sites/default/files/world_report_download/hrw_world_report_2020_0.pdf

Jaffee, A. T. (2016). Social studies pedagogy for Latino/a newcomer youth: Toward a theory of culturally and linguistically relevant citizenship education. *Theory & Research in Social Education, 44*(2), 147–183. https://doi.org/10.1080/00933104.2016.1171184

Kolata, G. (2020, December 9). Social inequities explain racial gaps in pandemic, studies find. *The New York Times*. https://www.nytimes.com/2020/12/09/health/coronavirus-black-hispanic.html

Ladson-Billings, G. (2004). Culture versus citizenship: The challenge of racialized citizenship in the United States. In J. A. Banks (Ed.), *Diversity and citizenship education* (pp. 99–126) Jossey-Bass.

Landorf, H., & Doscher, S. (2015). *Defining global learning at Florida International University*. Association of American Colleges and Universities. http://www.aacu.org/diversitydemocracy/2015/summer/landorf

Landorf, H., Doscher, S., & Hardrick, J. (2018). *Making global learning universal: Promoting inclusion and success for all students*. Stylus.

Lee, S., & Wehrli, Z. (2020). *COVID-19 brief: Impact on refugees*. U.S. Global Leadership Coalition. https://www.usglc.org/coronavirus/refugees/

Letzing, J. (2020). *How COVID-19 is throttling vital migration flows*. World Economic Forum. https://www.weforum.org/agenda/2020/04/covid-19-is-throttling-vital-immigration-flows/

Lourenço, M. (2018). Global, international and intercultural education: Three con-
    temporary approaches to teaching and learning. *On the Horizon, 26*(2), 61–71.
    https://doi.org/10.1108/OTH-06-2018-095

Loweree, J., Reichlin-Melnick, A., & Ewing, W. (2020). *The impact of COVID-19
    on noncitizens and across the U.S. immigration system.* American Immigra-
    tion Council. https://www.americanimmigrationcouncil.org/research/impact-
    covid-19-us-immigration-system

McAvoy, P., & Hess, D. (2013). Classroom deliberation in an era of political polar-
    ization. *Curriculum Inquiry, 43*(1), 14–47. https://doi.org/10.1111/curi.12000

McCarthy, C., Giardina, M. D., Harewood, S. J., & Park, J. K. (2003). Contesting
    culture: Identity and curriculum dilemmas in the age of globalization, postcolo-
    nialism, and multiplicity. *Harvard Educational Review. 73*(30), 449–465.

Merryfield, M. M., & Subedi, B. (2006). Decolonizing the mind for world-centered
    global education. In E. W. Ross (Ed.), *The social studies curriculum: Purposes,
    problems, and possibilities* (pp. 283–295). State University of New York Press.

Merryfield, M. M., & Wilson, A. (2005). *Social studies and the world: Teaching
    global perspectives. NCSS Bulletin 103.* National Council for the Social Studies.

Mitchem, M., Shatara, H., Kim, Y., & Gaudelli, W. (2020). Global education in
    neoliberal times: A comparative case study of two schools in New York. *Journal
    of International Social Studies, 10*(1), 92–112.

Myers, J. P. (2006). Rethinking the social studies curriculum in the context of glo-
    balization: Education for global citizenship in the U.S. *Theory & Research in
    Social Education. 34*(3), 370–394. https://doi.org/10.1080/00933104.2006.10
    473313

National Council for the Social Studies. (2013). *The college, career, and civic life
    (C3) framework for social studies state standards.* Author.

Nganga, L., Roberts, A., Kambutu, J., & James, J. (2020). Examining pre-service
    teachers' preparedness and perceptions about teaching controversial issues in
    social studies. *The Journal of Social Studies Research, 44*(1), 77–90. https://doi.
    org/10.1016/j.jssr.2019.08.001

Obenchain, K. M., & Morris, R. V. (2014). *50 social studies strategies for K–8
    classrooms.* Pearson.

Ogedegbe, G., Ravenell, J., Adhikar, S., Butler, M., Cook, T., Francois, F., Iturrate,
    E., Jean-Louis, G., Jones, S. A., Onakomaiya, D., Petrilli, C. M., Pulgarin, C.,
    Regan, S., Reynolds, H., Seixas, A., Volpicelli, F. M., & Horwitz, L. I. (2020).
    Assessment of racial/ethnic disparities in hospitalization and mortality in pa-
    tients with Covid-19 in New York City. *JAMA Network Open, 3*(12), 1–14.
    https://doi.org/10.1001/jamanetworkopen.2020.26881

Pais, A., & Costa, M. (2020). An ideology critique of global citizenship education.
    Critical Studies in Education, 61(1), 1–16. https://doi.org/10.1080/17508487.
    2017.1318772

Parker, W. C. (2004). Diversity, globalization, and democratic education: Curricu-
    lum possibilities. In J. A. Banks (Ed.), *Diversity and citizenship education* (pp.
    433–458). Jossey Bass.

Rapoport, A. (2009). A forgotten concept: Global citizenship education and state
    social studies standards. *Journal of Social Studies Research, 33*(1), 91–113.

Rodríguez, N. N. (2018). From margins to center: Developing cultural citizenship
    education through the teaching of Asian American history. *Theory & Research*

in Social Education, 46(4), 528–573. https://doi.org/10.1080/00933104.2018.1432432

Steenburgen, B. (1994). *The condition of citizenship.* Sage.

Suárez-Orozco, M. M., & Michkiyan, M. (2016). Introduction: Education for citizenship in the age of globalization and mass migration. In J. A. Banks, M. M. Suárez-Orozco, & M. Ben-Peretz (Eds.), *Global migration, diversity, and civic education: Improving policy and practice* (pp. 1–28). Teachers College Press.

Subedi, B. (2010). Introduction: Reading the world through critical global perspectives. In B.Subedi (Ed.), *Critical global perspectives* (pp. 1–18). Information Age.

Torres, C. A. (2017). *Theoretical and empirical foundations of critical global citizenship education* (Vol. 1). Taylor & Francis.

United Nations High Commissioner for Refugees. (2020). *Figures at a glance.* Author. https://www.unhcr.org/figures-at-a-glance.html

Weill-Greenberg, E., & Corey, E. (2020, December 15). *Researchers estimate mass incarceration contributed to more than half a million additional cases of Covid-19 over the summer.* The Appeal. https://theappeal.org/covid-19-community-spread-mass-incarceration-prison-policy-institute-report/

White, G., & Myers, J. P. (2016). The changing role of citizenship education in a globalizing society. In J. A. Banks, M. M. Suárez-Orozco, & M. Ben-Peretz (Eds.), *Global migration, diversity, and civic education: Improving policy and practice* (pp. 179–201). Teachers College Press.

Woetzel, J., Madgavkar, A., Rifai, K., Mattern, F., Bughin, J., Manyika, J., Elmasry, T., diLodovico, A., & Hasyagar, A. (2016). *Global migration's impact and opportunity.* McKinsey Global Institute. https://www.mckinsey.com/featured-insights/employment-and-growth/global-migrations-impact-and-opportunity

World Nomads. (2020). *COVID-19 travel alert: Which countries have open borders?* Author. https://www.worldnomads.com/travel-safety/worldwide/worldwide-travel-alerts

Yayboke, M. (2020, March). *Five ways COVID-19 is changing global migration.* Center for Strategic and International Studies. https://www.csis.org/analysis/five-ways-covid-19-changing-global-migration

CHAPTER 16

Teaching Federalism

Investigating Federal vs. State Power in the Wake of a Pandemic

Karon LeCompte, Brooke Blevins, and Kevin R. Magill

The year 2020 will long be remembered as a year of momentous challenges. COVID-19 surfaced in the United States, and our nation's response to the disease has been controversial and inconsistent, revealing deep fissures in our nation's infrastructure and political structures. This chapter illuminates the concept of federalism and how the balance between federal and state authority manifested during the pandemic. We explore how federal and state governments have collaborated and collided in their responses to COVID-19. Additionally, we discuss ideas for teaching the concept of federalism using responses to the COVID-19 pandemic.

Federalism is a way of organizing a nation's government in which different levels of government share authority over the same land and people (Fraga, 2012). It is touted in the social studies curriculum as one of the most significant aspects of American democracy. However, the COVID-19 pandemic has exposed significant fractures and limitations in this system of government, particularly within our polarized political environment.

Structural issues, often linked to our federalized system, have limited the U.S. response to the pandemic. Reactions to the COVID-19 pandemic from federal and state governments have been inconsistent due to the overlap in jurisdictions and to mixed messages, often divided along political lines. Confounding the situation is that our nation's first defense against the virus, our public health service, "is divided among 2,684 state and local public health departments" (Price, 2020, p. 1). Although the federal government issues some health guidelines, states can choose to ignore those rules or propose other measures. Such flexibility makes creating a national strategy all the more complicated (Fernandez, 2020). Moreover, the federal government has fueled conspiracies and used the virus to sway public opinion for political gain rather than working to protect Americans.

We proceed by first examining the legacy and history of federalism as well as how it functioned during the pandemic. We then provide considerations for teaching federalism against the backdrop of the COVID-19 pandemic.

THE LEGACY OF FEDERALISM

The primary question under federalism is, "Who has the power?" While federalism is one of the basic principles of the U.S. Constitution, it is also a complex concept to understand. Our current conception of federalism was born out of the failure of the Articles of Confederation to provide for a strong national government. Approved in 1777, the Articles of Confederation bound the states together in a loose "league of friendship" that allowed the states to retain nearly all governmental power. The Articles of Confederation created a confederacy in which states essentially acted as independent entities linked together for limited purposes, such as national defense. State governments had the sovereignty to rule within their territories, while the national government had few powers. In 1787, the Constitutional Convention would convene to consider the need for a stronger national government, but there was disagreement on how strong it should be.

The Federalist framers argued that a new, stronger federal government would provide three significant advantages. First, it would ensure that changes to government or laws would not swing based on popular whims. Second, it would require that power remained with a privileged, educated few (without the tyranny of a king). Third, it would allow for a centralized response to concerns shared by states. Decisions in this system would be made "by passing them through the medium of a chosen body of citizens, whose wisdom may best discern the true interest of their country" (Hamilton et al., 1787/2021, para. 16) and thus "protect[ing] the minority of the opulent against the majority" (Farrand, 1987, pp. 430–431). These Federalist foundations would also allow Alexander Hamilton to establish U.S. financial systems that provided long-term financial stability to the country by assuming and consolidating some parts of state debts. The new federal government would work across state lines to provide a centralized mechanism for quick federal responses to shared concerns. In 1789, the Articles of Confederation were replaced with the U.S. Constitution, which established a stronger national government and the concept of federalism as we now know it.

Given these foundations, federalism is a system of government in which two levels of government control the same territory, with the national government having responsibility for broader governance of these areas and states and cities governing issues of local concern. The relationship between and power given to federal and state governments was central to the framers' thinking as they articulated an amended structure of government in the U.S. Constitution. Not only did the Constitution divide authority between national and state governments, but the framers also established a system of checks and balances to separate powers within the national government. These divisions of power were supposed to create clear lines of responsibility for each level of government by promoting local control and preventing the concentration of power within one level of government. The U.S. Constitution established a system of "dual sovereignty" in which authority is shared between the federal and state governments, with each entity providing checks for the other.

In the U.S. Constitution, enumerated or expressed powers are granted to the federal government in Article 1, Section 8, and include the following: Establish a postal system, coin money, maintain the military, declare war, set standards for weight and measurement, regulate trade, regulate copyright and patents, and conduct diplomacy. In addition, the federal government has implied powers to make laws that are necessary and proper for carrying out the express powers. Matters that are not articulated in either the federal government's expressed or implied powers are reserved for the states to regulate. The Tenth Amendment of the Constitution provides these reserved powers to states: "The powers not delegated to the United States by the Constitution nor prohibited by it to the States, are reserved to the States respectively, or to the people."

States, then, have the right to oversee a number of essential functions, such as establishing local government, creating educational standards, conducting elections, overseeing civil and criminal law, and regulating trade within the state. Reserved powers allow states to legislate and regulate to protect their citizens' health, safety, and welfare. The federal and state governments share some powers, such as taxing, regulating elections, building roads, establishing courts, and providing for citizens' welfare; these are known as concurrent powers.

Making federalism even more complex is the fact that federalism in the United States has gone through several phases during which the relationship between the national and state governments has varied. Federalism grew from specific and well-defined powers that belonged to the national government and state governments, often described as the "layer cake" model, to a model in which the powers of the national and state governments became more interwoven, or similar to a "marble cake" (Grodzins, 1966). The following section explores the historical changes in the concept of federalism and how current conceptions of federalism may have complicated national and state responses to COVID-19.

PHASES OF FEDERALISM

The early years of federalism were marked by the constant struggle between national and state powers as the national government sought to establish its role within the newly created federal design. The newly defined powers of the federal government often provoked states to resist in order to protect their interests (see, for example, the *McCulloch v. Maryland* [1819] and *Gibbons v. Ogden* [1824] Supreme Court cases). During the early phases of federalism, the supremacy clause (Article VI, Paragraph 2, of the U.S. Constitution) that establishes the Constitution, and federal law, as supreme over state laws and constitutions was the subject of much debate. The Civil War was the ultimate showdown between national and state power and ultimately helped to solidify the power of the national government.

Dual federalism (1870–1930) reified the legal conception of "states" and a "national" government, treating each as if it were a discrete political actor. In the era of dual federalism, both levels of government stayed within their jurisdictional spheres. Dual federalism had four main characteristics: The national government had only enumerated powers; the purposes that the national government promoted constitutionally were few; within their respective "spheres," the two governments were equal in sovereignty; and the relations between national and state governments was one of tension and not collaboration (Corwin, 1962).

Under dual federalism, programs and authority were clearly divided amongst the federal, state, and local governments (Grodzins, 1966). The dominance of the national government in areas like military, banking, foreign policy, antitrust laws, fair-trade practices, and direct regulation of railroads were markers of a new emergence of power at the national level and led to the development of federal agencies. As the number of agencies grew, the national government grew. Although the national government retained regulatory functions, operational functions happened at the state and local levels (Walker, 2000).

Cooperative federalism grew out of necessity and in response to the Great Depression. During the era of cooperative federalism (1930–1970), national and state governments coordinated efforts to address national problems. Cooperative federalism blurred the lines of power between state and national governments (Grodzins, 1966). During this era, the federal government became active in policy areas previously handled by the states. While the era of cooperative federalism led to a broadening of federal powers in concurrent and state policy domains, it was also the era of deepening coordination between the states and the federal government. Nowhere was this clearer than with respect to the social welfare and social insurance programs created during the New Deal and Great Society eras, most of which were administered by both state and federal authorities and were jointly funded.

The 1970s ushered in an era of New Federalism that attempted to decentralize policy management and reduce the increasing federal power that emerged during cooperative federalism (Marbach et al., 2006). The Nixon and Reagan administrations primarily sought to restore states' power in policy areas into which the federal government had moved during the previous 40 years. New Federalism was premised on the idea that the decentralization of policies enhances administrative efficiency, reduces overall public spending, and improves policy outcomes. Reagan coupled New Federalism with austerity politics leading to the privatization of certain services and the relaxing of select government regulations.

However, in between the Nixon and Reagan administrations, Jimmy Carter was engaged in more cooperative federalism efforts to revitalize urban communities that relied on "new partnerships" and cooperation between the federal, state, and local governments. In addition, Carter established the Department of Education, making it a cabinet-level department. In so doing, he expanded the federal role in education, a power that was traditionally reserved for the states.

Since the 9/11 attacks, the United States has experienced increasing centralization of national power with the establishment of agencies and policies designed to protect the health, safety, and well-being of its citizens, such as the establishment of intergovernmental agencies such as the Department of Homeland Security and Transportation Security Administration and new federal policies in areas of education (e.g., No Child Left Behind) and healthcare (e.g., the Affordable Care Act). There are numerous intergovernmental task forces or ad hoc groups, often resulting in a mismatch of conflicting powers (Turnock & Atchison, 2002). However, New Federalism is still alive and well, as evidenced by the current response to the COVID-19 pandemic; the federal government refused to make national policy decisions, leaving the states to determine their responses to the pandemic.

FEDERALISM AND COVID-19

When the pandemic hit, the Trump administration failed to announce a clear national strategy regarding COVID-19, instead leaving decision-making largely to state and local governments (Rozell & Wilcox, 2020). Some state and local leaders relied on the Constitution's federal structure by making decisions to close schools and nonessential businesses, implement stay-at-home orders, and provide funding relief for food and housing. Others resisted such measures, waiting for more direction and more precise federal health and safety authority guidelines. In an article in *The Atlantic*, Professor of American History Gary Gerstle (2020) noted, "In a crisis defined by erratic leadership in Washington, D.C., the states, as much out of desperation as by design, find themselves asserting long-dormant powers. A new era of federalism is unfolding before our eyes." This patchwork of state-based responses has significant implications for our country's long-term health (Knauer, 2020).

As state authorities responded to the COVID-19 crisis, we witnessed the polarized political environment's impact on these decisions. Decisions about how and when to "shut down," "open up," and "return to normal" often followed party affiliation, with "red" and "blue" states making markedly different decisions (Kettl, 2020). Decisions related to lessening the spread of the virus were confounded by other ideological considerations such as economics, health and safety, individual rights, and educational access, to name a few. Many people, including state and local leaders, struggled to make sense of the ideological tensions associated with freedom, liberty, and civic responsibility. For some, the idea of freedom is to exist as a healthy citizen, which for others comes into ideological conflict with the freedom to make choices about wearing masks or socially distancing. These ideological tensions and differing responses made the enforcement of specific policies difficult.

Many states required limits on social gatherings, added other states to travel quarantine lists, issued overnight curfews, mandated face masks, and encouraged citizens to stay home (Hauck & Woodyard, 2020). Some states also included rules like only takeout and delivery service for restaurants, closure of or limited capacity for gyms and salons, and reduced capacity in retail businesses. Many also chose to implement tiered rules based on the severity of the outbreak in a given county. Certain states even required local governments to enforce the rules or risk being fined.

In the midst of these state-based responses, the Trump administration chose to continue with deregulation and austerity policies, which considerably weakened our ability to combat COVID-19 through a national strategy. In just the first few weeks of the Biden administration, there were considerably more national leadership and policy decisions aimed at managing the COVID-19 crisis at the national level. Some of these responses came as executive orders, and others were bills considered by Congress. Below, we describe examples of various federal, state, and local responses to the pandemic as a way of highlighting the tension that occurred with respect to federalism.

State of Emergencies

Several federal acts ensure that the President has access to resources to help the nation address a public health crisis. Invoking a state of emergency at the federal level gave the President emergency powers via executive order under the Defense Production Act. In essence, this power allowed "the federal government to deliver virus response funds and other assistance to state and local governments in an effort to reduce the spread of the virus and protect the economy against its mounting impact" (National Council of State Legislatures, 2020, para. 1). On March 13, 2020, President Trump invoked the National Emergencies Act, which allowed him to temporarily waive or modify certain requirements of the Medicare, Medicaid, and State Children's Health Insurance programs. The Public Health Service Act established the Coronavirus Task Force and issued policy modifications and waivers in support of response efforts to assist the health care community. The Defense Production Act allowed President Trump to ask private companies to prioritize and execute government contracts to allocate materials, services, and facilities to battle the virus. The Stafford Act COVID-19 emergency declaration provided states with professionals with expertise in operations, logistics, planning, and recovery to assess conditions. It also provided seven billion dollars in loans and support to small businesses, authorized the Treasury and Internal Revenue Service to ease citizens' tax burdens for a year, and required states to declare a state of emergency to access additional federal funds (National Council of State Legislatures, 2020, para. 1).

States also have the power to implement certain rules when a state of emergency is issued. For example, in early March 2020, Governor Mike DeWine of Ohio issued an executive order declaring a state of emergency. Through this order, he authorized the Ohio Department of Health to implement rules designed to protect the general public. The Health Department then issued an order requiring people to stay at home unless engaged in essential work or activities.

Stay-at-Home Orders

In March 2020, California became the first state to issue a statewide shelter-in-place order after six Bay Area counties had already issued local orders. At the same time, other states such as Texas, Florida, and Georgia, all red-leaning states, left decisions for stay-at-home orders up to local municipalities, creating a patchwork response plan. Not only did contiguous counties implement varied responses, so did contiguous states such as North Carolina, which issued a stay-at-home order, and South Carolina, which did not. This fractured response plan meant that residents who lived just a few miles from one another experienced different restrictions based on their county or city response plan.

States differed sharply in the timing, extent, and duration of lockdown orders and exceptions, and some never issued stay-at-home orders at all. As the pandemic wore on, some states and local governments relaxed or removed stay-at-home orders based on economic or political reasons, such as getting businesses and schools back open. To complicate matters, President

Trump often encouraged those in states with lockdown measures, such as Michigan and Wisconsin, both with Democratic governors, to reject such policies. As infection numbers fluctuated, some states reissued stay-at-home orders, curfews, and gathering size restrictions.

Mask Mandates

Despite evidence from the Centers for Disease Control and Prevention (CDC) about the efficacy of mask-wearing in preventing the spread of COVID-19, many states were slow to adopt such statewide mandates. At the time this chapter was written, 38 states had adopted statewide mask mandates, but many states allowed individual municipalities to exempt out of these mandates based on local infection rates. For instance, in July 2020, the governor of Kansas issued an executive order requiring wearing masks in public spaces, but county authorities could opt out of this policy. After July 3, COVID-19 incidence decreased in 24 counties with mask mandates but continued to increase in 81 counties without mask mandates.

When masks were mandated, they were not always enforced with the same rules. For example, some states required masks for children under 10, and others did not. Some states required masks when outdoors and not socially distanced, while others only mandated them indoors. At the federal level, the Trump administration failed to issue a national mask mandate, and administration members often refused to wear masks in social gatherings, including an event held in honor of the nomination of Supreme Court Justice Amy Coney Barrett at which numerous White House officials, including President Trump, were infected with COVID-19. In one of his first executive orders, President Biden issued a mandate requiring face masks be worn inside buildings and on lands controlled by the federal government, as well as during interstate travel aboard trains, buses, and planes. While Biden's policy did not have the authority to change masking policies in individual states or cities, Biden did call on governors, local city leaders, business leaders, and others to implement masking policies and social distancing measures to control the spread of COVID-19.

Testing

The United States saw a slow response to COVID-19 testing in comparison to other developed nations despite passing the Families First Coronavirus Response Act in March 2020. The bill ensured that COVID-19 tests were free to anyone in the United States without a co-pay. However, former White House chief of staff Mick Mulvaney called the U.S. coronavirus testing capabilities at the time "simply inexcusable" because, initially, certain people could not qualify for a test, the tests took too long to report results, and there were not enough tests (Vazquez, 2020). The ideological-political battles, misinformation, and failure to work with the World Health Organization caused increased difficulties, which saw the United States lag behind most developed nations in testing. This lag meant that states were also slow to respond with critical supplies and robust testing plans. Further, states tested at dramatically different rates and reported infections and deaths differently, making nationwide inferences difficult.

As the pandemic continued, testing by both private and public entities increased, though few testing mandates have been ordered. Backed by the federal government's power, the Americans with Disabilities Act allowed employers to require mandatory employee medical testing if interacting closely with people is a business necessity. Therefore, many employers have begun requiring weekly COVID-19 tests when employees are at a reasonable risk of infection. Effective January 26, 2021, flying internationally requires passengers to demonstrate that they are COVID-19–free by documenting that they have taken a test within 3 days of departure or showing proof of recovery from the virus within the last 90 days when trying to enter the United States.

Vaccines

The federal government implemented "Operation Warp Speed" to "produce and deliver 300 million doses of safe and effective vaccines with the initial doses available by January 2021, as part of a broader strategy to accelerate the development, manufacturing, and distribution of COVID-19 vaccines, therapeutics, and diagnostics" (U.S. Department of Health and Human Services, 2020, para. 1). To achieve this goal, the federal government chose drug companies, provided funding, and expedited trials to support vaccine development and manufacturing. Unfortunately, while Operation Warp Speed called for 20 million vaccines to be distributed by the end of 2020, only about 2 million vaccines had been taken by the end of the year, largely because the federal government failed to provide clear direction and funding for successful and far-reaching vaccine distribution.

While the CDC issued guidance about vaccine priority, including prioritizing health care workers, first responders, and the elderly, states could develop their own vaccine priorities. For example, Florida vaccinated long-term care residents prior to first responders. In other states such as New York, teachers were considered frontline workers and were vaccinated in Phase 1B, while in other states, like Texas, they were not. In some states, people waited in incredibly long lines for a chance to receive the vaccine, while other states were more strategic and created online waiting lists. In some states, confusion over vaccine priorities and failure to administer doses in a timely fashion led to the disposal of expired vaccines.

Schooling

As states returned to school in Fall 2020, the politically polarized environment played out as red and blue states made different decisions about students returning to face-to-face instruction. In general, red states and counties were quicker to reopen schools than blue-leaning states and counties. A Brookings Institution report found that there was no relationship "between school districts' reopening decisions and their county's new COVID-19 cases per capita," but rather, "Districts located in counties that supported Trump are much more likely to have announced plans to open in person" (Valant, 2020, para. 7). Districts were also faced with pressure from the Trump administration to open schools or risk losing funding (Gaudiano et al., 2020).

Complicating matters is the fact that school boundaries are not always the same as county boundaries, which raises questions about who has jurisdiction to make decisions about school reopenings. Because of local decision-making, one school district may have opened for in-person learning, while another, adjacent school district may have elected to learn remotely. Additionally, in some states, private and religious schools were exempt from county and state regulations and could make their own decisions about reopening. In some instances, wealthier families pulled their students from public schools with remote instruction and put them into private schools with in-person instruction.

Beyond students' health, the pandemic illuminated the longstanding educational divide between those with the best educational opportunities, often wealthy, White children, and those without, mainly low-socioeconomic students of color. Parents, teachers, staff, state, and national governments all became entangled in a complex, politically polarized struggle. Many low-income students suffered due to the lapse of in-person time in school, while other children in rural areas or children who did not have access to technology fell behind because they did not have adequate Internet or computers. While wealthier families may have had the ability to have a parent at home or hire someone to help with remote instruction, many students from low-income families found themselves navigating remote instruction by themselves as their parents went to work.

The Biden administration vowed to reopen the majority of elementary and middle schools for in-person learning during his first 100 days in office. However, there was confusion within the administration about what counts as "in-person" learning (New York Post Editorial Board, 2021). The task of reopening schools is complicated by the fact that the federal government has little jurisdiction in schooling decisions. School districts operate and are funded differently from one another, have differing resources, and are impacted by differing political ideologies.

COVID-19 AND THE *RETEACHING* OF FEDERALISM

The complex and shifting conceptions of federalism are rarely explored as currently conceptualized in history textbooks. Instead, federalism is uncritically promoted as a pillar of American democracy without examination of the strength and weakness of this concept and how it has evolved over time. Therefore, we suggest that federalism should be approached in a more critical fashion that explores both its affordances and constraints. COVID-19 serves as a robust case about which to teach the nuances of federalism. Teaching about COVID-19 allows teachers and students to examine the complex matrix of federal and state responsibility and explore how federalism may prove problematic when addressing issues of national health. Critical inspection of federalism, including our fascination with it and our reliance on this structure of government to protect our nation's freedom and health, is a worthwhile endeavor. It also allows us to reconsider our nation's values and civic approaches.

There are several elements to focus on when teaching federalism in a more nuanced fashion. First, teachers can focus on the complex ecology of the political system. Students and teachers need to understand who has the power to do what, what the implications of these power structures are for citizens, and how the private sector and international relationships influence power dynamics and social relations. The examples of federal and state responses described above provide evidence of federalism's complex structural, logistical, and political realities. Teachers will also want to consider the ideological, ethical, and communal aspects associated with the federalist response. A teacher might begin with the premise that in a democracy, the federal government's primary function is to serve the people's will and tackle issues that individuals, private industry, local governments, and state governments cannot. Federalist interventions should then support the nation's general preparedness for the nation's welfare and ensure that policies exist to combat issues of broad and grand concern like global warming, pollution, and the COVID-19 outbreak.

Second, we argue that understanding federalism's history and its use as a tool of political power is vital to discussing its place within a constitutional republic with democratic values. Achieving this level of understanding involves the study of political decision-making, historical/economic contextualization, and our values as a community, state, and nation. Because federalism is, in essence, the power to decide who controls public capital (e.g., transportation and healthcare systems), we need to teach students about how and why political battles occur. Throughout U.S. history, contentions over control of public capital have defined the ways citizens understood the government and society.

Teaching federalism might also include considering its purpose, history, context, and design as a prerequisite for understanding its complexities and constraints. The lack of a national response to COVID-19 has illuminated the social and economic inequities in our way of life. The lack of coordinated national response has disproportionately affected the poor; Black, Indigenous, and People of Color; those with preexisting conditions or disabilities; and the elderly. Studying the differential impact of COVID-19 on various groups can help students understand the implications of an often-inequitable system and how the system's interventions may or may not work to meet citizens' needs. This is not to say that federalism is bad, but rather that political values are amplified through federalist interventions and in the ways in which they are used as tools for political power.

Third, we argue that teachers should consider utilizing inquiry-based case studies to help nuance the teaching of federalism. Inquiry allows students to see both the complexity of federalism and how national, state, and local entities might operate given the particular case presented. Self-directed, structured inquiries require that students explore foundational knowledge about federalism, how it has been carried out in the past, and how it might be carried out in other situations. Such educational experiences can foster understanding about federalism as well as help students envision how they would like the system to function for citizens. Student inquiry related to aspects of the COVID-19 pandemic, such as school opening/closing policies, eviction protections, or international travel restrictions, can help students explore elements of federalist interventions that are most important to them while also helping them to learn about federalist structures. Students can make reasoned arguments about public policy, capital allocation, and shared decision-making through inquiry.

CONCLUSION

In theory, federalism is a system that can make addressing issues of more universal concern more efficient than what a few individuals can accomplish alone; however, the pandemic has highlighted how this system can break down and make addressing issues more difficult. Our hope is that helping students understand both the affordances and constraints of the federalist system, as well as the implications of such a system, will help young people develop a deeper understanding of a system of government that impacts their own civic participation and the welfare of their community.

REFERENCES

Corwin, E. S. (1962). A constitution of powers and modern federalism. In R. G. McCloskey (Ed.), *Essay in constitutional law* (pp. 188–189). Knopf.

Farrand, M. (1987). *The records of the Federal Convention of 1787.* Yale University Press.

Fernandez, A. (2020, May 4). *Covid-19: A case study into American federalism.* FIU Law. https://law.fiu.edu/2020/05/04/Covid-19-a-case-study-into-american-federalism/

Fraga, L. R. (2012). *United States government: Principles in practice.* Holt McDougal.

Gaudiano, N., Perez, J., & Stratford, M. (2020, July 09). *Trump threatens to cut federal funds from schools that don't reopen.* Politico. https://www.politico.com/news/2020/07/08/trump-schools-reopening-federal-funding-352311

Gerstle, G. (2020, May 06). The new federalism. *The Atlantic.* https://www.theatlantic.com/ideas/archive/2020/05/new-federalism/611077/

Grodzins, M. (1966). *The American system: A new view of government in the United States.* Rand McNally.

Hamilton, A., Jay, J., & Madison, J. (2021). *Federalist Papers No. 10.* (Original work published 1787). https://billofrightsinstitute.org/primary-sources/federalist-no-10

Hauck, G., & Woodyard, C. (2020, December 08). New coronavirus restrictions: Here's what your state is doing to combat rising cases and deaths. *USA Today.* https://www.usatoday.com/story/news/nation/2020/11/13/Covid-restrictions-state-list-orders-lockdowns/3761230001/

Kettl, D. F. (2020). States divided: The implications of American federalism for Covid-19. *Public Administration Review, 80*(4), 595–602. https://doi.org/10.1111/puar.13243

Knauer, N. J. (2020). The Covid-19 pandemic and federalism: Who decides? *New York University Journal of Legislation and Public Policy, 23*(1). http://dx.doi.org/10.2139/ssrn.3599239

Marbach, J. R., Katz, E., & Smith, T. E. (2006). *Federalism in America: An encyclopedia.* Greenwood Press.

National Council of State Legislatures. (2020, March 25). *President Trump declares state of emergency for Covid-19.* Author. https://www.ncsl.org/ncsl-in-dc/publications-and-resources/president-trump-declares-state-of-emergency-for-covid-19.aspx

New York Post Editorial Board. (2021, February 17). Get schools open, President Biden. *New York Post.* https://nypost.com/2021/02/17/get-schools-open-president-biden/

Price, P. J. (2020, May 4). A coronavirus quarantine in America could be a giant legal mess. *The Atlantic.* https://www.theatlantic.com/ideas/archive/2020/02/coronavirus-quarantine-america-could-be-giant-legal-mess/606595/

Rozell, M. J., & Wilcox, C. (2020). Federalism in a time of plague: How federal systems cope with pandemic. *The American Review of Public Administration, 50*(6–7), 519–525. https://doi.org/10.1177/0275074020941695

Turnock, B., & Atchison, C. (2002). Governmental public health in the United States: The implications of federalism. *Health Affairs, 21*(6), 68–78. https://doi.org/10.1377/hlthaff.21.6.68

U.S. Department of Health and Human Services. (2020, December 21). *Fact sheet: Explaining Operation Warp Speed.* Author. https://prevention.nih.gov/news-events/news-releases/2020/06/fact-sheet-explaining-operation-warp-speed

Valant, J. (2020, July 29). *School reopening plans linked to politics rather than public health*. Brookings Institution. https://www.brookings.edu/blog/brown-center-chalkboard/2020/07/29/school-reopening-plans-linked-to-politics-rather-than-public-health/

Vazquez, M. (2020, July 13). *Ex-WH chief of staff calls U.S. coronavirus testing capabilities 'simply inexcusable'*. CNN. https://www.cnn.com/2020/07/13/politics/mick-mulvaney-coronavirus-testing/index.html

Walker, D. B. (2000). *The rebirth of federalism: Slouching toward Washington*. Chatham House.

CHAPTER 17

What Do We Leave Behind?

Assessment of Student Learning in Social Studies Post–COVID-19

Stephanie van Hover, Michael Gurlea,
Tyler Woodward, David Hicks, and David Gerwin

The COVID-19 pandemic disrupted public schooling in myriad ways, including how social studies is assessed. State after state cancelled high-stakes testing and asked districts and teachers to determine what students learned and how they met the expectations outlined in state policy documents. The cancellation of high-stakes tests and, in some instances, of grades altogether offers the opportunity to pause and reflect on the essential question that education scholar Gert Biesta (2009) raised: Are we "valuing what we measure, or measuring what we value?" (p. 43). Assessment informs instruction; how students are assessed and the stakes attached to those assessments matter a great deal *and* endorse a certain set of values surrounding social studies. Historically, state-level assessment has reified (and valued) students' ability to regurgitate factual content on forced-choice multiple-choice examinations (with some states requiring an essay). The content assessed is typically comprised of a bland, U.S./Eurocentric patriotic narrative of "progress" approved by committees of policymakers, ignoring current scholarship (van Hover et al., 2010).

In recent years, however, a slow shift has been taking place in social studies assessment as states eliminate high-stakes tests and replace them with some version of authentic or performance-based assessments (Darling-Hammond et al., 2016; Grant, 2017). These changes also reflect larger projects such as the *College, Career, and Civic Life (C3) Framework* (National Council for the Social Studies [NCSS], 2013) and Stanford's *Beyond the Bubble* project (Breakstone et al., 2013). COVID-19, however, interrupted all social studies assessment and raises many questions.

In a post–COVID-19 era, will states, concerned about "lost learning," return to an overreliance on high-stakes tests that privilege regurgitation of information? That is, will the disruption caused by COVID-19 lead to a mass retreat to "normalcy" and the familiarity of traditional assessment practices? Or will states trust that performance-based assessments or teachers' classroom-based assessments provide sufficient insight into mastery of content? If teachers are permitted more freedom and the social studies curriculum continues to transform, what will high-quality assessment look like post–COVID-19? What assessments might teachers use in their classroom that are similar to and different from the "normalcy" of high-stakes standardized tests? What knowledge, skills and understandings did COVID-19 surface as essential to social studies, and how are these assessed? What are the complexities involved in such a shift? In this chapter, we explore these, and other questions, framed within the argument that in order to reach excellence, individuals often need to "drop the tools" that comprise an essential part of their identity.

In a 2007 keynote at a conference exploring the theme "realizing human potential through teaching excellence," organizational psychologist Karl E. Weick (2007) shared the tragic story of two groups of firefighters who ignored the order to drop their firefighting tools as they tried to outrun wildfires and were killed before they reached the safe zones in the midst of canyon brush fires 45 years apart. He sought to highlight the idea that when literal tools (e.g., chainsaw, backpack, etc.) are an essential part of your identity, you might not know when or how to drop them even when leaving those tools behind could save your life. Weick argued that "people may refuse to drop their tools because of problems with hearing, trust, control, physical well-being, and calculation" as well as "social dynamics," a "reluctance to admit failure in a can-do culture," that they have "little familiarity with the alternative," and are hoping "the danger will pass and everything will work out" (pp. 7–8). While the issue we discuss here is clearly not equivalent to the life-or-death situation faced by smoke jumpers, we draw on this notion of "tools" to unpack what post–COVID-19 excellence in assessment could and should look like. We argue that old ways of assessing traditional knowledge, while sometimes comforting to teachers and administrators, weigh social studies education down, and that true change cannot take place until these old tools are dropped and replaced.

To further explore the need to "drop our tools" in a post–COVID-19 era, we begin by briefly synthesizing the literature on assessment. We then describe responses to school closures (and reopenings) during the COVID-19 pandemic in Virginia and New York City, drawing on data from research studies and our own experiences. We conclude by outlining some ideas to consider for social studies assessment in a post–COVID-19 era and parse out which tools we should drop, which we should keep, and why. It should be noted that our primary focus is on summative assessment, evaluation of student learning at the conclusion of a unit or course (Hattie & Yates,

Table 17.1. Defined Assessment Terms

Assessment Term	Definitions From the Literature
Authentic Assessment	"Performance tasks and activities designed to simulate or replicate important real-world challenges . . . [involves] realistic performance-based testing—asking the student to use knowledge in real-world ways, with genuine purposes, audiences, and situational variables" (Wiggins & McTighe, 2005, p. 337).
Performance Assessment	Allow students to demonstrate significant learning targets that are challenging to measure with other assessment formats (Resnick & Resnick, 1992); offer specific tasks that support learning as opposed to acting as indicators of learning (Bennett, 2010); enhance instructional practices by exposing to teachers what is important for students to learn (Lane, 2010).
Alternative Assessment	"Ask students to perform, create, produce, or do something; tap high-level thinking and problem-solving skill; use tasks that represent meaningful instructional activities; invoke real-world applications; and, require new instructional and assessment roles for teachers" (Herman, 1992, p. 13).

2014). Throughout this chapter we use a number of terms from the assessment literature, and Table 17.1 provides the definitions we are employing.

ASSESSMENT AND SOCIAL STUDIES

Most of the research on assessment in social studies explores the impact of the presence or absence of a high-stakes standardized end-of-course assessment or offers suggestions as to what high-quality assessment could be (Grant, 2006; Grant & Salinas, 2008; Shemilt, 2018). In the absence of state-mandated end-of-course assessments, research suggests that social studies may not be covered at all due to reductions in instructional time, particularly at the elementary level (Fitchett et al., 2014). The presence, however, of a high-stakes test at the end of a social studies course has an ambiguous and complicated relationship with student learning and can act as a lever on teachers' instructional practice (Au, 2007; Grant & Salinas, 2008). Studies indicate that when teachers make decisions about how to prepare students for high-stakes end-of-course assessments, they often focus on coverage and control of tested content (Au, 2007; Barton & Levstik, 2004). As Smith (2018) found in a study of the National Assessment of Educational Progress and California social studies examinations, these tests are uncertain measures of what students have learned. After analyzing student think-aloud data, he concluded that:

> [test] items typically elicited three construct-irrelevant processes: factual recall/ recognition, reading comprehension, and test-taking strategies. Further, findings revealed that although the items often prompted students to engage in factual recall, they were often not sound indicators of student knowledge. (p. 1256)

Recently, however, there has been an emerging assessment trend throughout the United States: new state-level innovations and policy shifts that eliminate high-stakes multiple-choice tests and replace them with some version of authentic or performance-based assessments (Grant, 2017). In Washington, for example, teachers are permitted to choose their class-room-based assessments from a state bank in which students create and answer a disciplinary question by writing a paper or crafting a presentation. In New York, a consortium of schools has created performance assessments to match the rigor of the state Regents exam (Grant, 2017). In Virginia, the state legislature is reducing testing in social studies and suggesting divisions replace high-stakes tests with locally developed alternative assessments (Gurlea et al., 2020). This push for authentic assessment is being enthusiastically endorsed as a move away from regurgitation of factual content and toward performance-based activities that recognize disciplinary skills and ways of knowing in the content areas that fall under the umbrella of social studies (NCSS, 2013; Shemilt, 2018; Torrez & Claunch-Lebsack, 2013; VanSledright, 2013).

While the impact of this shift is only beginning to be investigated empirically within the field of social studies, some research supports the power and potential of performance assessments. In 2011, the National History Day (NHD) project published the results of a longitudinal study indicating that students participating in the NHD project, which includes authentic disciplinary inquiry and original research, outperformed their peers on standardized tests (NHD, 2011). A study of short, constructed history assessments of thinking (HATs), compared to traditional multiple-choice versions of the same tasks, found that HATs better reflected student knowledge and elicited responses that were not as influenced by question format. These results support other studies that indicate multiple-choice tests tend to overestimate student knowledge (Reich, 2009; Smith, 2018). In addition, studies have shown that when students are exposed to a high-quality, student-centered, project-based methodology, they are still able to perform well on traditional metrics of assessment (Parker et al., 2011, 2013). These ambitious styles of instruction and assessment may also have broader consequences of greater political participation (see McAvoy & Hess, 2013).

In sum, the research on social studies assessment focuses on the high-stakes assessment context that emerged post–*No Child Left Behind* and what high-quality assessment *could* be. The current shift from testing controlled by the states to more local control over assessments is under way, and (very) preliminary research indicates the power and potential of performance assessments (Fitzpatrick et al., 2019; NHD, 2011; Smith et al., 2019). The pandemic struck during a complex, shifting policy context, and COVID-19 accelerated crucial conversations about the role, purposes, and values associated with assessment, particularly regarding racial/cultural biases, equity, access, inclusivity, and social justice. In fact, the reluctance to drop old tools has always exacerbated issues of equity in assessment (e.g., tracking, IQ testing, etc.). As educational scholars Erick Montenegro and Natasha Jankowski (2017) note,

> Assessment, if not done with equity in mind, privileges and validates certain types of learning and evidence of learning over others, can hinder the validation of multiple means of demonstration, and can reinforce within students the false notion that they do not belong in higher education. (p. 5)

These sentiments have never been more applicable to K–12 education, as means of instruction and students' demonstrations of knowledge have been narrowed to what is allowed by technology and creativity in a remote learning setting. The story of assessment during COVID-19 highlights these issues.

COVID-19: WHAT HAPPENED?

Both New York City and Virginia public schools closed for in-person instruction in March 2020, which had an immediate impact on social studies instruction and assessment. In this section, we share recollections about the school closures (and reopenings) from our perspectives. As context, New York City and the state of Virginia have roughly the same number of students enrolled in public schools.

In New York City, an epicenter of the pandemic, Mayor Bill de Blasio resisted closing schools because he feared that without schools open not enough workers would be available to keep the public hospitals or the transit system running, as parents would have to stay home with their children instead of going to work (Mays & Goldstein, 2020). When schools switched to virtual schooling after March 15th, social studies teachers who were enrolled in a graduate-level education class taught by one of the authors reported being required to keep students on pace—to continue covering the mandated curriculum to ensure students could take the New

York State Regents Exams. The examination was eventually cancelled by the state, but teachers reported continuing to enact the test-based curriculum, as all lessons and lesson materials were now fully online and available for administrators to review (and administrators could visit classrooms at any time). New York State suspended the Regents examination again for the 2020–2021 school year, but a number of schools are requiring that teachers use the "Passport for Social Studies," a set of Regents exam–focused, scripted demonstration lessons that are developed by the New York City Department of Education.

As part of a larger study of assessment in Virginia that three of us (van Hover, Gurlea, and Woodward) conducted, several school division social studies leaders were interviewed and asked specifically to reflect on assessment during and after the COVID-19 shutdown. Conversations reveal a chaotic response to the closure of in-person schooling, a response that varied by division and highlighted—and exacerbated—inequities in the system. As one division-level leader recalled:

> At the time we were not considered a one-to-one (computer) district, nor would we have had time to distribute devices . . . so we went into emergency planning mode. We had students with no device, no Internet access, no textbook and, in a lot of cases, no correct phone number.

This division responded by printing packets, and they "put [their] performance assessments in those packets," but this leader observed, "There was really no opportunity for assessment in our division" from the time schools closed, and "we didn't have any true assessment of learning, which is providing a conundrum as we return to school [in Fall 2020] because we're trying to figure out what students have retained." This leader went on to say,

> Reading level, math, where are they, what was the impact of the Covid slide? . . . not all kids had devices or Wi-Fi or parental support to be able to engage . . . so we're anticipating when we do get [assessment] data back, the achievement gap with our equity and opportunity students is going to have widened despite some of the best efforts of even our rock-star teachers.

The leader noted that given the sudden nature of the shutdown "it's really hard for us to hold anyone accountable for the learning that was supposed to take place . . . We didn't have a system." Similarly, a second division leader said that they also created a packet of work and some assignments for students. The requirement was that students had to submit three assignments, but failure to submit those three assignments had no impact. This division, and others, ceased requiring teachers to report grades.

A third division leader explained that "Whatever teachers did in any type of instruction and assessment, they were not allowed to take grades"; as for assessment, "pretty much everything shut down, there was no official assessment anymore." She described many teachers responding by becoming more innovative and told the story of one teacher who used the online space to invite guest speakers to present to the students, including a panel of Civil Rights activists. For this presentation, over Google Hangout, "there were 180 kids tuned in" who were engaged and asked questions, which she described as "the most amazing experience."

The shutdown of assessment and grading took place during the abrupt closure of in-person schooling from March to the end of the school year. The Virginia Department of Education (VDOE) did release "learning in place" documentation in the form of "tracking logs" that were developed "to assist teachers with determining which standards students have had sufficient exposure and experience with prior to the COVID-19 school closure" and to make decisions "regarding when and how experience with new standards might occur moving forward." These trackers asked teachers to check off standards that had been "sufficiently covered prior to March 13, covered sufficiently during closure, not yet sufficiently covered" (VDOE, n.d., para. 8). These documents, interestingly, were developed by the state math division and not mentioned in any of our interviews.

School started in early Fall 2020 with the pandemic showing no signs of abating, and seemed characterized by questions about how to move forward in a changed landscape and how to interpret directives from the VDOE. While the modality of instruction remained a division-level decision (in-person, virtual, or hybrid), the VDOE released a memo reminding divisions that "testing will go on." This directive has sparked fierce debate over what and how to assess—as this division leader noted,

> It needs to be a stimulus-based question where they look at a document, or apply outside knowledge. [Something] you can't just Google, and that's going to be a challenge and probably require additional professional development for teachers as we move forward in their ability to develop that type of assessment.

Similarly, another division leader said,

> I do think that the inquiries are well set up for a virtual environment because [students can access online] resources and [c3teachers.org] provides the primary sources for the students to access. So, I think there are going to be some great possibilities there. I am still going to move forward with promoting performance-based assessments.

This leader also said that perhaps divisions could do their "best intent" with assessment and not meet the "letter of the guidelines" because "localities are [not] meeting the guidelines, anyway" and "teachers are overwhelmed with the circumstances, and [assessments] would be more for them to deal with during an unusual time."

Teachers' and schools' responses to the pandemic exposed preexisting and deep-seated issues regarding assessment. Removing traditional avenues of numeric grading and high-stakes testing forces educators to ask themselves: To what extent were these true measures of student learning? What goals of social studies education did they measure? We see evidence of teachers who went above and beyond the call of duty and pursued student engagement, growth, and progress in creative ways that have the potential to reframe the narrative around assessment and legitimately get kids interested in social studies. As difficult as the pandemic has been on all of us, it provides a unique opportunity to ask, What assessment practices or tools are worth keeping? What creative work has been done in response to the pandemic that is worth capturing and highlighting to improve our practice in the future? What tools do we need to drop and never use again?

ASSESSMENT POST-COVID-19

The chapter opened by referencing Biesta's (2009) essential question—Are we "valuing what we measure, or measuring what we value?"—and Weick's (2007) argument that "dropping tools" is sometimes necessary to thrive and excel. What is it that the field of social studies values, and how can that be assessed? What old tools must we "drop" to achieve assessment excellence? The field has coalesced around the values of the C3 Framework, the importance of inquiry, and teaching disciplinary skills and ways of knowing. A growing number of scholars are raising critical questions about the content promoted in textbooks and standards documents (Journell, 2009a, 2009b; Shear et al., 2015). The pandemic itself highlights the vital role social studies can and should play in schooling by helping to ensure that participants in U.S. society are able to read critically and understand the evidentiary warrant behind information; that they can engage in civil discourse, understand systemic injustice and racism past and present, and work collectively to fix a broken system; and that they can critically examine U.S. society and its place in a global and interdependent world in order to understand the world they inhabit. Assessing this type of social studies education requires "dropping" multiple-choice tests that privilege regurgitation of random knowledge and shifting to high-quality performance-based assessments.

We know that high-quality performance-based assessments are possible. Students can participate in a yearlong project-based learning experience, gain disciplinary skills in government and civics, and still perform well on an Advanced Placement exam (Parker et al., 2011, 2013). Students can engage with disciplinary problems and be exposed to research and outperform their peers on traditional measures (NHD, 2011). Students do not have to be limited by test format, test question style, or traditional measures of knowing in order to show knowledge in social studies (Smith et al., 2019). These examples are just the beginning of what we know to be possible through ambitious performance-based assessment.

In a summer planning meeting of South Bronx public schools participating in the New York State (NYS) Performance Assessment Consortium, teachers debated whether they should focus on the theme of the 2020 presidential election or police brutality; they chose police brutality, as they saw great connections to historical topics required by the state standards. These teachers had received a waiver from the high-stakes NYS Regents examinations, had participated in extensive professional development in high-quality assessment, had been given time and money to collaboratively plan (with one another and with college and university content and assessment experts), and shared the belief that history should be connected to the world in which students live. A sample of these teachers scored higher on Authentic Intellectual Work rubrics than any other teachers observed in a national study (Saye et al., 2018). These are teachers dropping old tools in favor of new ones and, in doing so, supporting high-quality social studies education.

It is important to recognize that not all performance assessments are of high quality. We have seen a range of performance assessments, from those that mimic problematic classroom practices and promote misconceptions and anachronistic understandings of history to those that teach students to analyze historical evidence and investigate provocative, authentic, and critical questions about the past and present. The shift to performance assessment is complex and requires attention to equity, access, resources, professional development, and quality.

In a study conducted by three of the authors (Gurlea et al., 2020), we explored the shift from a high-stakes test to a performance assessment in Virginia and found the process of change to be uneven across the state. Themes from our analysis indicate that division leaders reported that their and teachers' ability to implement local alternative assessments was impacted by how well-resourced the division was, as well as by how much guidance and support they received from the state. Findings also indicated that the ability to enact these assessments also varied based on who was trusted to create, implement, and grade them. Some well-resourced divisions used preexisting performance-based assessments constructed by third parties, some divisions banded together with state-level consortia to collaborate, and other divisions relied solely on teachers to create these tasks and fulfill the state requirement. The findings also highlighted two critical needs:

high-quality professional development for teachers and time for teachers to pivot. Otherwise, a new assessment becomes one more thing for teachers to deal with in a time of extraordinary stress. Further, these findings agree with Weick's (2007) assertion of the need to drop tools that have become burdens. In order for teachers and administrators to change their practice, we need to do more than just legislate new assessment requirements. A mandate from the state will not immediately cause teachers to drop their tools. Important work must be done to dismantle the culture that has placed so much value on antiquated and inequitable assessments.

Ambitious performance-based assessment requires change; it should also be noted that, given the extraordinary stresses of COVID-19, there is the possibility that a craving for normalcy will compel states, division leaders, and teachers to cling to familiar tools. COVID-19 disrupted the rhythm of schools, the cadence, the expected patterns of semesters, graduation, sport seasons, class schedules, and end-of-year assessments. Schools are made up of "chronological codes," or "known trajectories of events which have been selected and labeled because they are anticipated to unfold in a more or less similar sequential manner in the future" (Clark, 1990, p. 143), and COVID-19 interrupted this familiar pattern. As we write this chapter, the first vaccines are being distributed and headlines are cautiously predicting when life will "return to normal." Everyone wants "normal"—to feel safe and secure, to return to familiar chronological codes and ways of living.

This need for normalcy could portend a retreat to the familiar, conservative grammar of schooling in which the old tools—multiple-choice tests—feel comfortable, affordable, and doable. It may feel risky to drop the old tools because there is little familiarity with alternatives, little trust in policymakers removed from the classroom, and deep exhaustion from the hard work of supporting students during a global pandemic. The pandemic has exacerbated budget shortfalls in education, and assessment done well is expensive. Will states be able to afford state-level testing? Or will they let the assessments be determined by schools? Multiple-choice testing is typically the fallback tool because it feels familiar, is easy to use, and is simple to implement and score. The pandemic has left educators (and the general public) exhausted. Headlines and social media posts highlight the challenges of online school, reporting that students are falling behind or simply not attending. Our concern is that state Departments of Education, districts/divisions, and schools might succumb to the idea that they need to "catch up," so they go in search of a baseline that is easily captured in the tests of old.

It is also evident that despite the cancellation of grades and state-mandated assessments during COVID-19, the education of children continued and that "rock star teachers," untethered by a state-mandated multiple-choice test, taught in "innovative" ways that reflect best practice in social studies instruction and assessment and that incorporate many of the tenets of culturally sustaining pedagogy. The pandemic has, in some cases, forced divisions to adopt new tools of assessment. As one division leader in Virginia pointed out, "You can't just have recall test questions, you know, multiple-choice, because the kids can Google. I mean, we've given them a device to Google!"

CONCLUSION

In his article, Weick (2007) quoted a text from Lao Tzu, who stated: "In the pursuit of knowledge, every day something is acquired; In the pursuit of wisdom, every day something is dropped" (p. 5). We argue that rather than go down the comfortable path of least resistance, the post-COVID period should be seen as a generator of opportunity to re-envision the landscape of learning and assessment in social studies education and focus on the pursuit of new tools. This opportunity will require social studies researchers to collaborate and support teachers; help replace increasingly discredited high-stakes multiple-choice social studies tests; and provide state agencies and school divisions the data, incentives, and professional development to substitute authentic inquiry and assessment. As sociologist Ron Westrum (1993) observed, "a system's willingness to become aware of problems is associated with its ability to act on them" (p. 340). The COVID-19 pandemic has only increased our awareness of the problems with our systems of assessment and accountability and exacerbated the need to enact change. It would be all too easy to ignore these problems, to hold tightly to the tools that are a part of us, and to return to the comfortable march of time through schooling.

REFERENCES

Au, W. (2007). High-stakes testing and curricular control: A qualitative metasynthesis. *Educational Researcher*, 36(5), 258–267. https://doi.org/10.3102/0013189X07306523

Barton, K. C., & Levstik, L. S. (2004). *Teaching history for the common good.* Routledge.

Bennett, R. E. (2010). Cognitively based assessment of, for, and as learning: A preliminary theory of action for summative and formative assessment. *Measurement: Interdisciplinary Research and Perspectives*, 8(2–3), 70–91. https://doi.org/10.1080/15366367.2010.508686

Biesta, G. (2009). Good education in an age of measurement: On the need to reconnect with the question of purpose in education. *Educational Assessment, Evaluation, and Accountability*, 21(1), 33–46. https://doi.org/10.1007/s11092-008-9064-9

Breakstone, J., Smith, M., & Wineburg, S. (2013). Beyond the bubble in history/social studies assessments. *Phi Delta Kappan*, 94(5), 53–57. https://doi.org/10.1177/003172171309400512

Clark, P. (1990). Chronological codes and organizational analysis. In J. Hassard & D. Pym (Eds.), *The theory and philosophy of organizations* (pp. 137–163). Routledge.

Darling-Hammond, L., Bae, S., Cook-Harvey, C. M., Lam, L., Mercer, C., Podolsky, A., & Stosich, E. L. (2016). *Pathways to new accountability through the Every Student Succeeds Act*. Learning Policy Institute.

Fitchett, P. G., Heafner, T. L., & Lambert, R. (2014). Assessment, autonomy, and elementary social studies time. *Teachers College Record*, 116(10), 1–34.

Fitzpatrick, C., van Hover, S., Cornett, A., & Hicks, D. (2019). A DBQ in a multiple-choice world: A tale of two assessments in a unit on the Byzantine Empire. *Journal of Social Studies Research*, 43(3), 199–214. https://doi.org/10.1016/j.jssr.2018.09.004

Grant, S. G. (Ed.). (2006). *Measuring history: Cases of high-stakes testing across the U.S.* Information Age.

Grant, S. G. (2017). The problem of knowing what students know: Classroom-based and large-scale assessment in social studies. In M.M. Manfra & C.M. Bolick (Eds.), *The Wiley handbook of social studies research* (pp. 461–476). Wiley-Blackwell.

Grant, S. G., & Salinas, C. (2008). Assessment and accountability in the social studies. In L.S. Levstik & C.A. Tyson (Eds.), *Handbook of research in social studies education* (pp. 219–236). Routledge.

Gurlea, M. P., Woodward, T., & van Hover, S. (2020, November 30—December 4). *Top down, bottom up . . . and then what happened?: Assessment policy change in middle school history classrooms* [Paper presentation]. College and University Faculty Assembly of the National Council of the Social Studies Annual Meeting, Washington, D.C., United States.

Hattie, J., & Yates, G. C. (2014). *Visible learning and the science of how we learn*. Routledge.

Herman, J. L. (1992). *A practical guide to alternative assessment*. Association for Supervision and Curriculum Development.

Journell, W. (2009a). An incomplete history: Representations of American Indians in state social studies standards. *Journal of American Indian Education*, 48(2), 18–32.

Journell, W. (2009b). Setting out the (un)welcome mat: A portrayal of immigration in state standards for American history. *The Social Studies*, 100(4), 160–168. https://doi.org/10.3200/TSSS.100.4.160–168

Lane, S. (2010). *Performance assessment: The state of the art*. Stanford University, Stanford Center for Opportunity Policy in Education.

Mays, J.C., & Goldsten, J. (2020, March 16). Mayor resisted drastic steps on virus. Then came a backlash from his aides. *The New York Times*. https://www.nytimes.com/2020/03/16/nyregion/coronavirus-bill-de-blasio.html

McAvoy, P., & Hess, D. (2013). Classroom deliberation in an era of political polarization. *Curriculum Inquiry*, 43(1), 14–47. https://doi.org/10.1111/curi.12000

Montenegro, E., & Jankowski, N.A. (2017). *Equity and assessment: Moving towards culturally responsive assessment* (Occasional Paper, 29). National Institute for Learning Outcomes Assessment.

National Council for the Social Studies. (2013). *College, career, and civic life (C3) framework for social studies state standards.* Author.

National History Day. (2011). *National history day works: National program evaluation.* Author. https://www.nhd.org/why-nhd-works

Parker, W. C., Lo, J., Yeo, A. J., Valencia, S. W., Nguyen, D., Abbott, R. D., Nolen, S. B., Bransford, J. D., & Vye, N. J. (2013). Beyond breadth-speed-test: Toward deeper knowing and engagement in an Advanced Placement course. *American Educational Research Journal, 50*(6), 1424–1459. https://doi.org/10.3102/0002831213504237

Parker, W. C., Mosborg, S., Bransford, J., Vye, N., Wilkerson, J., & Abbott, R. (2011). Rethinking advanced high school coursework: Tackling the depth/breadth tension in the AP US government and politics course. *Journal of Curriculum Studies, 43*(4), 533–559. https://doi.org/10.1080/00220272.2011.584561

Reich, G. A. (2009). Testing historical knowledge: Standards, multiple-choice questions and student reasoning. *Theory & Research in Social Education, 37*(3), 325–360. https://doi.org/10.1080/00933104.2009.10473401

Resnick, L.B., & Resnick, D.P. (1992). Assessing the thinking curriculum: New tools for educational reform. In B.G. Gifford & M.C. O'Conner (Eds.), *Changing assessment: Alternative views of aptitude, achievement and instruction* (pp. 37–55). Kluwer.

Saye, J. W., Stoddard, J., Gerwin, D. M., Libresco, A. S., & Maddox, L. E. (2018). Authentic pedagogy: Examining intellectual challenge in social studies classrooms. *Journal of Curriculum Studies, 50*(6), 865–884. https://doi.org/10.1080/00220272.2018.1473496

Shear, S. B., Knowles, R. T., Soden, G. J., & Castro, A. J. (2015). Manifesting destiny: Re/presentations of Indigenous peoples in K–12 U.S. history standards. *Theory & Research in Social Education, 43*(1), 68–101. https://www.doi.org/10.1080/00933104.2014.999849

Shemilt, D. (2018). Assessment of learning in history education: Past, present, and possible futures. In S.A. Metzger & L.M. Harris (Eds.), *The Wiley international handbook of history teaching and learning* (pp. 449–471). Wiley-Blackwell.

Smith, M. D. (2018). New multiple-choice measures of historical thinking: An investigation of cognitive validity. *Theory & Research in Social Education, 46*(1), 1–34. https://doi.org/10.1080/00933104.2017.1351412

Smith, M. D., Breakstone, J., & Wineburg, S. (2019). History assessments of thinking: A validity study. *Cognition and Instruction, 37*(1), 118–144. https://doi.org/10.1080/07370008.2018.1499646

Torrez, C. A., & Claunch-Lebsack, E. A. (2013). Research on assessment in the social studies classroom. In J. H. McMillan (Ed.), *Sage handbook of research on classroom assessment* (pp. 461-472). Sage.

van Hover, S., Hicks, D., Stoddard, J., & Lisanti, M. (2010). From a roar to a murmur: Virginia's History and Social Science standards, 1995 to the present. *Theory & Research in Social Education, 38*(1), 80–113. https://doi.org/10.1080/00933104.2010.10473417

VanSledright, B. A. (2013). *Assessing historical thinking and understanding: Innovative designs for new standards*. Routledge.

Virginia Department of Education. (n.d.). *History & social science*. Author. https://www.doe.virginia.gov/instruction/history/

Westrum, R. (1993). Thinking by groups, organizations, and networks: A sociologist's view of the social psychology of science and technology. In W. Shadish & S. Fuller (Eds.), *The social psychology of science* (pp. 329–342). Guilford.

Weick, K. E. (2007). Drop your tools: On reconfiguring management education. *Journal of Management Education, 31*(1), 5–16. https://doi.org/10.1177/1052562906293699

Wiggins, G., & McTighe, J. (2005). *Understanding by design* (2nd ed.). Association for Supervision and Curriculum Development.

Afterword

The nation's quest to become a more perfect union has always been fraught with triumphs and tragedies, successes and setbacks. That is the American way. History has revealed our unrelenting quest to be better in the face of adversity, resistance, and difference. What that perfect union looks like has often been shaped by different realities, varied experiences, and diverse perspectives of what these United States of America should look like, how we as a nation-state should be governed, whose voices should be heard, and whose rights should be upheld and protected.

We are aware that 400 years of history leave behind actions and attitudes that we must reckon with in order to actualize a better future. How do we address the tragedies around the theft of lands from Indigenous peoples? How can we make amends for the enslavement of millions of people of African descent? How do we create equitable immigration laws that provide hope and prosperity, and don't criminalize people seeking opportunity? How do we create laws, structures, and systems to ameliorate or replace those that have long kept us a divided and fractured nation-state? These are just some of the questions that constantly loom over us as we seek that more perfect union.

The year 2020 will go down as one of the most monumental, historical, and trying years in U.S. history—one that will be in the history books for decades to come. Along with the direct health impact of the COVID-19 virus—which has claimed the lives of more than 4 million people worldwide and over 700,000 Americans—we have endured isolation, exasperation, anxiety, a profound economic downturn, and great uncertainty about the future. These challenges have been compounded by racist violence, ethnic hostility, political turmoil, and even armed insurrection at the start of 2021. We are all, understandably, tired.

A multitude of challenges lie before us, and much of the work will take place in schools. We look to the hope, promise, and possibility that can come from schools in this trying moment in our nation's history. Social studies educators in particular can and must play an important role in helping students make meaning of what we have all witnessed and experienced over the last year. An impressive chorus of scholars have researched and written about the importance of engaging in controversial issues (Hess &

McAvoy, 2015; Journell, 2017), creating more critical approaches to civic education (Crocco et al., 2018), and centering youth voices in much of the discourse around social studies education (Payne & Journell, 2019). Yet this moment feels different, because it is different.

The magnitude of massive loss of life in a short span of time, the economic fallout, and the accompanying racial strife and polarized political climate have created a confluence of circumstances that many adults are seeking to understand; so where might our students be on this matter? This is a time when the scholarly community and the practitioner community must come together to bridge the theory-to-practice divide in a robust and more transformative manner. The collection of chapters in this book help to provide us a healing roadmap—a roadmap that explicitly names the challenges, emotions, and pain that many Americans have encountered historically and contemporarily. The authors in this work also provide us with critical and evidence-based directions, recommendations, resources, and hope for how we can move forward.

To be clear, our goal is to help provide young people with the knowledge, skills, resources, and dispositions to live in an increasingly diverse and democratic society. Many young people continue to question the utility of our democracy. If that questioning leads to broad rejection of democracy, we will all be in peril. We must walk a fine line, an intellectually honest balance of uncovering the sins of a nation whose lofty ideals of justice, freedom, opportunity, and equal protection under the law have not been met for millions of minoritized Americans. Yet many of the Americans who have been most excluded from the American dream have been the Americans who believe most in the hope and possibility of a better America, a more inclusive America, and a more loving America. Chants and protests around racial and economic inequality should not be seen as un-American; to the contrary, these are vociferous appeals for America to be her better self—to live up to the principles of egalitarianism and opportunity.

Over the past several months, I have heard from a number of middle and high school students who have said that they desperately wanted to discuss, debate, and analyze the events at the Capitol on January 6th, but that the riot was largely ignored or given only scant attention by most of their teachers, which is deeply troubling and sorely disappointing. Social studies should play a vital role in filling a massive void in many classrooms. The Capitol insurrection represented a moment that many students wanted to discuss with their teachers, but teachers were either unable or unwilling to do so. Talking about insurrection, democracy, race, protest, hate, and education is what many of our students want in this moment. Teachers may be unsure how to lead, structure, or facilitate these difficult discussions. How, then, do we help students become participatory citizens in a diverse democracy? We should consider discussing the following:

- *The importance of peaceful protest.* The United States prides itself on the importance of the First Amendment, the right to free speech and peaceful protest. The First Amendment guarantees freedoms concerning religion, expression, assembly, and the right to petition. It guarantees the right of citizens to assemble peaceably and to petition their government. The events of January 6th demonstrated destruction of a sacred building, the occupation of the place where the nation's most important business is held, and violence and harm to people who are given the responsibility of protecting the Capitol. Educators can be integral in helping to guide students in how to debate, discuss, and dissect the importance and value of free speech and peaceful protest, and then to determine if the events of January 6th meet that criteria of what should constitute free speech or assembly under the First Amendment.
- *The value of controlled classroom conversation on controversial subjects.* In this moment of change, complexity, grief, and suffering, teacher silence is complicity. A robust body of literature speaks to the importance of discussing controversial issues in classrooms. Scholars Diana Hess (2009) and Rebecca Geller (2020) have offered important frameworks, strategies, and approaches that teachers can use to engage students in current events that are not easy to discuss. Teachers must recognize that silence on matters tied to protest, race, and education renders them complicit in contributing to the divisive racial climate that exists in our society and ultimately permeates into our schools. Teachers need to equip themselves with knowledge, strategies, and skills to engage age-appropriate, civil, respectful, and multiperspective discourses, which will assist students in coming to their own understanding and positions on these issues. In short, silence on racial justice matters is not a good option.
- *What teachers and students can do to preserve democracy in these challenging times.* Threats to democracy have been ever-present over the course of the two and a half centuries of our country's existence. To be clear, attacking science, questioning truth, challenging democratic rights to votes, and disputing outcomes of elections are contemporary efforts to undermine our democracy. Social studies educators have a vital role in this moment of helping our future legislators and leaders recognize the importance of civil discourse, respectful debate, and the utility of country before party. We seem to be teetering further away from the notion of civil disagreement and how we peacefully articulate views with contradictory opinions. The strength of our democracy fundamentally rests on coexisting peacefully even when we do not agree on issues of the day.

Schools continue to be more racially diverse with each passing year. Students see, hear, and feel many of the racially charged issues that are part of schools and society writ large. Kristen Duncan and Amber Neal poignantly historicize protests in the wake of COVID-19 in Chapter 10. How are people using their voices this moment? How are citizens mobilizing for a more just nation in the midst of a global pandemic? Why are people willing to put their lives at risk to achieve racial justice? These are just some of the pressing issues of the day that social studies educators can engage with students.

Our classrooms can and should be spaces that are safe, supportive, and racially inclusive. As we seek to prepare our students to become democratic citizens in an increasingly diverse society, quests for racial justice cannot be ignored, pleas for inclusion must be honored, and our willingness to talk race, justice, and democracy is essential to creating what our students need and deserve in this moment. Our time is now. The challenge is clear and the task may seem daunting, but in many ways, we sit in a moment for potential transformation. We sit in a moment where we may have the opportunity to center hope, possibility, and opportunity as more than just hollow words and empty concepts, but as a reality in our schools and a staple in our nation.

—*Tyrone C. Howard*

REFERENCES

Crocco, M. S., Halvorsen, A.-L., Jacobsen, R., & Segall, A. (2018). Less arguing, more listening: Improving civility in classrooms. *Phi Delta Kappan, 99*(5), 67–71. https://doi.org/10.1177%2F0031721718754818

Geller, R. C. (2020). Teacher political disclosure in contentious times: A "responsibility to speak up" or "fair and balanced"? *Theory & Research in Social Education, 48*(2), 182–210. https://doi.org/10.1080/00933104.2020.1740125

Hess, D. E. (2009). *Controversy in the classroom: The democratic power of discussion.* Routledge.

Hess, D. E., & McAvoy, P. (2015). *The political classroom: Evidence and ethics in democratic education.* Routledge.

Journell, W. (2017). Framing controversial identity issues in schools: The case of HB2, bathroom equity, and transgender students. *Equity & Excellence in Education, 50*(4), 339–354. https://doi.org/10.1080/10665684.2017.1393640

Payne, K. A., & Journell, W. (2019). "We have those kinds of conversations here . . . ": Addressing contentious politics with elementary students. *Teaching and Teacher Education, 79*, 73–82. https://doi.org/10.1016/j.tate.2018.12.008

About the Editor and Contributors

Wayne Journell is professor of Secondary Social Studies Education at the University of North Carolina at Greensboro. He is the editor of the Research and Practice in Social Studies book series for Teachers College Press.

Sohyun An is professor of Social Studies Education at Kennesaw State University.

Varenka Servin Arcos is a teacher and adviser in the General Baccalaureate subsystem of upper secondary education in Veracruz State, Mexico.

Brooke Blevins is the Conwell G. Strickland Endowed Chair of Education and chair of the Department of Curriculum and Instruction at Baylor University.

Lisa Brown Buchanan is associate professor of Education in the Department of Education and Wellness at Elon University.

Yun-Wen Chan is assistant professor in the Department of Curriculum and Instruction at Texas State University.

Ya-Fang Cheng is assistant professor in the Division of Education and Leadership at Western Oregon University.

Rebecca C. Christ is assistant professor of Social Studies Education in the Department of Teaching and Learning at Florida International University.

Christopher H. Clark is assistant professor of Secondary Education at the University of North Dakota.

Kristen E. Duncan is assistant professor of Social Studies Education at Clemson University.

Leonel Pérez Expósito is professor of Education and Sociology at Universidad Autónoma Metropolitana, campus Xochimilco, and member of the Technical Council of the National Commission for the Continuous Improvement of Education (Mejoredu) in Mexico.

Anna Falkner is assistant professor in the Instruction and Curriculum Leadership Department at the University of Memphis.

David Gerwin is professor of Secondary Education at Queens College, City University of New York.

Maggie Guggenheimer is a math lecturer in the Watson College of Education at the University of North Carolina–Wilmington.

Michael Gurlea is a PhD student in the Department of Curriculum, Instruction, and Special Education at the School of Education and Human Development, University of Virginia.

Tracy Hargrove is associate professor in the Early Childhood, Elementary, Middle Level, Literacy and Special Education Department at the University of North Carolina–Wilmington.

Jennifer Hauver is associate dean of Education Programs at Trinity Washington University.

Mark E. Helmsing is assistant professor in the School of Education and Affiliate Faculty in the Folklore Studies Program and Department of History and Art History at George Mason University.

David Hicks is professor of history and Social Science Education in the School of Education (College of Liberal Arts and Human Sciences) at Virginia Tech.

Tyrone C. Howard is professor, Pritzker Family Endowed Chair, and the director and founder of the Black Male Institute at the University of California, Los Angeles.

Karon LeCompte is associate professor of Social Studies Education at Baylor University.

Kevin R. Magill is assistant professor of Secondary Teaching at Baylor University.

Catherine Mas is assistant professor of History at Florida International University.

Sarah A. Mathews is associate professor of Curriculum and Instruction and Social Studies Education within the Department of Teaching and Learning at Florida International University.

Carly Muetterties is the director of Learning Design at Newsela.

Amber M. Neal is a PhD candidate in the Department of Educational Theory and Practice at the University of Georgia.

Katherina A. Payne is associate professor of Curriculum and Instruction at the University of Texas at Austin.

Noreen Naseem Rodríguez is assistant professor at the University of Colorado–Boulder.

Sandra Schmidt is associate professor of Social Studies Education at Teachers College, Columbia University.

Lynn Sikma is associate professor in the Department of Early Childhood, Elementary, Middle, Literacy, and Special Education at the University of North Carolina–Wilmington.

Amy Taylor is professor of Science Education at the University of North Carolina–Wilmington.

Stephanie van Hover is professor of Social Studies Education and Chair, Department of Curriculum, Instruction, and Special Education at the School of Education and Human Development, University of Virginia.

Cathryn van Kessel is associate professor in the Faculty of Education at the University of Alberta in amiskwacîwâskahikan (Edmonton, Canada).

Bretton A. Varga is assistant professor of History-Social Science at California State University, Chico.

Cara Ward teaches a variety of elementary and secondary education courses in the Watson College of Education at the University of North Carolina–Wilmington.

Joel Westheimer is the University Research Chair in Democracy and Education at the University of Ottawa.

Tyler Woodward is a PhD candidate in the Department of Curriculum, Instruction, and Special Education at the School of Education and Human Development, University of Virginia.

Holly Wright is the social–emotional learning specialist at Gradient Learning.

Index